Jesuit Studies

Contributions to the arts and sciences

by members of the Society of Jesus

Jesuit Studies

The Churches and the Schools
FRANCIS X. CURRAN

Deception in Elizabethan Comedy
JOHN V. CURRY

Bishop Lancelot Andrewes
MAURICE F. REIDY

Master Alcuin, Liturgist
GERALD ELLARD

Theodore Dwight Woolsey
GEORGE A. KING

The Praise of Wisdom
EDWARD L. SURTZ

The Wagner Housing Act
TIMOTHY L. MCDONNELL

JESUIT STUDIES

The Honor of Being a Man

THE WORLD OF ANDRE MALRAUX

Edward Gannon, S.J.

LOYOLA UNIVERSITY PRESS

Chicago, 1957

IMPRIMI POTEST: Stephen F. McNamee, S.J.
Vice-Provincial of the Maryland Province
October 22, 1957

IMPRIMATUR: ✠ Samuel Cardinal Stritch
Archbishop of Chicago
November 13, 1957

It is always a risky thing to do a book on a man who is still alive, and André Malraux is at this moment very much alive. I have nevertheless run the risk, because the man is important already, and because what he has written so far will remain important no matter what else he may write.

The order of the book is the only thing it can be, chronological. It is always a mistake to draw indiscriminately from the works of an author in an attempt to present his thought, and when the author is highly philosophical the procedure would be disastrous. A philosopher, after all, keeps developing and even changing his thought during his dialogue with life, and Malraux is at heart a philosopher. He has written nothing important since 1954. If anything else appears (and there are promises), it will almost certainly be in the field of the philosophy of art. There are few men in history so devoted to art as Malraux.

I wish to thank Professor Alphonse de Waelhens of the University of Louvain for introducing me to the work of Malraux, my superiors for their encouragement, Clayton E. Hudnall for working painstakingly on the proofs, and Reverend William F. Troy, S.J., dean of Wheeling College, for allowing me the time needed to see this book through the press.

EDWARD GANNON, S.J.

WHEELING COLLEGE
October 15, 1957

CONTENTS

Whoever wishes passionately to change for the better the world in which he lives has intuitions that underlie all his thought and all his strivings. The contemporary French writer who is the subject of this study is not an exception. "One can live accepting the absurd," he says; "one cannot live the absurd."[1] As men we may have been "flung at random between the profusion of the earth and the galaxy of the stars, but in that prison we can fashion images of ourselves to deny our nothingness."[2] Thus the basic intuitions of André Malraux.

The purpose of this book is to trace the evolution of a thought which was first the awakening of a serious young man to what he saw as the bankruptcy of European man (and of Oriental man, to the extent that he was Europeanized),[3] along the tortuous course of almost four thousand pages of his writings, to his daringly triumphant discovery that Europe need not remain bankrupt at all, that there is not only something to be salvaged, but a new world to make. The resurgence of Europe is possible with a belief in world humanism, one avenue to

---

[1] André Malraux, *Les conquérants* (henceforth cited as *Conq.*; see p. 224), version définitive, pp. 230-31. Paris: Grasset, 1949.

[2] André Malraux, *Les noyers de l'Altenburg* (henceforth cited as *N.A.*; see p. 224), pp. 98-99. Paris: Gallimard, 1948.

[3] André Malraux, *La tentation de l'Occident* (henceforth cited as *T.O.*; see p. 224), pp. 179-89. Paris: Grasset, 1926.

which is the resurrected art of all history, of which Europe is the first inheritor.[4] With this heritage Europe can thrill once more with the "force and honor it is to be a man."[5]

This gospel took over twenty years to fashion. There had always been some hope from the beginning. Lucidly aware that, if God is dead, man is lost in an individualism that reaps the absurd,[6] Malraux first preached the one thing still possible— action, the exercise of liberty, the employing of the one life a man has; the chance to defy the absurd. In *Les conquérants* and *La voie royale* adventurers and revolutionaries drown themselves in action, without regrets. But all of this turns out to be incomplete. When, in *La condition humaine*, the first limning of redemption from the absurd begins to appear, it is as though action has done better than it knew. A sense of fraternity among men of action becomes a good worth achieving, a new value to hurl at the absurd. *Le temps du mépris* advances it, and *L'espoir* is its incarnation. In *Les noyers de l'Altenburg* fraternity has reached out from the present to call in the community of men of all times, and in *Les voix du silence*, as in *Le musée imaginaire de la sculpture mondiale*, absurdity is reduced to a more clearly defined fatality, which, made man-sized, can be kept at a distance by the victorious presence of the great styles in art—

---

[4] For Malraux "America is simply one part of the West. The Americans, as Faulkner just said, do not advance an ideology distinct from our own. They belong to the mind of Europe, while remaining Americans" (In "What Stand Will You Take?" speech delivered before the Congress of Cultural Freedom, June 6, 1952, following Faulkner's: published in *Confluence*, September 1952, p. 4). Also: "There is no specifically American culture. That idea is an invention of Europeans. . . . [America] has always thought herself part of *our* world" ("Address to the Intellectuals," in the Salle Pleyel, March 5, 1948, published as postface to *Les conquérants*, pp. 252-53).

[5] André Malraux, *Les voix du silence* (henceforth cited as *V.S.*; see p. 224), p. 640. Paris: Gallimard (Galerie de la Pléiade), 1951.

[6] André Malraux, "D'une jeunesse européenne" (henceforth cited as *J.E.*; see p. 224); in *Ecrits*, with essays of other young Frenchmen; Vol. 70 of *Cahiers verts*, pp. 133-44. Paris: Grasset, 1927.

each an *Anti-destin*.[7] European man can once more believe in man.[8]

There is a great deal more to say. If the "most vigorous, the greatest, the most wholesome of French novelists"[9] is to be understood and weighed for his gold, it is high time that his whole thought be presented as an organic thing. It is as much a sense of justice, which would save Malraux from the superficial treatment he has too long received from too many critics, as a desire to help make clear the reasons for his present importance in the world of thought, that has prompted this book.[10] His novels and writings on art may, or may not, warrant the judgment that he is at present the "only writer who has been able to express in its entirety and in its full depth the fundamental drama of our civilization."[11] In any case, we would like to know why such things are said.

Actually, Malraux keeps increasing in importance. The latest example of how seriously he is considered is an impassioned three volumes (the third a volume of reproductions of works of painting and sculpture from all ages: a Malraux tech-

---

[7] *V.S.*, pp. 637-40.

[8] Malraux is conversant with world culture, participated in a Chinese and in the Spanish "Revolution," collaborated with the British in World War II, leaned long in the direction of world communism—but wrote no novel about France. He is, however, intensely French. In the "Address to the Intellectuals" already cited he says: "We know that from now on a man is not more of a man for being less French . . . but would simply be more Russian" (p. 249). "When was France great? When she was not turned in on herself. She is universalistic. For the world, the great France is more than the France of the cathedrals or of the Revolution, than that of Louis XIV. There are countries like Great Britain which are greater as they are more alone, and that is perhaps their honor. France has never been so great as when she spoke for all men, and that is why her silence now is so poignant" (*ibid.*, p. 273).

[9] Emile Rideau, *Paganisme ou Christianisme*, p. 141. Tournai: Casterman, 1953.

[10] Of the books written on Malraux, I would single out two as doing a careful job of work: W. M. Frohock, *André Malraux and the Tragic Imagination* (Stanford: Stanford University Press, 1952) and Gaëton Picon, *André Malraux par lui-même* (Paris: Editions du Seuil, 1953).

[11] Marcel Savanne, *André Malraux*, p. 117. Paris: Richard-Masse, 1946.

nique) entitled *Le musée inimaginable.*[12] The author, Georges Duthuit, is almost too studied in his merciless attack, but that such a huge arsenal be brought out against Malraux is proof enough that his prestige is great. Rarely, too, do books on art now appear without some references to Malraux. And it is not surprising to hear that he is currently the idol of the young university students in Paris.

Whether or not this importance is permanent cannot be now determined. But in any history of culture that includes our time, his voice will be recorded as one many men listened to, and there were some who did not walk away unimpressed.

---

[12] Georges Duthuit, *Le musée inimaginable.* Paris: Librairie José Corti, 1956.

PART I

The Plight
of Modern Man

CHAPTER I

The Death
of the Absolute

Twentieth-century Western man, according to Malraux, is deprived of God, and many values once worth fighting for, were there a God, have now also disappeared. Although Nietzsche's "God is dead" will always defy statistical analysis, there have at all times been men without faith, even in the Middle Ages;[1] and today the number of those who possess no faith has become so great that the times can very truly be called "godless." In the former Christian world death fitted into the concept of life. Now things are reversed, and life, to very many, is part of death.[2]

In *Les conquérants* Garine, the leading character, wills to die merely because death comes. He is never convinced that his death will bring forth a better world, nor is he at all interested in a better world. Indifferent to systems, he chooses that system which circumstances force on him. He is contemptuous of those who think they work for the good of humanity, as if it were desirable that one should work for humanity or as if there were hope of accomplishing anything by working for what is said to be the common good. "Those cretins insist they are right. Actually, there is only one thing that is right, that is not a parody:

---

[1] *N.A.*, p. 145. [2] *Ibid.*, p. 141.

7

the most efficacious use of force."[3] Force, however, can never result in victory, except the victory over the sense that one should be victorious,[4] and suffering only confirms the fact that life is derisive.[5]

There are no ultimates. Tchen, in *La condition humaine*, determined to kill Chiang Kai-Shek, sees action as a stimulant, as that which gives him a deep consciousness of his estrangement from the life of values, and insists on doing the murder for only one reason: "I dislike the idea of *my* women receiving kisses from others."[6]

And even when, in *Le temps du mépris* and *L'espoir*, all the heroes fight with belief in justice and a better world, it is a world here and now, the world of men, where what counts is "the quality of man."[7] In the last of Malraux's novels, *Les noyers de l'Altenburg*, a tankman's son is "all that stands for the absolute in this degrading, gloomy, troublesome adventure called life."[8]

Yet, despite this pessimism, from one end of the work of Malraux to the other, men live in a more or less uplifting world of men. Many of the characters in his books are noble by any standard. Many die for their belief in man. In other words, what the Christian world once called the "gifts of the Holy Ghost," the world of Malraux's books portrays as the "quality of man." The death of the heroes does not therefore involve despair: it means "humanism" with all the resonance that term has today, because Malraux preaches "man" with his own peculiar form of allegiance to Nietzsche's declaration of independ-

---

[3] *Conq.*, p. 62.
[4] *Ibid.*, p. 99.
[5] *Ibid.*, p. 258.
[6] André Malraux, *La condition humaine* (henceforth cited as *C.H.*; see p. 224), édition revue et corrigée, p. 181. Paris: Gallimard, 1946. (First published in 1933.)
[7] André Malraux, *L'espoir*, p. 233. Paris: Gallimard, 1937.
[8] *N.A.*, p. 265.

ence from God: *"If* there were gods, how could I endure not to be a god? *Therefore* there are no gods."[9]

1. MALRAUX'S RELIGION

In what is by far the most penetrating study on Malraux to date, André Blanchet's "La religion d'André Malraux,"[10] the author calls Malraux a "being as religious as a Hindu or Christian monk, but one who refuses God."[11]

We know very little of the life of Malraux, and less of his religious training or of the influences of religion on him.[12] If *Les noyers de l'Altenburg* is to be taken as partly biographical, his father was a Catholic who made his first Communion.[13] But his father is so much T. E. Lawrence that this is scant evidence indeed. His grandfather in the same book is such a good Catholic that he goes to Rome to see the pope, in protest against ecclesiastical malpractice in Reichbach, but becomes disgusted with Rome and for the rest of his life considers himself "cut off from the Church but not from Christ."[14]

---

[9] Friedrich Nietzsche, *Thus Spake Zarathustra (Also Sprach Zarathustra)*, translated by A. Tille and revised by M. M. Bozman, p. 76. London: J. M. Dent and Sons, 1950.

[10] André Blanchet, "La religion d'André Malraux." *Etudes*, June 1949, pp. 289-306; July-August-September 1949, pp. 45-65.

[11] *Ibid.*, June 1949, p. 289. See *V.S.*, p. 341: "On conçoit mal un esprit religieux sans Dieu." Had Malraux read Blanchet in the meanwhile?

[12] Writers on Malraux are reduced to the annoying necessity of reconstructing his life from fragments found in his writings, in newspapers and recollections of acquaintances, as though he were long dead. Frohock in *André Malraux and the Tragic Imagination*, pp. 3-20, has a chapter called "The Legend of a Life of Action," painstakingly working through evidence which Malraux could easily rectify if he had half a mind to do so. In "The Human Condition" (*New Yorker*, November 6, 1954, pp. 45-75; November 13, 1954, pp. 46-92) there are more details about Malraux's personal life, and the author, Janet Flanner, has packed into the article more data than is found printed anywhere about Malraux's political meanderings. I consider this work by Flanner essential to any understanding of Malraux. See also A. T. Baker, "Man's Quest" in *Time*, July 18, 1955, pp. 24-30.

[13] *N.A.*, p. 79.

[14] *Ibid.*, p. 39.

François Mauriac, brilliant Catholic novelist known and respected for the sincerity of his religious convictions, recalls in his *Journal* the young Malraux of eighteen coming to see him to discuss Christianity. "Malraux," says Mauriac, "does not treat religion with disdain. He hates, perhaps, but he does not despise. This rebellious eighteen-year-old already knew the one he was talking about. There was nothing in him of that horrible species of old radical Freemason who would become soft all over when he thought of the sweet vagabond of Judea. Malraux knew Christ: the sweet vagabond of Judea is always his stern adversary."[15]

The young Frenchman corresponding with the young Chinese in *La tentation de l'Occident*, in his last letter, which is an implicit surrender to all the Chinese criticisms of Western culture, writes: "There is no ideal to which we can sacrifice ourselves, because all we know is lies, and we do not know what truth is. The earthly shadow that spreads behind the marble gods is enough to separate us from them. With what an embrace man hugs himself. *Patrie*, justice, greatness, truth—which of their statues does not bear such traces of human hands that it arouse in us the same sad irony aroused by the old faces we once loved? . . . and yet what sacrifices, what unjustified heroism sleep in us!

"Certainly there is a higher faith: that proclaimed by all the village crosses. . . . It is love, and peace is in it. I will never accept it; I will never bow to ask of it the peace to which my weakness beckons me."[16]

There is defiance here, as there is in many things said by the characters in Malraux's earlier books. But it is difficult to read all his work, up to 1956, and not detect a softening toward Christianity, coincident with his growing understanding of

---

[15] François Mauriac, *Journal*, p. 220. Paris: Grasset, 1937.
[16] *T.O.*, pp. 216-17.

Christian values as found especially in medieval art. If Malraux were to be classified in any known category in regard to his religious position, he should be called what he says he is, an agnostic,[17] but (something he does not say) bred of postulatory atheism. This atheism, as will become clear, is the only position compatible with his belief in the autonomy of man, and is a familiar thing nowadays, ever since Feuerbach first gave man back to man by finding that "the divine being is nothing but the being of man . . . nothing but that being objectivized, i.e. contemplated and adored as a being apart."[18] Nietzsche lyricized it all with his "God is dead: I teach you now the Superman,"[19] and "The creating, willing, valuing *I* is the measure and value of things."[20] Henri de Lubac, S.J., wrote recently in his study of atheist humanism that it was nothing other than this urge to achieve complete freedom which "inspired the ideas of men like Dietrich Kerler, for instance, who declared in a letter to Max Scheler that 'even if it could be proved by mathematics that God exists, I do not want him to exist, because he would set limits to my greatness. . . .' And in a study which caused a great stir in Germany not long ago, Max Scheler went so far as to speak of postulatory atheism as the essential characteristic of modern man."[21]

The doctrinaires of this position, up to Sartre, who finds existentialism a humanism precisely because without God man

[17] André Malraux, *Le musée imaginaire de la sculpture mondiale* (henceforth cited as *M.S.*; see p. 224), p. 60. Paris: Gallimard (Galerie de la Pléiade), 1952.

[18] Ludwig Feuerbach, *Essence du Christianisme (Das Wesen des Christentums)*, authorized translation by Joseph Roy, p. 38 (Paris: Librairie Internationale, 1864). "L'être absolu, le Dieu de l'homme, c'est l'être même de l'homme" (p. 27). "Dieu est l'être de l'homme contemplé comme la plus haute vérité" (p. 44). Homo homini deus!

[19] Nietzsche, *Zarathustra*, p. 5.

[20] *Ibid.*, p. 24.

[21] Henri de Lubac, S.J., *The Drama of Atheist Humanism*, translated by Edith M. Riley, p. 27. London: Sheed and Ward, 1949.

must be more "human," more responsible, are many and quietly blasphemous.[22] But though Malraux could well be classed with them as a consequence of his own furious humanism, his tone, when he speaks with his own voice, is never blasphemous: if anything, it is nostalgic. Even the most violent of all his heroes, Garine, sends warnings of impending danger to missionaries laboring nearby, so that they can leave a troubled area in time. Claude is reminded of the face of an intelligent priest when he gazes at Perken, whose eyes "are firm and lost, full of memories."[23] The Christian doctrine of charity is beautifully told in *La condition humaine*.[24] In *L'espoir* the Catholic Loyalists are allowed a touching kind of eloquence. The pages on Romanesque and Gothic art in *Les voix du silence* are among Malraux's most poignant.[25] And all his virulence against the false values of the times is prompted as much by his anger at the modern betrayal of Christ as at the bourgeois usurpation of other real values. Malraux could accept Sartre's "il est très gênant que Dieu n'existe pas"[26] as his own, but for different reasons. It is as though it has never occurred to him that he could be a "croyant": the believer's world just does not happen to be his own. He has no thought of asking the believer to give up the things in which he believes; he allows a believer his own solution to the problem of fatality,[27] as, early in life, he had allowed the Catholic his Catholic answer to the modern world.[28] He has

---

[22] Their blasphemy is a more chastened thing, however, than Heine's "Don't you hear the bell? Down on your knees. The sacrament is being carried to a dying God" ("D'Allemagne depuis Luther," *Revue des Deux Mondes*, 1834, p. 408).

[23] André Malraux, *La voie royale* (henceforth cited as *V.R.*; see p. 224), p. 52. Paris: Grasset, 1930.

[24] *C.H.*, p. 76.

[25] *V.S.*, pp. 215-49. The tone of his *Le monde chrétien* (Paris: Gallimard [Galerie de la Pléiade], 1954) is almost worshipful.

[26] Jean-Paul Sartre, *L'existentialisme est un humanisme*, p. 35. Paris: Nagel, 1952.

[27] *V.S.*, p. 639.

[28] *J.E.*, p. 137 note.

no desire to be the cause of any doctrinal clash. He respects all
sincerity, no matter in whom it is found. He just does not happen to be Christian.[29]

2. MODERN CIVILIZATION AND RELIGION

Modern Western civilization, for Malraux, has lost a belief
in God, and with it has gone hope and strength. Europeans are
tired of themselves, tired of their crumbling individualism, tired
of their exaltation.[30] The absolute reality was God, then man;
but man died, after God, and Europeans are anxiously looking
for someone to whom they can entrust his strange inheritance.[31]
The power of the pope and of the king would today be vanity.[32]
In the face of its dead gods the whole West, after exhausting the
joy of its triumph, is getting ready to conquer its own enigmas.
"The West is stubborn, but sad, in search of its unity."[33]

The characters in the novels speak an almost strident form
of disbelief. Hong the terrorist has learned by heart a poem
recited by an old Chinese of the north:

> Je combats seul et gagne ou perds
> Je n'ai besoin de personne pour me rendre libre
> Je ne veux pas que nul Jésus-Christ pense
> Qu'il pût jamais mourir pour moi.[34]

---

[29] In his preface to Manès Sperber, ". . . qu'une larme dans l'océan," p. xiii
(Paris: Calmann-Lévy, 1952), Malraux writes: "Manès Sperber est israélite
d'héritage comme je suis catholique; non de foi. L'héritage rend fraternelles
à cet agnostique la grandeur et les failles laissées par l'incarnation d'une
grande forme de pensée." The Catholic religion is still "la nôtre," he says
in M.S., p. 13. Taking Marcel's classifications (Gabriel Marcel, Being and
Having (Etre et avoir), translated by Katherine Farrer, p. 205. Westminster:
Dacre Press, 1949), I would put Malraux in the second class, as one of those
who "will say that faith is a boon to its possessor, but that this boon is
denied to himself."

[30] T.O., p. 139.

[31] Ibid., p. 174.

[32] Ibid., p. 209.

[33] J.E., p. 134.

[34] Conq., p. 156.

Perken in *La voie royale* remarks: "Je n'aime pas qu'on soit dupe de Dieu."[35] In *La condition humaine* Tchen, first educated by missionaries, had quickly lost interest in any existing values and had sought to create his own. The old Gisors had taught him to think of that period of his life as no more than a cultivation of his sense of the heroic: "How shall a soul justify itself, if neither God nor Christ exist?"[36] When Tchen has started his plan to kill Chiang Kai-Shek, he meets the missionary Smithson, his former teacher, and to a question about what he has found to replace the faith he has lost, replies that he does not want peace but the opposite. And he resents the missionary referring things to God.[37] In *L'espoir* Ximenes, chief of the Civil Guard, a Catholic, finds an abyss between himself and Puig, an anarchist, who hates priests because he hates "a man who says that he forgives me for doing the best thing I have ever done. I don't want to be forgiven."[38] Later a peasant, violent against priests, shouts: "What does a priest tell you when he is confessing you? He tells you to repent. If so be there's a single priest who got a single one of us to repent of having defended himself—well, nothing's too bad for him. Because repentance— it's about the best thing a man has in him."[39] Ximenes reflects: "Why, oh why must people always confound the sacred cause of Him who at this moment watches us, with that of His unworthy ministers . . . of those among His ministers who are unworthy?" Manuel replies: "But Colonel, who but those unworthy ministers you speak of have made Him known to us?"[40]

The characters in *Les noyers de l'Altenburg*, none of them believers, listen rapt to the words of the savant Möllberg:

[35] *V.R.*, p. 20.
[36] *C.H.*, p. 79.
[37] *Ibid.*, pp. 198-99.
[38] Malraux, *L'espoir*, p. 31.
[39] *Ibid.*, p. 132.
[40] *Ibid.*, p. 130. See p. 220, the struggle of Guernico, the Catholic writer.

". . . from the Zend-Avesta to the Koran, man is incapable of being aware of the world except through a religion; in the twelfth century the whole known world thought religiously."[41] But they never solve the problem, "Existe-t-il une donnée sur quoi puisse se fonder la notion d'homme?"[42]

Briefly, in the novels the religious structure is dead; and except for a few Spaniards in *L'espoir,* the cast of characters is pitted against religion. It is in his great work on art, however, that Malraux describes with his own voice the decline of the religious absolute.

The pagan absolutes are obviously not what died in the West. It is Christianity that has paled, and Malraux's description of its decline is as follows:

The Romans had put value in mastery, and all Roman virtue was a form of constancy.[43] The Christian, on the other hand, even though capable of martyrdom, knew he was a sinner and needed grace to be constant. This grace had to be given to him personally: specific to the Christian religion is its individualization of the destiny of each man.[44] The variety of representations of Christ and of the Madonna in Christian art, for instance, is due to the fact that they are not natures, as Zeus and Venus, but particular persons, living particular events. "The Christian events are unique, and the Incarnation will not happen again. The Greek gods have attributes, the Virgin holds the Child and Christ carries His cross."[45] Hence the personal relationship of man with God that reconciles man to the absolute. "If the anguish of Medea, the grief of Niobe concern only

---

[41] *N.A.,* pp. 133-34.
[42] *Ibid.,* p. 150.
[43] *V.S.,* p. 215. See *T.O.,* pp. 53-59.
[44] See André Malraux, "Laclos"; in *Tableau de la littérature française,* pp. 417-28 (Paris: Gallimard, 1939). "Les péchés permettent à la vie chrétienne de n'avoir pas besoin des types, à travers quoi l'Occident ira de l'âme à l'individu" (p. 419).
[45] *V.S.,* p. 218.

themselves, the grief of the Virgin concerns all men. Christianity has not invented the scene, but it has invented this, that the
spectator be involved."[46] Redemption, a restoration of meaning
into life which gives importance to the individual, is the meaning of Christianity, and it lasted until the Renaissance.

Then, though in a Christian framework,[47] man became dis-
rupted with wars, with the discovery of Greece, the first "questioner of the universe,"[48] with Protestantism, with the craving
for new worlds.

Protestantism had its first fervor, but "l'éclair protestant"[49]
soon lost its force. The Protestant illumination was reduced to
candlelight . . . and in the Catholic world continued the dissolu-
tion of the divine, begun with the Greek questioning of the
universe.[50] The Jesuits could not save the divine, because they
substituted piety and means of propaganda for faith and evan-
gelical preaching.[51]

To replace the divine in their lives Europeans set out to
conquer the world. "Europe is going to separate itself from
Being, and become mistress of the world."[52] "A Christianity as
incapable of answering the timeless questions posed to man by
old age, by death and by all forms of destiny, as those Jesus

---

[46] *Ibid.*, p. 222.

[47] *M.S.*, p. 45; *V.S.*, p. 268.

[48] *V.S.*, p. 72.

[49] *Ibid.*, p. 466.

[50] *Ibid.*, p. 478.

[51] *Ibid.*, pp. 88-89. Baroque, for Malraux, "entendait moins . . . montrer ou rendre
témoignage que séduire." He therefore thinks unkindly of Jesuits, at least in
their influence on art, because baroque is, for him, pure Jesuit. See *ibid.*,
pp. 499, 528, 574. His distaste for any art of "propaganda" is clear in his
condemnation of Russia's prostitution of art: "There is no psychological
technique which is not, basically, a contempt for the buyer or the voter:
otherwise it would be useless" (postface to *Conq.*, p. 267). His ideas are
very close to those expressed by Marcel in *Les hommes contre l'humain*
(Paris: La Colombe, 1951) in the chapter entitled "Les techniques d'avilisse-
ment," pp. 33-46.

[52] *V.S.*, p. 466.

had posed, was going to try to forget them."[53] "The man once orientated by Being is going to be replaced by a man susceptible to ideas and to actions: the coordinating Value is broken into fragmentary values. What is in process of disappearance from the Western world is the absolute";[54] and for the first time in history a religion is not put to the test by another, but by a negation—by reason.[55] The eighteenth century has dawned.

As in the attack of Protestantism, there is an initial exaltation in the assault by reason[56] (and a communion of peoples because of the French Revolution). But it dies, and the most disastrous event in modern history takes place: the rise of the bourgeoisie. Had Napoleon been able to establish a real nobility and work out a real peace with the Church, he would have restored a hierarchy that could reach the souls of men, and have allowed reason a humble function.[57] But he failed, and the bourgeoisie are left to re-establish order.

The bourgeoisie becomes a caste, but is the first caste *sans valeurs*. They want a world of "facts, ordered by no transcendence, and subjecting them to nothing."[58] Man becomes a miserable offscouring who refuses demons and gods, heroism and pity.[59] The universalism of the Church, the heroism of soldiers and citizens, are of no interest to the bourgeois.[60] Now, for the first time in history, there is no noble goal for man: "La bourgeoisie ne suscitait aucune expression suprême particulière de l'homme."[61] The result? An agnostic civilization comes to

---

[53] *Ibid.*
[54] *Ibid.*, p. 479.
[55] *Ibid.*, p. 478.
[56] *Ibid.*, p. 480.
[57] *Ibid.*, p. 481.
[58] *Ibid.*, p. 490.
[59] *M.S.*, p. 41.
[60] *V.S.*, pp. 480-82.
[61] *Ibid.*, p. 485. One could add that the bourgeoisie is simply not interested in expressing itself at all.

term, the first. Agnosticism is not new, but never before did we see an entire civilization that was agnostic.[62]

Men of "facts" are men absorbed by science. But science answers no important question, and we are today left with the "débris" of the "progress" of the nineteenth century.[63] The old questions are more insistent than ever, and we have no answers: it has become clear that what the nineteenth century called progress demanded a heavy ransom. The world became dualistic again, the devil re-entered; and "the immense hope that man had put in the future was no longer valid."[64] We know now that "our peace is as vulnerable as the preceding ones, that democracy carries in it capitalism and totalitarian police, that science and progress permit atomic bombs, that reason fails to give an account of man."[65] The transforming power of man began by putting the world in the workshop, and ends by putting man himself in question. "Too strong to be a slave, and no longer strong enough to be a king, the individual . . . ceases to find [in his conquest] his *raison d'être.*"[66]

The eternal has left the world. Our generation is deaf to the Christian voice,[67] and modern civilization is in a paralysis that makes it incapable of giving any form to Christian values.[68]

3. MALRAUX AND CHRISTIANITY

Thus far Malraux's general survey of the decline of Christianity. There is nothing particularly new in it, and the lines

---

[62] *Ibid.,* p. 494. "L'agnosticisme n'est pas une nouveauté: le nouveau, c'est une civilisation agnostique." Malraux seems to contradict himself when he says (*ibid.,* p. 479) that our civilization "n'est pas celle de notre agnosticisme, mais celle de notre conquête du monde."

[63] *M.S.,* p. 60.

[64] Postface to *Conq.,* pp. 259-60.

[65] *V.S.,* p. 538.

[66] *Ibid.,* p. 601.

[67] *Ibid.,* p. 479.

[68] *Ibid.,* p. 493.

are so broad that there is little fault to find. To the careful reader, however, there is a point that is troubling, and that is that Malraux, though he understands how Christianity brought God into the world, does not seem to understand that Christianity also preserves God's transcendence. In *Le musée imaginaire de la sculpture mondiale* he finally makes a distinction that seems implicit in much of *Les voix du silence:* that there are religions in which God is an absolute, and there is one in which He is a Creator.[69] He has never really spoken of the God of Christianity as an absolute.

Egypt submitted itself to the irreducible order of the heavens[70]—an absolute; China to a force that dominates, that is jealous of individuality: a Chinese means to make himself a place rather than a means of action. All action is the penetrating presence of being, to accept which is to be serene:[71] again an "absolute." Buddhism aims at uneventful meditation.[72] The Fayum had a religion of death.[73] Byzantium, with a religion that was "almost ours," saw the world as mystery,[74] and Christ as "le Prophète absolu."[75] There is in these civilizations, as in African and all other civilizations until Christianity, except in Greece, "whose art is the first that seems to us profane,"[76] what Malraux never tires of calling "la paralysie sacrée."[77] They are religions where man is fixed, subject to an impersonal absolute, by yielding to which man both loses his individuality and finds his peace.

Christianity changes all this: not as Greece, but as irreducibly itself. There is a personal Redeemer, and the individual becomes important. "Profound though the Christian experience of the world be, it ends always in a solitude."[78] It is a sense

---

[69] *M.S.*, p. 60.
[70] *V.S.*, p. 72.
[71] *T.O.*, pp. 49-50.
[72] *V.S.*, p. 151.
[73] *Ibid.*, p. 187.

[74] *Ibid.*, p. 210.
[75] *Ibid.*, p. 212.
[76] *Ibid.*, p. 73.
[77] *Ibid.*, p. 79.
[78] Malraux, "Laclos," p. 419.

"of possessing a personal life, distinct in the eyes of God, which gives Christianity its force."[79]

In other words Christianity is, for Malraux, the first religious rupture with the absolute. A proof would be in Romanesque art, which, when compared to Byzantine (for him more Oriental than Christian), is a humanization of the divine; though still profoundly religious, it is no longer sacred.[80] "Le gothique commence aux larmes," and finally "le sourire va retrouver son droit d'accès à la cité de Dieu."[81] Giotto, caught by the Franciscan fraternity, expresses the love in Christianity, and in doing so "il est le Christianisme même."[82] And the day that Nicholas of Cusa[83] wrote that "Christ is perfect man," a Christian cycle closed at the same time as the gates of hell.[84] The result is that Western man is delivered into the individualism that finally played him false.

It would seem, then, that the Incarnation, for Malraux, finally ended in the triumph of man over God. To teach a man his worth as a man, because God thought him worth the price of His own Son, encouraged man's pretensions; and in man's gradual awakening God recedes into the world of dreams. "The delight of a god," says old Gisors in La condition humaine, "is to become man and yet to know that he can always reassume the power of his godhead; whereas man's dream is suddenly to become a god, and yet not to lose his personality—le rêve de l'homme, de devenir dieu sans perdre sa personnalité."[85]

Certainly we can admit that this can and does happen. It is, to talk in rawest terms, the old story of pride. But to blame

---

[79] *Conq.*, p. 121.
[80] *V.S.*, p. 230.
[81] *Ibid.*, p. 242: the smile of Rheims, for example.
[82] *Ibid.*, p. 259.
[83] Nicholas of Cusa (1401-1464), a German cardinal, who sustained ecumenical councils as against the power of the pope.
[84] *V.S.*, p. 84.
[85] *C.H.*, p. 273.

belief in the Incarnation for individualism of the sterile sort is to confuse a doctrine and a heresy. Surely, that man suddenly realize his worth in God's sight and become brother to Christ in the Incarnation is to become an individual in the authentic sense. To forget where this new value comes from, and focus on it to blur out the source, is to exaggerate one aspect of the truth, and is the *choosing* that is literally heresy. To exalt this personal value further, so that it becomes, though initially derived, now an absolute in its own right, is the mystery of the first sin. And, as Malraux sees vividly, in becoming a god man has betrayed man into the bankruptcy of values that is the modern world into which he was born. Nietzsche knew what it meant to the world when he spoke of the "death of God." There is no reason for absolute values when there is no absolute. Culture rests on valuations, and European cultures were Christian. Hence the breakdown of culture, and the loss of man's belief in himself, and the new kind of skepticism that is the mark of the twentieth century.

It is sad, however, to find that Malraux hears in "Christ is perfect man" the death sentence of God: for him it is the infiltration of freedom into the absolute, to such an extent that God is no longer seen as the giver of liberty, but as its enemy. It is seemingly contradictory that a man so passionate for freedom as Malraux must find in the death of the Christian God man's loss. It is melancholy that he will find a new absolute in the "quality of man," free from the bourgeois degradation of the individual. It is as though the first Christian reconciliation of God and man was only an illusory thing, only an uneasy truce until the human should gather its forces and slay the deliverer. Quite possibly, Christianity over the long centuries could be for Malraux "a liberator which raises up the means to free men from itself."[86]

---

[86] *V.S.*, p. 167.

Is it not closer to the truth that the Christian "grille" through which we still, despite ourselves, view the world[87] is wide enough to keep our vision alive to man's value? We have the scar of Christianity still in our flesh,[88] and it is the symbol that we are still eager to do battle for human liberty. Is it not these Christian values that keep the world restlessly in flames, vividly transformed though they be into such shapes as dialectic materialism and some forms of democracy? And it is Europe, the center of Christendom, which forged the formulas, though they be on Chinese or African or American or Russian banners.[89]

---

[87] *J.E.*, p. 137.
[88] *Ibid.*, p. 135.

[89] See *T.O.*, pp. 180 ff.

CHAPTER II

The Weight
of Destiny

With the demise of the absolute, enter *le destin*, *l'absurde*, and *l'angoisse*. *Le destin* is Malraux's word for all that we cannot escape and crave to escape: it is fatality, necessity, all the forces of deriding determinism.[1] It has many faces, but each age finds one pushed close to its own, and men have either fled into religion to escape it or have turned boldly to slay it, only to find it impervious to human weapons. Then, since all our actions, especially our thinking, are directed against it, our actions become absurd, because the absurd is the contradiction, the "divorce between man and his life, the actor and the set."[2] Finally, it is because we sense that we are acting absurdly that we experience what Sartre called "la nausée"; Malraux, eschewing the clinical, calls it, simply, *anguish*.[3]

---

[1] I shall usually translate the word *le destin* as "destiny," but the reader is warned to clear it of any of the pleasant overtones it can have in English. Malraux once uses it for a benign providence (*M.S.*, p. 60); normally it is fatality, even when he substitutes *la destinée* as in *V.S.*, p. 538.

[2] Albert Camus, *Le mythe de Sisyphe*, édition augmentée, p. 18. Paris: Gallimard, 1942.

[3] Emmanuel Mounier ("Interrogation à Malraux," *Esprit*, October 1948, p. 476) remarks of Malraux that "tous les thèmes que Sartre, quinze ou vingt ans plus tard acclimatera sous un plus lourd appareil, fulgurent déjà dans son oeuvre avec une étonnante précision."

What Malraux means by destiny is little discussed by French writers, doubtless because the theme is so current in so much European literature today. The idea bears examining, however, if only because so much of what Malraux writes depends on his understanding of what it means for man to be a creature of destiny.

The impact of destiny for Malraux is coincident with the resurgence of the irrational as a force in life. The rationalism of the eighteenth century ended in scientism, which has now proved false. The culture of the eighteenth century, therefore, had sought whatever might enforce its rationalism; we of the twentieth century are interested in "what reinforces our irrationalism."[4] We are caught by the deep and mysterious elements in man.[5] "The devil," as an idea possessing content, is now recognized again,[6] and Europe, "dying or not, but openly threatened . . . tends to think itself less in words of liberty than in terms of fatality."[7]

In *La tentation de l'Occident* the young Frenchman A. D. analyzes Western man, his dreams, his frenzy for action, and his passion for reality: his delirious craving "être quelqu'un,"[8] all in an effort to defend himself against that to which he has been promised, a "most bloody destiny."[9] The European, he says, hurls an *esprit* against the world, and is thereby duped. He would do much better to cultivate an Oriental *sensibilité* (an irrational), a sentiment of the secret rhythms that throb beneath his conscious life, which would deliver him from his unspoken fear of destiny by helping him yield to it—because, despite himself, Western man, after the treason of science, has found

---

[4] *V.S.,* p. 494.
[5] *Ibid.,* p. 535.
[6] *Ibid.,* p. 539.
[7] *Ibid.,* p. 540.
[8] *T.O.,* p. 101.
[9] *Ibid.,* p. 103; note that this was written in 1926.

an inevitable discord between his thought and his sensibilities.[10] "The world is reduced to an immense play of relations which no intelligence can fix, since it is their nature to change, to be constantly renewed. . . . To try to make the needs of the soul disappear . . . to rear a domain of the spirit and of the emotions which moves and changes in new relations and new births, in a life that belies all actions and all calculations" is the melancholy task of modern man.[11]

Even our ideas of ourselves are useless as a basis of judgment. We may try to judge another by his acts alone; we cannot do the same in our own case, because we all dream grand dreams which, leaving traces in our memories, fragmentize our waking thought, depriving it of coherence. There is not a European who has not conquered the world in his dreams, and all of this is a way of forming images of ourselves, so invading our consciousness that the mind can no longer grasp itself. There is nothing definite by which we can define ourselves. "Miserable actors who do not want to relinquish glorious roles, we are, for ourselves, beings in which sleeps the confused, formless cortège of our possible actions and of our dreams."[12] No matter how much I crave consciousness of myself, I know I am subject to a disordered series of sensations I cannot comprehend, which depend solely on my imagination, and the reactions they evoke. To think the sheer *moi* is to be obfuscated: what is elementary in our involuntary life links us to the universe, and on it depends a whole order of sensations which we have only guessed at so far.[13]

The Catholic religion, says Malraux, had taught that a man can judge his own acts, but that was not in order to understand them; the preoccupation was moral. "It is less important to know why a man kills another" for a Catholic, "than to know

---

[10] *J.E.*, p. 145.
[11] *Ibid.*, pp. 152-53.

[12] *T.O.*, p. 101.
[13] *J.E.*, pp. 139-44.

if the victim died saved."[14] But, up to 1957, Malraux maintains that there is no real way to know ourselves in our deepest
wellsprings: "We know that man does not have the same sort
of consciousness of himself that he has of the world, and that
each of us is for himself *un monstre de rêves.*"[15]

Hence the irrational makes nonsense of our attempts to
analyze ourselves. "Self-examination doesn't teach us about
man, but merely about the man who is in the habit of examining himself."[16] We are too much victims of an unintelligible
"historicity" (as the philosophers would put it) to hope for
"total reflection." "To wish to give precision to the self is to
scatter oneself in probabilities."[17]

What is this "irrational" that is so clamorous within the
individual nowadays, and so rife in our general culture?
Spengler, well known to Malraux, has described it in terms that
would be very acceptable to him. The "causality principle,"
based on clear concepts, and a systematization of the "idea of
nature" (the world as nature) is now yielding to the "destiny
idea." "The destiny idea demands life experiencing and not
scientific experience, the power of seeing and not that of cal-
culating, depth and not intellect. . . . Causality is the reasonable,
the law-bound, the describable, the badge of our waking and
reasoning experience. But destiny is the word for an inner certainty that is not describable. . . . Destiny itself (passed over
in silence by Kant and every other builder of rational world
systems with their armoury of *abstractions* because they could
not touch *life*) stands beyond and outside all comprehended
nature."[18] It is as though Garine is summing all this up when

---

[14] Malraux, "Laclos," p. 419.
[15] *V.S.,* p. 628. In *C.H.,* p. 68, each being is for himself "un monstre incomparable."
[16] *N.A.,* p. 115.
[17] *J.E.,* p. 143.
[18] Oswald Spengler, *The Decline of the West,* translated by C. F. Atkinson,
    Vol. 1, pp. 117-19. London: George Allen and Unwin, 1926.

he sighs: "Ah! Cet ensemble *insaisissable* qui permet à un homme de *sentir* que sa vie est dominée par *quelque chose.*"[19]

That "destiny is the irrational," that which cannot be reduced to human terms, is, of course, another way of saying that there is always mystery in life, something beyond the human grasp, because there is too much reality around us, and in us, and/or because we know that even to possess it all would not satisfy. Even the most lucid of Christians is by that fact the more dazzled by the mystery that is God: the difference in his life is that he knows that all its unintelligible elements are directed by a higher providence, which does not allow that he be just an accident in the universe.[20] The modern agnostic is also lucid: he knows what he does not know, but decides by that fact that it is all irrational. The tragedy is that his lucidity is in the service of the anti-intellectual.

Malraux is therefore fascinated with the unknowable, and so is our epoch, which "wishes to find in the arts of savages not only the expression of another world, but also the monsters of the depths in which psychoanalysis fishes."[21] There is in man "sa part nocturne,"[22] "la part de ténèbres,"[23] "la part obscure,"[24] "les profondeurs saturniennes,"[25] all summed up by Malraux in the expression *les mères (die Mütter).*

In discussing the feminine nude in Greek art he says that with it "the order of the stars to which it is linked had ceased to be fatality to become harmony. . . . The earth can be saved and extend to the cosmos its triumph over what had been the terrifying royalty of the Mothers."[26] Mystery, cosmic rhythms, the "quivering of the universal"—all of that is the domain of *les mères.*[27]

---

[19] *Conq.,* p. 170. (Italics mine.)
[20] *M.S.,* p. 61.
[21] *V.S.,* p. 573.
[22] *Ibid.,* p. 556.
[23] *Ibid.,* p. 574.
[24] *Ibid.,* p. 588.
[25] *Ibid.,* p. 622.
[26] *Ibid.,* p. 79.
[27] *M.S.,* p. 50.

Malraux is obviously referring to Goethe's *Second Faust* in speaking of the Mothers. Mephistopheles sends Faust to *die Mütter* to bring back Paris and Helen. "Descend, then," he says, "I could also say, Ascend. 'Twere all the same.

> Escape from the created
> To the shapeless forms in liberated spaces,
> Enjoy what long ere this was dissipated.
> There whirls the press, like clouds on clouds unfolding.
> Some in their seats, the others stand or go
> At their own will: Formation, Transformation,
> The Eternal Mind's eternal recreation.
> Forms of all creatures, they are floating free.[28]

There is more than poetry in all this. Whatever else "the Mothers" may mean, one thing is clear: they are goddesses in a realm of wraiths, of movement, of the irrational, beyond intelligence, and in the depths of nature—our own and the world around us. They are what Malraux calls the "organic and subterreaneous part of men."[29] They are symbols of the inhuman, such as that which, with the death of Greek harmony in the Far East, "burst out on the desert and found again the night of the sacred caverns";[30] and even modern psychology has not hesitated to use symbolisms of the feminine element to portray the unconscious, all that goes back into the womb, the biological, all that springs from collective human experience,[31] all that cannot be put into concepts.

---

[28] *Faust*, translated by Bayard Taylor, Part II, Act I, Scene 5, pp. 201-02. Oxford: Oxford University Press, 1952.

[29] Malraux, "Laclos," p. 420.

[30] *V.S.*, p. 167.

[31] See Jolan Jacobi, for example, in *La psychologie de C. G. Jung*, translated by Baillods, pp. 20-29 (Switzerland: Delachaux et Niestlé, S.A., 1950). Jung's psychology is illustrated by the use of the symbol Tai-ki-tu, the fundamental symbol of Chinese philosophy, made up of light and shadow. The light shows the masculine principle. All in it is directed, conscious. The dark is the feminine principle, the realm of the unconscious.

What has brought on this fascination with the irrational? *a movement that began again @ Romanticism*
Precisely the crumbling of any mental structures able to make
sense out of life. The modern obsession with psychology is not
a scientific luxury; the elements of the unconscious, of the inherited, of the obscurely felt, of, if you will, the *biological*—
all spring into agitated life when the mind can no longer give
the will a clear path to follow. It is not conscience that any
longer "doth make cowards of us all." It is consciousness: the
sense of being at the play of irrational forces, of the unconscious. "In accepting the notion of the unconscious," says Malraux, "Europe is deprived of its best arms."[32]

The Oriental man makes the effort to achieve an effortless
surrender to the irrational. But the Christian man of the West,
craving personal immortality and hopelessly committed to a
hope of making a meaning out of his life, yearns to transcend
it.[33] "With quiet distress, we are conscious of the way our
actions are opposed to our deeper life. This life, in its intensity,
cannot belong to the spirit. . . . For this deeper life is also
rudimentary, and its power, though giving the lie to the arbi-
trariness of our spirit, cannot deliver us from it. It says to the
spirit, 'You are a lie, the fabricator of lies, the creator of realities.' And the spirit answers, 'Yes, but at all times, when the day
ends, men have thought they saw riches in the shadow, and your
riches are only the last reflections of the day that is dying.' "[34]
Despite himself Western man cannot yield to the irrational.

The sense of personal fatality is strong in Malraux's novels.
In *Royaume farfelu* the army against Ispahan fails, not because
of any defense put up by the city, but because of scorpions:
even action without obstacles is blocked by irrational forces.[35]
In *Les conquérants* Garine, the man of action, knows that there

---

[32] *T.O.*, p. 94.
[33] *V.S.*, p. 628.
[34] *T.O.*, p. 215.
[35] André Malraux, *Royaume farfelu*. Paris: La Nouvelle Revue Française, 1928.

is in this life "a certain rhythm, a personal fatality, if you will, which I cannot escape." For him it is the urge that makes him play a dangerous game precisely because it is dangerous.[36] Clappique, in *La condition humaine,* gambling away the money that could save Kyo, experiences the "passive sensation of collapse he was looking for; again he seemed to be taking hold of his whole life, and suspending it above this derisive roulette ball. With its aid he satisfied, both at once, and for the first time, the two Clappiques that went to make up himself: the one that wished to live and the other that longed for destruction."[37] Kyo, in the beginning of the book, wants "to retain complete control of his life,"[38] and later in prison means to make dying an exalted deed, "the supreme expression of a life to which this death was so similar," in order to cheat the tragic indifference of death in snatching our masks from us.[39] But it is Kyo who, deceived in May, calls himself "a kind of absolute affirmation, the affirmation of a fool."[40] In *L'espoir,* Moreno, escaping prison, reports immediately back for duty. Later he says: "Now I know better. No one on earth can escape what's coming to him, *his truth,* and it isn't death, no, it isn't even suffering. It's the spin of a coin, of a penny."[41]

At times destiny takes more concrete forms, readily apparent. It can be, and often is, death. "You know as well as I do," says Perken in *La voie royale,* "that life has no sense; and living alone does not eliminate the preoccupation with one's own destiny. . . . Death is there, you understand . . . as the irrefutable proof of the absurdity of life."[42] As Perken dies,

---

[36] *Conq.,* p. 216.
[37] *C.H.,* p. 288. The scene is possibly the best example of the force of blind destiny in Malraux: see pp. 283-90.
[38] *Ibid.,* p. 52.
[39] *Ibid.,* p. 362.
[40] *Ibid.,* p. 67.
[41] Malraux, *L'espoir,* p. 166.
[42] *V.R.,* p. 157.

Claude, face to face with the futility of being a man, reflects that "almost all the bodies lost in the night of Europe or the day of Asia are crushed with the vanity of their lives, and full of hate for those who will awaken in the morning and console themselves with the gods. . . . No thought of the divine, no future reward, nothing can justify the end of a human life."[43]

In *Les noyers de l'Altenburg* Pascal's prison comes to Malraux's mind. "Imagine a large number of men in chains, and all condemned to death, every day some of them being butchered before the eyes of the others, and the others seeing their own plight in the plight of their fellows. . . . This is the picture of man's estate."[44]

But it is in *Les voix du silence* that Malraux gives a direct description of destiny. It is the consciousness of human servitude. "The word gets its accent from the fact that it expresses the mortal part of everything that has to die. There is in us a 'fault' that is sometimes glaring; the Saints called their despair 'aridity,' and 'Why hast thou forsaken me?' is, for Christianity, the cry of man himself. Time runs perhaps to eternity, certainly towards death. But destiny is not death, it is all that is imposed on man by the consciousness of his estate: even the joy of Rubens knew it, because destiny is deeper than misfortune. That is why man so often takes refuge in love against it;[45] that is why religions defend man against it, even though they do not defend him against death. . . . The consciousness we have of destiny, as profound as that in the East . . . is the Apparition of the Twentieth Century."[46] It is old age,[47] death without

---

[43] *Ibid.*, p. 268.
[44] *N.A.*, p. 289; see also p. 97. The quotation is from Pascal's *Pensées*, II, Chapter VIII, 13 in the original Port-Royal 1670 numbering. Pascal found his answer in the Gospel. Not so Malraux.
[45] For a particularly violent form of this see *V.R.*, pp. 230-32.
[46] *V.S.*, pp. 628-29.
[47] *J.E.*, p. 149; *V.R.*, p. 53; *C.H.*, p. 214.

meaning,[48] the multitudinous meanings in life that are incomprehensible to man,[49] a consciousness of the irremediable,[50] the sense of being a burdened inhabitant of an absurd universe,[51] the need to question everything.[52]

With destiny, the absurd. "The sickness of believers evokes God; that of agnostics, the absurd."[53] To act as though there are goals, to desire as though there is fulfillment, to think as though there are meanings (or at least as though they can be understood together: "to understand is above all to unify," says Camus),[54] all the time knowing the calloused intransigence of destiny—that is the absurd. "We know we did not choose to be born, and we do not choose to die. That we did not choose our parents, that we can do nothing with the passage of time. That between us and universal life, there is a sort of . . . gulf. When I say that every man is deeply conscious of the existence of fate, I mean he is conscious—and almost tragically so, at certain moments at least—of the world's independence of him."[55] As Camus says, "This thickness and strangeness of the world, this is the absurd."[56] (Yet, as man climbs out of his place in the universe, he is that much more slave to its laws.)

---

[48] *V.S.*, p. 466; see also p. 538.

[49] *Ibid.*, p. 322.

[50] *Ibid.*, p. 416.

[51] *Ibid.*, p. 523.

[52] *Ibid.*, p. 539. In the light of the above, Roger Stéphane in *Portrait de l'aventurier*, pp. 86-88 (Paris: Sagittaire, 1950) could not be more correct when he insists that the notion of destiny is important in Malraux, but he is inexact in seeing it as including an individual will to elaborate one's life in order to give it a fullness not due to external things. All men do not, according to his interpretation of Malraux, have a destiny—the irresolute man, for example. Rather we would say that for Malraux destiny is a given and belongs to every man. It does, for some, serve as a haircloth (as Stéphane suggests), though as a haircloth to be thrust off.

[53] *V.S.*, p. 416.

[54] Camus, *Le mythe de Sisyphe*, p. 32.

[55] *N.A.*, p. 127. In *T.O.*, p. 168, the absurd is the "point extrême du particulier."

[56] Camus, *Le mythe de Sisyphe*, p. 29.

The blinded Grabot in *La voie royale* does not answer the
question of Perken and Claude, "Qu'est-ce que vous êtes? Quoi?
Quoi?" He does not turn his face to Perken, who was near to
him, but to the light. Finally "his cheeks contracted; he was
going to speak. Claude waited for that voice, terrified. At last
he answered, . . . Rien. . . . He was a man who said his truth."[57]
(Camus remarks that when a man is asked what he is thinking,
and says "Nothing," he is expressing a void in him that is eloquent of a state of soul which is the first sign of absurdity.)[58]

And with the absurd, as is evident from the previous quota-
tions, anguish *(l'angoisse)*. "My father," says Kyo, "thinks
that anguish, the consciousness of one's own fatality, lies at the
roots of man, and is the source of all fears, even of that of
death."[59] His father's remedy was opium. "Fundamentally, the
mind only conceives of man as eternal, and so all consciousness
of this life can be nothing but anguish. Life should not be
thought by the mind, but by opium."[60] Nowhere is the keenness
of this anguish more brutally sharp than at Perken's death, when
he cries: "Il n'y a pas . . . de mort. . . . Il y a seulement . . .
moi . . . moi . . . qui vais mourir."[61]

The *condition humaine*[62] is a word, a cry, with no recourse
to philosophical arabesques: man cannot live according to
his hopes.[63]

In the modern literature which leans heavily on destiny, the
absurd, and anguish, the medium is most often the novel, the

---

[57] *V.R.*, p. 175.
[58] Camus, *Le mythe de Sisyphe*, p. 27.
[59] *C.H.*, p. 180.
[60] *Ibid.*, p. 400.
[61] *V.R.*, p. 268.
[62] *La condition humaine* and *la condition de l'homme* are phrases too frequent
   in Malraux to enumerate. *La condition de l'homme* appears first in *Royaume
   farfelu*, p. 81; the narrator had passed through a terrifying night trying
   to forget it.
[63] *Conq.*, p. 231.

play, or the poem, because this sad trio cannot be expressed conceptually, and must be lived in a full human context. This makes sense, if we remember that basically these ideas are negations. Kurt Reinhardt in *The Existentialist Revolt* points out that *l'angoisse* for the existentialists cannot be fully understood or explained, because "in Existential anguish man is not threatened by something definite (as is the case with 'fear'), something that could be named or defined. If the object of anguish could be thus determined, man might be able to rise in defense, ward off the danger and regain his security."[64] It is more the sense of the nothingness of things in our regard, the deception in formulas, that brings on the anguish; and in it all is what one might term the modern mystery of negation.

The theme of the anguish of man, conscious of the fortuitous and the fragile of his life, is not new, however, to literature or to philosophy. It is the stuff of tragedy, and enters philosophy with each assertion of *limit*, which is a profoundly negative concept. "You do not know," says Perken, "what a limited, irrefutable destiny is. It falls on you as a regulation falls on a prisoner: the certitude that you will be this and not something else, that you will *have been* this and not something else, that you will never have what you have not had. And behind you, all your hopes."[65]

Is all of this black pessimism? Should we not rather say that it is all so basically the human experience that it would be naive or unintelligently pious to reject it? Limit, negation, evil, mortality, are all necessary in the present *condition de l'homme.* The important thing, as a matter of fact, is not in what terms

---

[64] Kurt F. Reinhardt, *The Existentialist Revolt,* p. 234 (Milwaukee: Bruce Publishing Company, 1952). According to A. de Waelhens in *La philosophie de Martin Heidegger,* p. 121 (Louvain: E. Nauwelaerts, 1942), Heidegger would distinguish: the object of anguish is definite, always a *this* or *that,* but we cannot define the *this* or *that* in itself.

[65] *V.R.,* p. 85.

Malraux or any other modern has presented man's estate: what counts is what they offer as a retaliation to that estate—or as a way of transcending it. The sense of *angoisse* can, for example, goad the agnostic into finding some other higher value as a redemption: even the search of scientific knowledge seems to keep some men relatively balanced, and certainly in the full fervor of activity. It can drive the victim of modern society, the depersonalized man, into the tired old escapes—and the seven capital sins. The radio and the press, the cinema, pleasure, and all the *arts d'assouvissement* so scored by Malraux can take up his time and divert him from recognition of his unhappiness. It can gird the modern young European into arbitrarily choosing some such world concept as communism; the young American into hanging on, for example, to his youth and its privileges. It is unhappiness with incompleteness, the need of something that is not negation, the old instinct to "make something out of one's life" before it is too late: the recognition that self-possession is possible only with the possession of some truth and some love. If neither is possible, life is unbearable.

And for the Christian, or the man searching for God, anguish can be defined as the impulse of our natures which are restless until they rest in God.

It is stupid to say that to answer anguish with a value is the refuge of the weak: because each man will inevitably forge his own answer, despite the dare to imagine Sisyphus happy.

The irony, in Malraux's case, is that he should, despite himself, be such a creature of his times that his own acute sense of history does not attract his allegiance to the vitality of the religious past, not in order to live in an archaism, but to find a vision for the future, a possibility for the new world he so passionately desires to construct. But, individualist extraordinary, he must find a new absolute. It is his search, and his discovery of a new absolute, which will occupy us for the rest of this study.

A word more about the *destin-absurde-angoisse* chain. When all the poetry is stripped away and all the modern descriptions of *destin* are reduced to their quintessential element, there emerges the oldest and most recurrent of human themes: that the immortal will ever be stranger amid the mortal, that the finite cannot ever be filled except (paradoxically) with the infinite, that unhappiness is precisely not having what we are made for, and that happiness, even now, is only partially attainable, and that precisely in being sure that we are on the way to what we are made for. It could be that Malraux and other moderns say this better than it has ever been said, but one is annoyed with the suspicion that they frequently prefer the saying of it all to the solving of it.

PART II

L'anti-destin

CHAPTER III

Intoxication
with Action

Suicide could be one answer to the hopelessness of modern man as just described, one solution of the problems to which hopelessness gives birth. Camus has posed the question, "Does this absurdity call for suicide, or is there some hope on which to found an escape?"[1] All of the characters of Malraux would answer with Perken, "Suicide does not interest me, although death interests many of them."[2]

In fact, the very pressure of destiny feeds Perken's passion to live. "You do not know the exaltation that springs from the absurdity of life. . . . It is not to die that I think of my death; it is to live. Accepting the possibility even of losing my death has made me choose my life."[3] And Garine says, "There is no force, not even true life, without the certitude, without the obsession of the vanity of the world."[4] A tessera for Malraux's heroes could be Garine's "A life is worth nothing,—but nothing is worth a life."[5]

Orientated by the sense of death, the thought of Malraux is far from a call to annihilation; it is rather an invitation to

---

[1] Camus, *Le mythe de Sisyphe*, p. 21.   [4] *Conq.*, p. 229.
[2] *V.R.*, p. 20.   [5] *Ibid.*, p. 216.
[3] *Ibid.*, pp. 160-61.

furious activity—even to what one author calls *le paroxysme*,[6] a paroxysm, however, of intense consciousness.

1. "LES CONQUERANTS"

Les conquérants, which appeared in 1928 and which is Malraux's first serious novel, is cast in southeast Asia.[7] The action is the Chinese Revolution, under Sun Yat Sen. Garine, an adventurer, a *conquérant,* after a nonconformist past joins the Bolsheviks, comes to the Orient to support the Revolution, and as a propaganda expert works hand in glove with Borodin, a member of the Internationale. Sickness eats away his strength; and as the obsession of the need of activity against all forms of the absurd keeps mounting in him, plans go against him, terrorists complicate things, and, as the book ends, he arranges to go to England for his health, knowing all the time that he is going to die.

Garine is a man of action, a good organizer, with power to influence men.[8] He hunts trouble spots as a release of his force.[9] Brought to trial in Switzerland as a young man for financing a number of abortions, he is stupefied with the possi-

---

[6] Pierre-Henri Simon, *L'homme en procès,* troisième édition, p. 33. Paris: A la Baconnière, 1950.

[7] Malraux's *Lunes en papier* (Paris: Simon, 1921) is a fantasy in which little men, taking the names of the seven deadly sins, journey to the kingdom of death through all sorts of surrealist adventures. *Royaume farfelu* appeared in the same year as *Les conquérants,* and Malraux seemingly took it seriously himself for a while, because it was included last in his *Oeuvres complètes,* published by Skira in 1945. It is again "dream stuff," however, though the characters are this time normal humans. Pierre de Boisdeffre in *André Malraux,* p. 33 (Paris: Editions Universitaires, 1952) calls these two books "l'aventure imaginaire," whereas Malraux's friend Bernard Groethuysen, in reviewing *Royaume farfelu,* refuses to take it seriously (*La Nouvelle Revue Française* [henceforth cited as *N.R.F.;* see p. 224], April 1, 1929, pp. 558-63). In any case, the two works are not to our purpose in this book.

[8] *Conq.,* p. 49.

[9] *Ibid.,* p. 62. Years later Malraux was to write: "La patrie d'un homme qui peut choisir . . . c'est où viennent les plus vastes nuages" (*N.A.,* p. 66).

bility of condemnation, and fights his case. "To play his life on that dirty, ridiculous map, which he had not chosen, was intolerable to him."[10] He is disgusted with the trial and its participants, experiencing the kind of disgust one feels before all the great manifestations of human absurdity.[11] Finally, in China, he works for the Revolution, not because he loves mankind (the Chinese Tcheng-Daï finds him dangerous because he does not love the people),[12] but because the proletariat are so far the losers. He craves one thing, a certain form of power.[13] "There is a passion that is deeper than others . . . a passion that is perfectly desperate . . . one of the most powerful supporters of force."[14] And his strength comes from putting "a complete absence of scruples at the service of something other than his immediate interests."[15]

As he grows ill, the memory of his trial in Switzerland becomes keener, and through the last third of the book he muses more and more on his past life. He realizes that the absurdity he has found in it, in men trying to judge other men, in the whole social order, has spread for him to almost everything that is human.[16] But there is one thing in life that counts— "C'est de ne pas être vaincu."[17] His action has rendered him listless in regard to everything that is not action. He had joined the Revolution because success was far away: "Basically, I am a gambler. And like all gamblers I think only of gambling,

---

[10] *Conq.*, p. 65. The idea of a man consciously playing his life, writing his biography, occurs more than once in Malraux's early works. "Quels livres valent d'être écrits, hormis les mémoires?" says Garine (*ibid.*, p. 162). See *ibid.*, pp. 63, 99; *V.R.*, pp. 18, 24, 52, 264.

[11] *Conq.*, p. 169.

[12] *Ibid.*, p. 147.

[13] Vincent Berger (*N.A.*, p. 43) says: "L'autorité c'est bien, mais le pouvoir c'est mieux."

[14] *Conq.*, p. 68.

[15] *Ibid.*, p. 79.

[16] *Ibid.*, p. 170.

[17] *Ibid.*, p. 211.

stubbornly and passionately."[18] The Revolution disgusts him, especially when Borodin orders him to speak at Klein's funeral. "He [Borodin] is dominated by the intolerable Bolshevik mentality, by a stupid exaltation of discipline. That's his business. But I did not leave Europe in a corner like a bag of rags . . . only to come here to teach the word obedience, nor to learn it."[19] And he knows that the orderliness of thinking and the careful planning of the Revolution will finally make him *passé*,[20] because individualism is a "bourgeois malady." He is an individualist; and precisely because he is an individualist he is only temporarily useful.

At last, in a burst of lucidity, Garine explains his life. There is no force, not even *real life*, without the certitude, without the obsession, of the vanity of the world. His friend comments, "I know that the very meaning of his life is attached to that idea, that it is from the deep sensation of absurdity that he draws his force: if the world is not absurd, all his life has been spent in vain gestures."[21] The death of Klein had awakened in him something like a laugh—a sad comparison for an emotion in the presence of the death of a friend; "But there is no deep comparison possible for those whose lives have no meaning. They are walled lives. The grin of the world is reflected in them, as in a twisted mirror."[22] No! Force is the only thing: "On ne se défend qu'en créant."[23]

Is Garine the usual man without beliefs, and hence without scruple, who can therefore play the game of action, creating his own truth as he chooses? Partly. But so is the American gangster of the cinema. Garine is more. He is also part philosopher, and knows that, if life is absurd, then his actions against it are not. The fact that he is aligned with a "humanitarian" cause

---

[18] *Ibid.*, p. 216.
[19] *Ibid.*, p. 222.
[20] *Ibid.*, p. 223.

[21] *Ibid.*, p. 229.
[22] *Ibid.*, p. 230.
[23] *Ibid.*, p. 231.

does not change things: the Revolution is not for him a means to a better world. It is, for Hong and all terrorists,[24] as it is for Borodin and the party-line communists, a chance to seize power.[25] But for Garine the Revolution is simply a place for action, nothing more. The action happens to be against a state of affairs, which, like all states of affairs, is absurd. When the new Roman type of communist, already defending the gains of the Revolution at Moscow, comes to take over,[26] Garine will be left with nothing to do—except instigate a revolution against the Revolution—because, like Garcia in *L'espoir*, he knows that a "popular movement, or a revolution, or even a rebellion can hold onto its victory only by methods directly opposed to those which gave it victory."[27] His comparison of himself to a gambler is apt: the man with gambling in his blood is restless for action, as Malraux says through the words of Clappique in *La condition humaine*: "It is remarkable that it should so often have been said that a gambler's thrill at the tables lies in the hope of winning. It's as though you said that men fight duels so as to become champion fencers."[28] The thing that men seek in gambling is not the winning of a wager; what appeals to the gambler is the intensity of experience that the very risk of gambling involves.

Does this book contribute anything to Malraux's armory against destiny? I think not. We are not, of course, to look for a solution of the problem of destiny: were there a solution, there would be no destiny. Garine lives *with* absurdity in this book, acts fiercely and freely, jealous of not being conquered, even by his fears of destiny. Yet without *La voie royale* as a commentary one cannot escape taking Malraux seriously when he called *Les conquérants* "ce livre d'adolescent."[29] It is Perken

---

24 *Ibid.*, p. 120.
25 *Ibid.*, pp. 226-27.
26 *Ibid.*, p. 226.

27 Malraux, *L'espoir*, p. 90.
28 *C.H.*, p. 291.
29 Postface to *Conq.*, p. 247.

in *La voie royale* who will say clearly the things Garine is trying to say.[30]

2.   "LA VOIE ROYALE"

La voie royale has the same theme fundamentally as *Les conquérants*, though it is not the story of a revolution but of two Europeans plunging into the jungle along the Royal Road of Cambodia on the search of some Khmerian bas-reliefs, of their success, and of its fateful aftermath. In both novels, however, the chief character is a man of force, utterly lucid in the face of the absurd, who is overcome in the end by sickness. In *La voie royale* another character shares the stage, Claude Vannec; and there is in the character of Grabot, whom we meet only near the end of the book, the lurking presence of a twisted form of *Ubermensch*.

This is the best novel of Malraux in which to learn his *action* answer to destiny. Destiny and the absurd focus here on death. Claude "discovered what linked him to this man [Perken] who had accepted him for some reason he could not understand: it was the obsession of death."[31] The two share that obsession: Claude in a more frightened way than Perken, who, like Garine, is of the family of those who are hostile to established values, indifferent to society,[32] energetic,[33] with a taste for actions "liées à la conscience de leur vanité."[34] His motto is in the word *refus*[35]—and he lives in the keen awareness of death. He accepts

---

[30] Malraux has always included *Les conquérants* in collections of his work, but dropped *La voie royale* from the Pléiade edition in 1947, allowing it back in the Gallimard (1951) edition. He was right to do so. Without it the stammerings of Garine never become really intelligible.

[31] *V.R.*, p. 53.

[32] *Ibid.*, p. 20.

[33] *Ibid.*, p. 18: "C'était la seule personne du bateau qui prononçait le mot: énergie, avec simplicité." *Conq.*, p. 222: "Garine ne croit qu'à l'énergie."

[34] *V.R.*, p. 25.

[35] *Ibid.*

in life the vanity of his existence, as a cancer; he lives with this *tiédeur* of death in his hand.[36] There is no finality in life; that is the condition of his action.[37] And Claude has left Europe to escape hope and dreams[38] because he has the same kind of mentality.[39]

They go off into the insect-infested jungle, struggling against the subhuman.[40] Finding their sculptures, they head on toward the region where Perken had created a kingdom,[41] but are doomed never to get there. Reaching a Moi village, they join in the ritual of friendship with the natives, only to discover that another European, Grabot, is already there, held captive by the Mois after they had cruelly blinded him and put him to a tread-mill. The name of Grabot has been mentioned already, and in ominous terms, in the earlier action of the book. He is the equiv-ocal symbol of all that Perken envies and of all that Perken secretly fears.

Possibly Grabot is the only person Perken had ever ad-mired. He was a man of such fierce will power that he had blinded one of his eyes while in military service, to show up a doctor who had accused him of malingering.[42] Wild stories were spread about him in the East, maybe all true. Perken sus-pected that they might find him on their trip: he could be in the

---

[36] *Ibid.*, p. 55.

[37] *Ibid.*, p. 54.

[38] *Ibid.*, p. 58.

[39] Alvear remarks in *L'espoir:* "Il y a un sentiment très profond à l'égard de la mort, que nul n'a plus exprimé depuis la Renaissance. . . . la curiosité . . ." (p. 230).

[40] See W. M. Frohock, "Notes on Malraux's Symbols," *Romanic Review*, De-cember 1951, pp. 274-76, and *André Malraux and the Tragic Imagination*, pp. 52-55: a discussion on the force of insect life in Malraux's novels. See also *N.A.*, p. 91: "Mécanique et vivant . . . sur toute la terre s'étendait l'ordre des communautés d'insectes au-dessous de la mystérieuse liberté humaine. La mort était là . . ."

[41] *V.R.*, p. 86.

[42] *Ibid.*, p. 93.

region for purposes of eroticism, because power for him was defined by the possibility of abusing it. "Due to his courage," says Perken, "he is much more separated from the world than you or I, because he has no shadow of hope. . . . He is a man who is really alone—and like all solitaries, is obliged to furnish his solitude: he does it with courage."[43]

Grabot is, however, a shattered relic as he walks the tread-mill. He is dehumanized, a picture of the same fate that could now be waiting for Claude and Perken. As they watch for the moves the Mois will make, they talk of Death, the genius of the story. Says Perken:

> "You know as well as I do that life makes no sense. Living alone is no cure for being preoccupied with one's own destiny. Death is there, you understand, as . . . as the irrefutable proof of the absurdity of life. . . ."
>
> "For each man?" asks Claude.
>
> "For nobody," replies Perken. "It exists for nobody. Not many could live. . . . All think of the fact of . . . oh! how can I make you understand? . . . of being killed. That's it. And that's not what's important. Death is something else: it's the opposite. You are too young. I understood first when I saw old age in a woman. . . . Then, as though that warning wasn't enough, when I found myself impotent for the first time. . . . What weighs on me is my *condition d'homme,* that I grow old, that that cruel thing, time, grows in me like a cancer. . . . All these filthy insects around this lamp are subject to the light. Those termites we saw live in their hill, subject to their hill. . . . Life is a stuff, you have to know what to make with it, though you never really make anything with it: but there are several ways of making nothing with it. . . .[44] To live *in a certain way* you have to discard threats, failure, other men."[45]

---

43 *Ibid.,* pp. 142-45.

44 Mounier ("Interrogation à Malraux," *Esprit,* October 1948, p. 483) writes: "L'anarchisme de Malraux est l'incessante sortie d'hommes prédestinés contre les fatalités qui les cernent, et dont ils pensent sourdement qu'elles ne leur laissent d'autre victoire qu'un changement de fatalités."

45 *V.R.,* pp. 157-59.

The escape from the Mois is ironic: Perken has fallen on an upturned spear, and the wound becomes infected. He dies at the end of the book, watched by Claude. His face ceases imperceptibly to be human, and he cries: "Il n'y a pas . . . de mort . . . il y a seulement . . . moi . . . moi qui vais mourir."[46] Perken dies as he has lived—alone!

3. LA VOLONTE LUCIDE

La voie royale is centered on the uniqueness, the meaninglessness, and loneliness of death, and the accent which that gives to old age and impotence.[47] It is a parable with the same moral, though more clearly comprehensible, as *Les conquérants:* one way to live the nothingness of life is to be alert to it, defy it, and then to meet it. The only evil is to be a dupe of dreams.[48]

If there is a serious ethic in these two books, it is in the value of a refusal of all values except that of sheer choice, with a courageous insistence with oneself that one keep clear on the meaninglessness of life. We could ask with a communist writer, "Of what use can action be if it is without content? Freedom, if it is without content? Existence . . . ?"[49] but the answer of a writer like Malraux, at this stage in his development, would be, "Have I not been saying that it is precisely in seeking content that men have been dupes?" Garine pleaded with Tcheng-Daï, the true Oriental, to start believing in *existences*,[50] not causes, not a new world of new mental structures, certainly not a God.

No, the Malraux hero at this point is after only one value: to be authentic in facing the absurdity of life. The only virtue is courage, and its expression is in lucidity in action. Things are

---

[46] *Ibid.*, p. 268.
[47] *Ibid.*, p. 53; see also p. 89.
[48] *Ibid.*, p. 20.
[49] Roger Garaudy, *Literature of the Graveyard*, p. 34. New York: International Publishers, 1948.
[50] *Conq.*, p. 119.

to be called by their right names.[51] "Many sick men," said Nietzsche, "have been amongst them that make poetry and languish after gods; these hate with a terrible hate him that knoweth, and that youngest of all the virtues which is honesty."[52] (Most rebels pride themselves on honesty!)

There is no *doctrine* worthy of adherence.[53] The young Malraux had already written of the youth scattered all over Europe, held to life by only one thing: the *volonté lucide* to do combat for want of a doctrine.[54] And he had told Julien Green that between the ages of eighteen and twenty-five life is a market where one buys not with money but with acts—and most men buy nothing.[55] This action is the one thing necessary. It is endowed with the fervor religion could give; it is free with the unscrupulousness of skepticism: but it is neither. It is simply action.[56]

The finality of individual actions may vary. That is unimportant. What is important is to choose, and no Malraux hero has any regrets. After all, any choice leads to absurdity. Life demands one thing: a taste for action linked to the deep consciousness of its vanity.[57] There is only occasional hostility toward those who have chosen otherwise, because all action is Manichean[58] and no one is to be blamed for the consequences of his choice: Garine says of Hong that there are few enemies

---

[51] If he is lucid enough, an assassin, for example, will speak of murder, not crime: see *Conq.*, p. 73. See Friedrich Nietzsche, *Par delà le bien et le mal (Jenseits von Gut und Böse)*, translated by G. Bianquis, p. 109 (Paris: Aubier, 1951): "Der Verbrecher ist haufig genug seiner That nicht gewachsen: er verkleinert und verleumdet sie."

[52] Nietzsche, *Zarathustra*, p. 25.

[53] Garine, in *Conq.*, p. 122: "Mon hostilité profonde va moins aux possesseurs qu'aux principes stupides au nom desquels ils défendent leurs possessions."

[54] *J.E.*, p. 148.

[55] Julien Green, *Journal*, Vol. 1, p. 23. Paris: Plon, 1930.

[56] Malraux, preface to Sperber, ". . . *qu'une larme dans l'océan*," p. xix.

[57] *V.R.*, p. 25.

[58] Malraux, *L'espoir*, p. 117.

he understands better.[59] Let each choose for himself; and if there is to be any talk of finality, let action be for this: to convert as wide a range of experience as possible into conscious thought—nothing else.[60]

In deciding to throw himself with the bomb under the car of Chiang Kai-Shek, Tchen feels a complete freedom and exhilaration. When asked if he wishes to make terrorism a kind of religion he answers: "Not a religion. The meaning of life . . . the complete possession of myself."[61] And Ferral looks for the same thing in *his* kind of action, eroticism.[62] "Action alone fulfills his life and satisfies a white man. What should we think of a painter of whom we are told that he had not painted any pictures?"[63]

The deep consciousness of the self that is bred of action haunts *La voie royale* in the equating of action and sexual experience. There is an erotic pleasure in trying to tear loose the stubborn bas-reliefs from the old temple,[64] a sexual fury in fighting failure.[65] Perken throws himself "sexually" into his advance against the Mois.[66] In fact, the atmosphere of sexuality

---

[59] *Conq.*, p. 157. Scali, in *L'espoir*, p. 107, before the dead enemy pilot, is suddenly silent: he and the man before him had each *chosen*. Kassner (André Malraux, *Le temps du mépris* [henceforth cited as *T.M.*; see p. 224]; in *Romans, André Malraux*, p. 544. Paris: Gallimard, 1951) and his Nazi questioner look at each other with tired disgust. Picon in *Malraux par lui-même*, p. 43, recalls that Malraux does not really describe the enemy in his books, suggesting as the reason, that he knows "qu'il est bien peu de routes sur lesquelles la noblesse humaine ne puisse pas s'engager." At this point "la noblesse humaine" is one thing: courage to face absurdity.

[60] Malraux, *L'espoir*, p. 282.

[61] *C.H.*, p. 221. Has Malraux forgotten that he wrote in *N.R.F.* for February 1, 1928, p. 251: "Il est à remarquer que les écrivains qui trouvent à la mort, ou plutôt au chant de la mort, un caractère voluptueux, se gardent bien de considérer la leur"?

[62] *C.H.*, p. 276.

[63] *Ibid.*, p. 271.

[64] *V.R.*, p. 127.

[65] *Ibid.*, p. 192.

[66] *Ibid.*, p. 197.

penetrating this book is proof enough that if there is any finality at all in action, it is "transformer en conscience une expérience aussi large que possible."[67]

Lucidity, action, live consciousness, possession of self. If the individual is thrown back on himself by the disappearance of all valid goals, then it is there that he is to make his peace. Claude reflects that Perken "said the word peace the way he would have said action [*agir*]."[68]

It is the function of death to make all of this clear. Death is, with a Satanic difference, what it is for the Christian: that which gives a sense to life. "If the world makes sense, death should find its place there, as in the Christian world . . . if not, life is part of death."[69] The Christian sees in his death a release to another life, and that new life gives meaning to this one. The hero of Malraux sees in it the substance of this life—and in facing it, finds a release from the stupid slavery of this life. "You do not know," says Perken, "the exaltation that comes from the absurdity of life. . . . There is something . . . satisfying in the extinction of a life."[70] (We have seen, however, that he found no satisfaction in his own death.)

Suicide is not the action called for: one would kill oneself only to exist,[71] and that would be futility confounded. "It is not to die that I think of my death: it is to live."[72] Memento mori!

Are we to find in all this merely the French preference, remarked on by Perken, for those who attach importance to playing their role,[73] and dismiss it out of court as nonsense?

------

[67] Malraux, *L'espoir*, p. 282. See also *V.R.*, pp. 108, 145, 156, 225; also *Conq.*, p. 214, and *T.M.*, p. 579: Kassner steels himself for a plane crash: "Tous ses sens étaient maintenant ramassés, de façon très précisément sexuelle."
[68] *V.R.*, p. 87.
[69] *N.A.*, p. 141.
[70] *V.R.*, p. 161.
[71] *Ibid.*, p. 20.
[72] *Ibid.*, p. 161.
[73] *Ibid.*, p. 18.

Does "an ethic of decadence rule over Malraux's world as it ruled over the Satyricon of Petronius?"[74]

Certainly Malraux is not constructing a philosophical system, and it would be unfair to judge him by a system. He is, however, in a philosophical climate, in what he is portraying in these two books. It is only necessary to glance at Heidegger, who antecedes Malraux, and Sartre, who follows him, to find serious attempts to justify an "authentic" life lived in the keen anticipation of death with no reference at all to a hereafter. To be "authentic" is to restore the real *I*, and release it from being a thing, the impersonal *man*, the *on*, of pedestrian, preoccupied existence.[75] This revitalization of the smothered self can be achieved by a lucid confrontation of my own death, a possibility where my full self is engaged, and an experience that is unavoidable, uniquely mine, and the end of all my other possibilities.[76] If I penetrate myself with the sense of death, and live in conformity with its meaning, I achieve validity as a man. Daily existences are a flight from it; authentic existence will be an unfaltering acceptance of it.[77]

My life is to realize possibilities. Not for a cause: Rachel Bespaloff says of Garine that the "cause" furnished him with but a pretext for accomplishing his fullest possibilities. "Consumed by the idea of a certain kind of power, this man, a profound stranger to the soul of the community, cannot feel he exists except by multiplying his own life in the lives of a great number of people, by fashioning the human material into a crowd that is on fire and yet subject to him."[78]

---

[74] Garaudy, *Literature of the Graveyard*, p. 37.
[75] See De Waelhens, *La philosophie de Martin Heidegger*, p. 72.
[76] *Ibid.*, p. 144.
[77] *Ibid.*, p. 146.
[78] Rachel Bespaloff, *Cheminements et carrefours*, p. 32 (Paris: J. Vrin, 1938), in *Notes sur André Malraux*, a perceptive examination of *Les conquérants, La voie royale*, and *La condition humaine*.

Whatever form the pursuance of the "possibilities" of life takes, the modern philosophers reject suicide as one of them. "Modern pessimism rejects suicide with a striking unanimity. Camus, as an absurd acquiescence to the absurd; Sartre as a contradiction, Malraux as a deception."[79] Heidegger rules it out because, although my death is the height of all my possibilities, it is also their effective annihilation. I must rather *await* my death, awake to the full nothing that it is. I can then see the profound emptiness there is in activity, accept this, and be free to act with a detachment that is unequaled. The supreme possibility of my existence is to exist no more. I therefore accept all possibilities, but no longer run the risk of being the dupe of any of them. I am consequently a *free* man, no longer haunted by regret, no more pressed down with any urgency in any jobs to do, completely myself.

This, in turn, gives me great tolerance toward the actions of others—because my liberty before death is untrammeled by other values.[80] I possess myself—with the courage of a man baptized by death and endowed, by that somber baptism, with the key of life.

Sartre has summed up the Malraux hero of these two books with praise. "He has lived out to the end an impossible condition: fleeing and seeking solitude, living to die and dying to live, convinced of the vanity of action and of its necessity, trying to justify his enterprise in assigning it a goal he does not believe in, seeking the total objectivity of the result only to dilute it into an absolute subjectivity. . . . At the price of an unbearable tension, this man has kept before him, simultaneously, and in their very incompatibility these [terms of contradiction]. He has been the permanent consciousness of their incompatibility. . . . He proves that it is the impossibility of existing that is

---

[79] Mounier, in "Interrogation à Malraux," *Esprit,* October 1948, p. 479.
[80] De Waelhens, *La philosophie de Martin Heidegger,* pp. 147-48.

the condition of his existence, and that man exists because he *is* impossible."[81]

I suppose that the best answer to the macabre cheerfulness of this whole philosophical climate is to say that a man cannot, simply cannot, live in it. Most men will either remain suffocated in the daily life Heidegger and Malraux decry, or look for other values than the existential *volonté lucide* for authenticity. The "doctrine" of action for authenticity as here described may sell books. It may even call for adherents for a while: but it will not call many to a new banner, because the banner has nothing written on it except *death*. Malraux himself, as a matter of fact, saw this in 1926 (four years before *La voie royale*) when he wrote: "In destroying God . . . the European spirit has anni- hilated all that could oppose man: but arrived at the end of its efforts, as Rancé before the body of his mistress, it finds only death . . . [and] it discovers it can no longer find anything worth having. Never has it made so troubling a discovery."[82]

Nietzsche had sung that he was a *creator* who had broken into pieces the tables of values of all creeds;[83] he proclaimed freedom "and an unholy Nay even to duty."[84] This was the first preachment of "authenticity" in the atheistic sense. "My destiny has decreed that I be the first honest man. . . . It is I who have discovered the truth, been the first to see a lie within a lie, to smell it with my nose."[85] But Nietzsche had to invoke something fantastic, his doctrine of the "eternal return" of the Superman, in order to save his song from trailing off into the desert. The argument of death was too strong even for him.

---

[81] Stéphane, *Portrait de l'aventurier*, précédé d'une étude de Jean-Paul Sartre, pp. 26-27.

[82] *T.O.*, pp. 215-16.

[83] Nietzsche, *Zarathustra*, p. 14.

[84] *Ibid.*, p. 20.

[85] Friedrich Nietzsche, *Ecce Homo*, translated by Alexandre Vialatte, p. 164. Paris: Gallimard, 1942.

The moderns are not nearly so romantic as Nietzsche, nor so triumphant in their accent. They have no belief in the unlimited "possibilities" of a Superman. They are attempting to do only one thing: to be honest in the face of all dead values, sterile though the heroism to which they call may be. With the one element in man that makes him a man, his liberty, they hope to achieve authenticity. But even liberty, Malraux says, "isn't a bargain; it's just liberty."[86]

The "First Immoralist" left an investment, but his descendants are receiving sorry dividends. There is courage in the attempts of modern atheists and agnostics to gather up the "small change" of the absolute, if only because that attempt lays them open to the charge of cheating: if life has no meaning—well, it has no meaning. Malraux never leaves them entirely. But *Les conquérants* and *La voie royale* are his only period of full endorsement of the tortured *non serviam* that is one type of authenticity. With *La condition humaine* he will begin to find meaning, not only in action as an expression of liberty, but in that expression of liberty as a contribution to a *cause* which offers some hope, something in the future.

When Sartre endorsed William the Silent's "You don't have to hope in order to act," he meant that the exercise of liberty is enough, without any hopeful prediction of the future. Malraux will not predict the future; but he will add to action the hope of a better world.[87]

---

[86] *C.H.*, p. 238.

[87] Sartre, *L'existentialisme est un humanisme*, p. 54. "D'abord je dois m'engager, ensuite agir selon la vieille formule 'il n'est pas besoin d'espérer pour entreprendre.' Ca ne veut pas dire que je ne doive pas appartenir à un parti, mais que je serai sans illusion et que je ferai ce que je peux. Par exemple, si je me demande: la collectivité, en tant que telle, arrivera-t-elle? Je n'en sais rien, je sais seulement que tout ce qui sera en mon pouvoir pour la faire arriver, je le ferai; en dehors de cela, je ne puis compter sur rien."

CHAPTER IV

Action with Content

Compared to his subsequent work, *Les conquérants* and *La voie royale* are a dry run for Malraux. *La condition humaine,* another series of days in the Chinese Revolution, is suddenly a work of stature. It established Malraux as a great French author, winning the Prix Goncourt the year it appeared, 1933. Our interest in it is not literary, but it would be misleading to work the kernel of thought out of it without reminding the reader that, though the process may not be one of falsification, it is necessarily one of abstraction. This is a work of Malraux which must be read and reread.

1. "LA CONDITION HUMAINE"

Death, that concretization of the absurd, had dominated *La voie royale*. It is shot through the whole fabric of *La condition humaine*. Boisdeffre calls it "le principal personnage de ce drame."[1] The book opens with a crime and ends with an execution, and for the leading characters death is the inevitable finish to all their acts—not the death of the ordinary man, in a hospital, or surrounded by loved ones (such scenes never occur in Malraux), but death by violence, surrounded by terror and cruelty and torture.

---

[1] De Boisdeffre, *André Malraux*, p. 49.

Yet there is an advance in the thought of this book over that of the two previous ones. Where Garine, locked in a sort of interior absolute, rejected all justification for being a revolutionary except the action of revolution itself, in which is to be found "the little known vice, courage,"[2] the revolutionaries in *La condition humaine* have goals that can be formulated. Where Perken was almost artificially made to die crying out his anguished "ma mort," the deaths in *La condition humaine* are sacrifices. It is not long that action can sustain itself in a vacuum: the great actions of this book, save one, are actions for ideals, consciously embraced. There is, of course, the continued presence of the absurd, of the *present* accent on human things, the impossibility of escaping meaningless situations; but none of that is any more the complete formula to sum up life. The characters have elected a cause, and human dignity begins to emerge as a *value*.

By the same token, the book is trying less to prove anything than to present life during a revolution.

It has one heretic, Tchen, the murderer of the opening pages. He had in the beginning given his allegiance to the Revolution in order to lessen the sufferings of the poor,[3] but his crime suddenly tears him from ordinary life, hypnotizing him with a new ideal, violence. He has ceased to be like the rest of men. "I'm unbelievably lonely," he blurts out to old Gisors. "The others don't understand. They don't know that it's the first time. . . . One may feel great contempt for the man one kills, but less than for other people." Gisors asks, "For those who do not kill?" He answers, "For those who do not kill, for the uninitiated." Finally choosing terrorism as his line of action, he says: "I know how to treat women when they develop proprie-

---

[2] *Conq.*, p. 149. Recall: "Il y a tout de même une chose qui compte dans la vie: c'est de ne pas être vaincu" (*ibid.*, p. 211), and Perken: "le courage compense" (*V.R.*, p. 156).

[3] *C.H.*, p. 200.

tary ideas: live with them. Does that apply to death? . . . Is that a kind of mating, too?" Gisors reflects that what Tchen wants more than anything else is to get himself killed;[4] his instincts now find satisfaction in nothing except destruction.[5] He finally gets his wish when, wounded in his unsuccessful attempt to assassinate Chiang Kai-Shek, he puts a revolver into his mouth and pulls the trigger "without knowing it."[6]

The absurd of death had become for Tchen a fascination, the call to a certain kind of ecstasy.[7] It is something like a sacrament of life; he who gives it receives from it the grace of election, as it were, and becomes one of the initiated, living intensely in the expectation of his own moment of destruction.[8]

We said that Tchen is a heretic: he is the only hero in the book who forgets that his death is to be in the service of a cause. Actually, Tchen is Malraux's last character to find in death the opportunity to achieve full freedom. And in this book, after his murder for the common cause, he slides into the margin of the activities of the others, permanently estranged. Malraux may understand such a character. But the "authenticity" it portrays blows up with the exploding bomb. He commits suicide "without knowing it."

There is one other marginal character, but he is a type of old Oriental rather than a real revolutionary. He is Gisors, Kyo's father. When his son's body is brought back to him, he finds "that there's something beautiful about being dead,"[9] and

---

[4] *Ibid.*, pp. 71-75.
[5] *Ibid.*, p. 171.
[6] *Ibid.*, p. 280.
[7] *Ibid.*, p. 179.
[8] Kassner (*T.M.*, p. 554) finds a strange exaltation when he is near death: it is like music. The idea of a man suddenly transformed by his crime came to Malraux early. In *T.O.*, p. 214, he writes: "Le meurtrier d'une vie, ou d'autres choses plus secrètes qu'ignore la main grossière des lois, peut se retrouver pénétré de son crime, ou du nouvel univers qu'il lui impose." See *N.A.*, p. 78.
[9] *C.H.*, p. 373.

keeping vigil, reflects that "men should be able to comprehend that there is no reality, but that only worlds of contemplation exist, either with or without opium, where all is vain."[10]

In Gisors Oriental detachment reasserts itself; he is almost a classical character. But for the others, for the heroes and the would-be heroes, death makes sense because there is something worth dying for. Hemmelrich, tied down by circumstances to his wife and child, curses the universe for "stripping him of the sole dignity he possessed, that he could possess, his death,"[11] his contribution to the Revolution. Kyo awaits death lying on a prison floor. He would die having fought for what

> in his own day would have possessed the strongest meaning and in-
> spired the most splendid hope. . . . What would have been the value
> of life for which he would not have accepted death? . . . This death
> of his was hallowed by the touch of common brotherhood, by con-
> tact with a gathering of broken men whom future multitudes would
> recognize as martyrs, whose bloody memory would bring forth
> golden legends.[12]

Katow, his friend, in the most moving of all the incidents in Malraux's work, suddenly terrified at being thrown alive into the boiler of a locomotive, overcomes his fear and gives the cyanide with which he has equipped himself to two fellow prisoners, rising superior to the "solitude that is the accent of death."[13]

What precisely is the value for which the heroes of *La condition humaine* are willing to die? It is the ideal of the Revolution, as they understand it. All the characters except Ferral, who in his craze for power is reduced to the stature of a little man pleading a tawdry case, are fighting on the commu-nist side. Not that the book is an argument for communism: Frohock remarks very wisely that "politically, *Man's Fate* is a

---

10 *Ibid.*, pp. 398-99.
11 *Ibid.*, p. 217.

12 *Ibid.*, pp. 361-62.
13 *Ibid.*, pp. 364-69.

very ambiguous book."[14] Rather, Malraux uses the action of the Revolution to say things about people who are working for a better world.

This world is defined as that in which *human dignity* is restored. It had been hinted at in *Les conquérants:* Hong gets his strength, not from hating the happiness of the rich, but because he despises the respect they have for themselves. "Un pauvre . . . ne peut s'estimer."[15] But Hong's sentiments are negative, and for him the Revolution becomes a fraternity of hate, "la haine . . . tenace, fraternelle."[16] Only in *La condition humaine* is the drive to revolution something positive.

In a rare passage at the end of the book old Gisors, who is as much Malraux's mouthpiece as any other character in any other of his books, says that

> a civilization is transformed when its most painful element, the slave's humiliation, the toil of the modern workman, suddenly becomes a value, when the victim no longer seeks to escape this humiliation but to find in it his salvation, no longer seeks relief from work but discovers in it his *raison d'être.* The factory, which is still so much like a church of the catacombs, should become what the cathedral was, and men should see there, instead of gods, the human force that is battling the earth.[17]

"There is no dignity, no real life possible for a man who works twelve hours a day without knowing what he's working for," says Kyo.[18]

---

[14] Frohock, *André Malraux and the Tragic Imagination,* p. 82.

[15] *Conq.,* p. 155.

[16] *Ibid.,* p. 154.

[17] *C.H.,* p. 394. In *T.M.,* p. 570, Kassner remembers a play "qu'on avait écouté jusqu'à la Caspienne et jusqu'au Pacifique, parce qu'elle donnait au travail son sens et sa dignité."

[18] *C.H.,* p. 80. See Malraux, *L'espoir,* p. 64, where Magnin says: "J'ai dirigé beaucoup d'usines; un homme comme nous, qui a toujours été intéressé par son travail, se rend mal compte de ce que c'est que passer une vie entière à perdre huit heures par jour. . . . Je veux que les hommes sachent pourquoi ils travaillent."

The value sought by the men of *La condition humaine* is therefore human dignity, which, negatively, is the opposite of humiliation,[19] or, positively, the recognition of those one loves.[20] It is also the right to "battle the earth."[21] Malraux will formulate this value later in his most famous phrase, "the honor of being a man,"[22] and, as we shall see, to "battle the earth" in a "communion of effort" (where each individual recognizes the worth of each other) is to live up to that honor. Gisors' words are the first hint of Malraux's future gospel.

Jean-Paul Sartre in his treatise on *Ma mort*[23] refers to Malraux's *humanization* of death with appreciation, but with a warning that death cannot, or at least should not, be looked on as a human or as a personal thing.[24] Death is not uniquely *mine*, because whether I die "to edify, to bear witness, to be patriotic, anybody else can die in my place. . . . In a word, there is no personalizing virtue that is particular to *my* death."[25] We are inclined to look on our deaths as personal only because of our unwarranted habit of giving a "subjectivity" to ourselves.[26] The possibility of death means one thing: "that I am biologically only a relatively closed system, something only relatively isolated, because my body belongs to the totality of existents."[27]

Sartre, of course, understands Malraux in this matter, and is perfectly right in saying he "personalizes" death. In *Les conquérants*, *La voie royale*, and *La condition humaine* each

---

[19] *C.H.*, p. 343.

[20] *Ibid.*, p. 56. See Valérie's complaint against Ferral (*ibid.*, p. 258).

[21] The reader's attention is called to the phrase, "battle the earth—en lutte contre la terre": an artistic "style" will be just such a battle in *Les voix du silence*.

[22] *V.S.*, p. 623; see also pp. 266, 417.

[23] Jean-Paul Sartre, *L'être et le néant*, vingt et neuvième édition, pp. 615 ff. Paris: Gallimard, 1950.

[24] Of Malraux's personalization of death Sartre remarks: "Une semblable théorie, à ce qu'il parait d'abord, ne peut que nous séduire" (*ibid.*, p. 616).

[25] *Ibid.*, p. 618.

[26] *Ibid.*, p. 619.

[27] *Ibid.*

death and each mention of death (except in the case of the Oriental Gisors) is something unique and terribly personal. In fact, if there is any constant rhythm to Malraux's work so far, it is the pulsing of individual consciousness through the whole being of every one of his characters. The previous chapter has shown this, and the section on "Eroticism" which follows will illustrate it further. Also, the intense sense of isolation that so many characters feel is another sign of the same thing. In *La condition humaine* at least six of the characters experience this *personal* estrangement. Not only Tchen feels apart; Kyo knows "la solitude,"[28] Gisors feels a "solitude totale,"[29] Ferral is crazed with the obsession of "une vie individuelle, isolée, unique, comme la mienne,"[30] for Katow "la pire souffrance est dans la solitude qui l'accompagne,"[31] Clappique has "une conscience aiguë de sa solitude."[32] Clearly, heightened self-consciousness is characteristic of Malraux's *dramatis personae*—and not a few have it excruciatingly, from remembering, like Garine, that they are going to die.[33]

Also, in giving meaning to the deaths in *La condition humaine* Malraux gives death what Sartre denies it ever has, "the character of an harmonious ending."[34] It may be, even for Malraux, absurd that we are born and absurd that we die;[35] even up to his most recent published writings he finds man an

---

28 *C.H.*, p. 67.
29 *Ibid.*, p. 84.
30 *Ibid.*, p. 144.
31 *Ibid.*, p. 250; see also p. 247.
32 *Ibid.*, p. 307.
33 "Toute l'Asie moderne est dans le sentiment de la vie individuelle, dans la découverte de la mort" (*Conq.*, p. 120).
34 Sartre, *L'être et le néant*, p. 617: "Ce qu'il faut noter tout d'abord c'est le caractère absurde de la mort. En ce sens, toute tentation de la considérer comme un accord de résolution au terme d'une mélodie, doit être rigoureusement écartée." Again: "[La mort] est l'inhumain par excellence puisque c'est ce qu'il y a de l'autre côté" (p. 615).
35 *Ibid.*, p. 631.

accident of the universe,[36] thrown at random between the earth and the stars,[37] granted an ephemeral moment called life.[38] But within this beginning and ending Malraux has started to find at least a temporary value, something that can justify a life. ("Time runs perhaps towards eternity; surely towards death."[39]) That value is human dignity. It is good that man is man; it is bad that he be dehumanized before his fellows. A man must take account of this: to take refuge in oneself alone is unendurable.[40] It is no refuge at all.

A careful thinker would ask whether Sartre is not more logical, since if he sees man as a "useless passion," then man's death is as meaningless as any ideal or value he may serve in life. Malraux says man is an accident of the universe, and hemmed in by the absurd and destiny; how, then, can he logically give his characters something to die for? Putting a meaning back into work, for example, is for the Christian a matter of seeing it as collaboration with the Creator or even the privilege of service, sanctified by the example of Christ; and the "opposite of humiliation" could be construed on the basis of the equal rights of man—again, before God. In 1950 Malraux drops a sentence that is revealing. Speaking of Goya, he says that it was to the gospel that he owed the conviction that man had the right to justice,[41] and he frequently says that it is Christianity that gives man a sense of having a personal value.[42] But in principle he can hold none of this as valid. One wonders therefore how his "values" can be values at all, torn, as they are, from their roots in Christianity.

---

[36] *V.S.*, p. 637.
[37] *N.A.*, p. 98.
[38] *V.S.*, p. 556.
[39] *Ibid.*, p. 628.
[40] *C.H.*, p. 293.
[41] André Malraux, *Saturne*, pp. 111-12. Paris: Gallimard (Galerie de la Pléiade), 1950.
[42] See, for example, *J.E.*, p. 135; *T.O.*, p. 150; *Conq.*, p. 121.

Is his stoicism before the absurd sacrificed to the exigencies of human sympathies? Sartre's stoniness is doctrinaire, almost prim. Malraux is not a doctrinaire, and the "logic" of the heart seems to be searching for a hearing as his work progresses. The heart is touched before human suffering, and for the heart no other argument is necessary. In fact, if a man has no "doctrine" he is, according to Malraux, more susceptible to appeals to his heart. "If one believes in nothing, precisely because one believes in nothing, one is obliged to believe in the qualities of the heart when one meets them."[43] Or again: "When a man who doesn't give a damn about anything meets genuine devotion or sacrifice, or something in that line, he's done for."[44]

The language of the heart? Sentimentalism, possibly; at the basis of much humanitarianism, certainly. It could be illogical, but agnostics are not always logical.[45] Malraux is another "agnostic with sympathies," and has never failed to rally to fineness in human beings wherever he has found it.

It should be remarked, also, that none of his appreciation of the human person is divorced from the spiritual element in man: the heart does not respond to the qualities of the flesh, but to the qualities of dedication, understanding, and sacrifice.

2.   EROTICISM

Surprisingly, it is in the erotic passages of his work that Malraux shows how uninterested he is in the sheerly sensual. There is, in fact, very little even of the sheerly instinctive in his characters; they are too conscious and too dedicated to "the always profound desire to act in control of their actions."[46]

---

[43] *C.H.*, p. 248.
[44] *Ibid.*, p. 247.
[45] Shade, a skeptical American newspaperman in Malraux, *L'espoir*, p. 43, "n'attachait plus d'importance qu'à ce qu'il appelait idiotie ou animalité, c'est-à-dire à la vie fondamentale: douleur, amour, humiliation, innocence."
[46] Malraux, "Laclos," p. 420.

Malraux rarely mentions even their physical appearances, though he can describe a countryside in Spain or a canvas of Tintoretto with haunting vividness. Gaëton Picon suggests that all of this is due to a kind of resentment in Malraux "against anything that could put an obstacle before the will or the spirit."[47] The body, linked as it is to death, is part of destiny— and to be resisted: Perken, advancing toward the Mois, "once more found himself on the ground, conquered by the flesh, by the intestines, by all that can revolt against man."[48]

There is no sensuality, "nullement une dimension sen-suelle," in Malraux's work. Even the French word *amour,* so often equivocal in its meaning, is defined by him as passion, not pleasure;[49] and he will condemn much of the cinema of today precisely because it works physically on the audiences.[50] Pinups are not Greek nudes: pinups are for sensations, and not an appeal to a higher value.[51] All such "arts" are "des arts d'assou-vissement" and create "complicity, not communion" among men, degrading and not ennobling them.[52]

There is, however, sexuality, but with this difference from much that is written today: it is always in the service of the will. It is precisely because he sees the writings of D. H. Lawrence as an "ethical affirmation" by means of sex that Malraux calls *Lady Chatterley's Lover* a work of art.[53] In his own work no character indulges in sex for sheer pleasure. For, as Perken remarks, the most stupid of prostitutes knows that the "irréguliers" are "des cérébraux," those with imaginations and

---

[47] Picon, *Malraux par lui-même,* p. 63.
[48] *V.R.,* p. 194.
[49] *V.S.,* p. 318.
[50] *Ibid.,* p. 521.
[51] *Ibid.,* p. 523.
[52] *Ibid.,* p. 528.
[53] André Malraux, preface to *L'amant de Lady Chatterley,* a translation by Roger Cornaz of D. H. Lawrence's *Lady Chatterley's Lover,* p. v. Paris: Galli-mard, 1932.

"l'inaptitude d'assouvissement";[54] and all Malraux's characters are "des cérébraux."

An idea that continues from *La tentation de l'Occident* to *La condition humaine* is that, for the man, the sexual act is the attempt to know the sensations of the woman. Ling writes A. D. that "Occidental love draws its force and its complexity from the need you feel, willingly or not, to make yourself like the woman you love."[55] A. D. agrees that "tout le jeu érotique est là, être soi-même et *l'autre;* éprouver ses sensations propres et imaginer celles du partenaire."[56] "How different the game of love would be if it did not imply the involuntary and constant imagination of the feelings of the person loved!"[57]

If Malraux has an "erotic" book, it would be *La voie royale.* Its eroticism, however, is never sheer sensuality. Perken considers "tout corps qu'on n'a pas eu" an enemy; for him the sexual act is to be used to unite the man to the sensations of the woman he takes, to imagine himself *her* without ceasing to be himself. "No, these are not bodies, these women . . . they are . . . possibilities."[58] And in the violent passage near the end of the book where, near death, he calls for a woman, he is shattered to realize that "never, never would he know the sensations of this woman . . . one possesses only what one loves."[59] In his quest for power he had forgotten love, which is possible only when sex is the complement of the woman, and never when the woman is the complement of her sex.[60] This insight robs his death of the triumphal note he had planned for it.

---

[54] *V.R.*, p. 16.
[55] *T.O.*, p. 89. The whole letter (pp. 75-89) is a comparison of Occidental and Oriental ideas of "amour," the Oriental insisting that the woman have no "personnalité particulière," the Occidental being linked to her individuality.
[56] *Ibid.*, p. 102.
[57] *J.E.*, p. 143.
[58] *V.R.*, p. 90.
[59] *Ibid.*, p. 232.
[60] *Ibid.*, p. 12.

There is a detailed study of the eroticism of another *conquérant*, Ferral, in *La condition humaine*. He is humiliated by Valérie, whom he had himself humiliated by making her a means of his will to dominate, so that he could possess her sensations. Ferral is the "cérébral" extraordinary, for whom intelligence is the possession of a method of imposing oneself upon people and things.[61] In his rage against Valérie he humiliates in turn a Chinese girl, and reflects before her that the pleasure of love involves the humiliation of oneself or of another— perhaps of both. "An *idea,* that's evidently what it is."[62] The pleasure consists in putting himself in the place of another constrained by himself; to possess another is self-possession.[63] He needs the eyes of others with which to know himself, the senses of another by which to know his own touch.[64] Obviously there is in all this the desire for sensation; but the sensation is a means to realize oneself, to experience one's autonomy, by dominating another. It is not an end in itself.

Malraux wrote *La condition humaine* seventeen years before Sartre wrote that the "sexual drive is the desire to appropriate to oneself another body, in as much as this body reveals to me my flesh as flesh."[65] But note the depersonalization again in Sartre. "My flesh as flesh" is not "self-possession." Malraux is on the plane of persons, egotistical though those persons be. Sartre remains, more often than not, "geometrical."[66]

The heavy accent of sadism in Malraux is evident. Sartre well says that sadism implies nonreciprocity in sexual relations,

---

[61] *C.H.,* p. 268.

[62] *Ibid.,* p. 275.

[63] *Ibid.*

[64] *Ibid.,* p. 276. "Il lui fallait les yeux des autres pour se voir" is to be lined up with Sartre's "La personne est présentée à la conscience en tant qu'elle est objet pour autrui. . . . Je ne suis pour moi que comme pur renvoi à autrui" (*L'être et le néant,* p. 318).

[65] Sartre, *L'être et le néant,* p. 458.

[66] Malraux (*N.R.F.,* June 1, 1928, p. 854) levels this criticism against Sade.

enjoying being the appropriating power and being free in the face of a liberty captured by the flesh.[67] It is this tone of sadism that gives the lie to a suspicion that *La voie royale* (or the Valérie-Ferral incident in *La condition humaine*) is dealing in sensuality for its own sake. Rather, the sexuality is depicted in order to show the fatality in any attempts to transcend oneself: and this idea is straight Malraux. For sadism is always doomed to failure because the other is still a person. The simultaneous attempt to have the greatest possible depersonalization[68] and the greatest possible personalization, the attempt to become the other in order to have a sharper sense of oneself, is to court a contradiction. Malraux says that it would be tragic if either carnally or spiritually one never lived except in the flesh of another,[69] and is, by that, saying that an attempt to do so is also tragic. The eroticism of the other sex is always a mystery.[70] How could it be anything else, given the uniqueness of each human personality and the psychological differences between the sexes? This craving to *use* the other for self-possession is perversion, as the words of Ferral indicate when he suddenly saw that his thirst for power was never quenched, was only kept alive by renewal . . . the only thing he hungered for was himself.[71] Sex is for other purposes.

It is worth noting that there are only two cases of real love in Malraux: in *La condition humaine* that between Kyo and May and in *Le temps du mépris* that between Kassner and his wife Anna.[72] There is one child, Hemmelrich's, though children flit through *L'espoir* as "gleams of light in a new world." Malraux's genius (or his interests) forbids the sympathy which

---

[67] Sartre, *L'être et le néant*, p. 458.
[68] *V.R.*, p. 15: "L'essentiel est *de ne pas connaître* la partenaire."
[69] *N.R.F.*, April 1, 1932, p. 916.
[70] Malraux, preface to *L'amant de Lady Chatterley*, p. iii.
[71] *C.H.*, p. 276.
[72] Katow had loved once (*C.H.*, p. 249) as had Perken (*V.R.*, p. 84).

has enabled other authors to bring to life "the most inaccessible of beings, the woman, the child, the humble, the insane."[73] None of these would be useful in novels of violence, especially when those novels are moving toward what is going to become a passion with Malraux, *la fraternité virile*. It has been suggested that the mystery of feminine love irritates Malraux, perhaps because it is too often caricatured as a drooping thing.[74] There are other explanations offered. All are equally unhelpful.[75] It is rather likely that the subject bores Malraux.

One word of caution. *La condition humaine* presents the ideal of relieving man's misery and restoring his dignity. That is not to say that Malraux has abandoned his notion of destiny. It is here, as in all his work, a shadow "erect, unique behind all these different and similar beings, like death behind a room of incurables."[76] As Gabriel Marcel remarks: "To a Malraux, man has not grown to manhood or reached his full stature until he has taken full account of his own tragic position. In the eyes of the author of *La Condition Humaine*, this alone makes heroism possible."[77] Real victory is far off, if at all possible. The conquerer will always say: "There is only one victory, and that is eternal. It is what I shall never have."[78] Even in *L'espoir* the tragedy of death is that it halts the process, once for all, irrevocably.[79] No; the characters of Malraux carry in their own flesh the heavy weight of their fatality. Man will always be defined

---

[73] Gaëton Picon, *André Malraux*, p. 116. Paris: Gallimard, 1945.

[74] Jean de Pontcharra, "André Malraux, révolutionnaire et romancier." *Etudes*, May 1938, pp. 455-56.

[75] Claude Mauriac, for example, in *Malraux ou le mal du héros*, pp. 73-150 (Paris: Grasset, 1946) has all sorts of analyses of the whole problem of sex and love in Malraux, with special emphasis on the arch megalomaniacs, Perken and Ferral. Most of it is uninspired.

[76] André Malraux, preface to William Faulkner, *Sanctuaire*, translated by R. N. Raimbault and Henri Delgove, p. ii. Paris: Gallimard, 1949.

[77] Marcel, *Being and Having*, p. 213.

[78] Camus, *Le mythe de Sisyphe*, p. 120.

[79] Malraux, *L'espoir*, p. 182.

as "the only animal that knows he is going to die."[80] As Frohock suggests, *"Man's Fate could have been called Of Human Bondage."*[81]

Two themes: the dignity of man, and his destiny. Within the shadow of destiny the first defense was action for self-possession's sake. In *La condition humaine* the demon of action has been exorcised and enlisted in the cause of human dignity. And coincident with that is Malraux's link with one of the present forms of humanitarianism, world communism.

---

[80] *N.A.*, pp. 202, 250; *V.S.*, p. 639.
[81] Frohock, *André Malraux and the Tragic Imagination*, p. 85.

CHAPTER V

Action with Others

André Malraux is still suspect in some quarters because he went through a communistic period. (Perhaps he would be a hero in those same quarters were he to become a professional ex-communist). What such suspicion fails to understand, or does not want to understand, is that sincerity and seriousness do not necessarily ride in the same saddle as clear thinking, and that the sincere and the serious are found in all sorts of causes. In fact, sometimes what annoys noncommunists is not the communism of communists, but the fact that they could be so unenlightened as to think that any cause claiming to have found an absolute is worth allegiance.

1. MALRAUX AND COMMUNISM

One of the purifying effects of militant communism, however, has been to provoke more and more men to line up behind a cause. The era of the "broad-minded" elite, intellectual or social, is swiftly disappearing, and there are few to mourn its passing. A man must have some form of transcendent reference, something bigger than himself to give himself to; otherwise he remains superficial, and what is deepest in him slumbers. A man who is at his best at a cocktail party is never at his best.

The existentialists have given vogue to a word that expresses the seriousness of the time: *l'engagement.* It is the word for a

choice each man must make in his present context, with full
responsibility, by himself, with full willingness to take the consequences. Part of the strength of existentialists, in fact, is their
ability to catch the seriousness of the time and to express it in
commanding ways: and this holds true of the whole group, be
they atheistic, agnostic, or Christian.

Not all men, however, are *engagés*. There are those, for
example, who still see some vague, undefined third alternative
between Christianity and communism, without taking the more
honest position of the philosophers of the absurd. They are dis-
tressed to find that Whittaker Chambers' *Witness,* for one, offers
a Hobson's choice.

At the time of his championing of the Loyalists in Spain,
Malraux put these words under the pen of an American newspaperman covering the Loyalist story:

> Let us find out what we want. When a communist addresses an
> international conference, he puts his fist down on the table. When
> a fascist addresses a national congress, he puts his feet on the table.
> A democrat, be he American, English, or French, when he addresses
> an international conference, scratches his neck and asks questions.
> . . . Let us find out what we want. Let us say to the fascists or, the
> next day, to the communists, if need be, "Get out of here. If not,
> you will have to deal with us."[1]

The sides are not now what they were in 1937. But, *mutatis
mutandis,* there are many who could listen to those words
with profit.

It is hard to say, however, which is more dangerous, pre-
tending that there is no position to take or taking the wrong
position. If communism is to do us any good (and there is no
wisdom if good cannot be occasioned by evil), it must evoke a
rebirth, not of belief in democracy (forms of government are
means, not ends, and the issue of communism is not only one

---

[1] Malraux, *L'espoir,* p. 275.

of the United States and her allies versus Russia and her satellites), but of belief in something worthy of the allegiance of a grown man with a sense of his own real value. George Orwell's *1984* seemed to see little else in democracy than a congenial atmosphere for sexual freedom. Some of our propagandists talk about central heating, plenty, and something vague called "humanity." The Voice of America is trying to create among people who know what suffering is an interest in the latest jazz. All of this will leave the serious young man of today stone cold. If communism has made us think, so far so good. If it makes us think only of the material blessings we will lose with a Russian victory, we have been thinking badly. It is time we were against communism for the right reason.

One of the more disastrous effects of communism has been to throw a political light around many issues which should be seen in their own light. The times have never been so politically conscious. Disguised as politics, communism has such missionary fire, and is such a religion, that its entrance into the world, *through politics,* has stimulated other equally intransigent forms of totalitarianism; the secularism of the times has taken refuge in other forms of politics that seem to be equally messianic, such as democracy or socialism, freedom for the blacks or *apartheid,* Hispanidad or North-Americanism. So much so that the old distinctions between religion and politics have either been sharply thrown into relief against each other, so that one seems forced to choose one or the other (as in America, where there are few writers anxious about the invasion of the state by the church who would seem to be unwilling to settle for the "American way of life" as the full way of life), or have become superimposed into one concept, as in totalitarianism. It is one of the exasperating but inevitable results of Marxism that we are forced to see any big issue silhouetted against its baleful light, and that we tend to be just as *simpliste* in our thinking against it as it is single-minded in its aims at world conquest.

To that extent communism has engaged the world: and to that extent it is dreadfully successful.

In 1948 a formidable group of French writers contributed a total of almost a hundred pages in criticism of a man who had broken with communism and openly committed himself to General de Gaulle. A. Rousseaux, A. Béguin, G. Picon, P. Debray, E. Mounier, and C.-E. Magny write on Malraux's new politics, drawing on all his work up to that point for material, because "tenant son oeuvre pour une des plus hautes de notre temps" they wish to fight "avec son choix à la hauteur de son oeuvre."[2] They say highly intelligent things about Malraux, but, to my mind, make a fundamental mistake in trying to explain M. Malraux the private citizen by André Malraux the writer. The latter is an artist, and like every artist is *one* thing in his world of art. Whether he is the same or something else outside of it is another question entirely. It is thus that, though the pages of these writers are frequently illuminating on Malraux the author, they cannot hope to throw much light on the decisions of his personal life.

The chief weakness of the criticisms is that they are based on a political assumption: that Gaullism is fascism.[3] That may or may not be true; but I submit that the question has little or nothing to do with what Malraux has been saying in his books. One is reminded of Klein's story in *Les conquérants*. During the Paris Commune a fat man was arrested. He protested, "But, sirs, I've never had anything to do with politics." "Justement,"

---

[2] "Interrogation à Malraux." *Esprit*, October 1948, p. 448.
[3] On Malraux, Gaullism, and fascism see Stéphane, *Portrait de l'aventurier*, p. 187. Stéphane quotes Malraux as saying to him: "Je sais ce que je suis, je sais que je ne serai jamais fasciste." See Malraux, *L'espoir*, p. 124: "Un homme actif et pessimiste à la fois, c'est ou ce sera fasciste, sauf s'il y a une fidélité derrière lui." A. Béguin ("Interrogation à Malraux," *Esprit*, October 1948, p. 451) writes: "Malraux est, en un sens, le seul authentique fasciste français." The reader is left to judge for himself, as this exposé of Malraux's thought continues, whether this is a just judgment.

answers an intellectual, and breaks the poor man's head.[4] Because Malraux was talking of communism in his books, he must have been talking politics: otherwise how explain his Gaullism? He does not seem to be allowed nonpolitical interest in what is *also* politics.

Our interest, therefore, is in Malraux's writings; and it is a fact that they were first sympathetic with communism and later become strongly anticommunistic. In neither is there a political issue at stake, whereas Gaullism was political. It may be that a man who makes an about-face on big issues has always been unconsciously against his own adherence to the first cause. There could be a dialectic of conversion. Often, as Malraux says in *Les voix du silence,* an artist breaks with his master, first in small and erratic ways, finally so completely that he ends up with a style defying that of his master.[5] There are converts from Anglicanism to Roman Catholicism who have ended up strongly anti-Anglican. (It is more true of ex-Catholics that they become violently anti-Catholic.) The modern ex-communist shows a singular virulence against communism. But to make rules out of this behavior is to try to work out a pattern for free choices; and that is impossible.

In his life, the little we know makes it clear that Malraux was active in Indo-China during the early thirties in the communist-tutored Jeune-Annam movement,[6] and that later in China he was in the Kuomintang. When the communists broke with Chiang Kai-Shek he did too. In 1934 he traveled to the Writers' Congress in Moscow, billed as a "Marxist humanist," and later in the same year went with Gide to Germany in behalf of the imprisoned Dimitrov.[7] He became actively anti-Nazi and antifascist; and when the Spanish war started in 1936 he imme-

---

[4] *Conq.,* pp. 56-57.
[5] See, for example, Latour and his "dependence" on Caravaggio (*V.S.,* pp. 373-94).
[6] Frohock, *André Malraux and the Tragic Imagination,* p. 5.
[7] See *T.M.,* p. 586, and postface to *Conq.,* p. 265.

diately joined the Loyalists, flying with their air force. He was wounded, and made a trip to America with Hemingway to enlist help for the Loyalists. With World War II (Russia and Germany had made a pact!) he enlisted in the French army, and after its defeat escaped, worked with the British Intelligence, and finally, at the time of liberation, took command of the Alsace-Lorraine brigade. After the war he emerged as a champion of De Gaulle and the secretary of his party.

When, some day, a definitive biography of Malraux appears, the author will have much to explain about his subject's shifting "political" allegiances, and there is an easy explanation which could exonerate Malraux from every charge of inconsistency. A man can hunt in many places for the same thing.

As to the communism in his writings, the rap on the knuckles administered by Trotsky in his criticism of *Les conquérants* says all that has to be said. Trotsky wrote that "a good inoculation of Marxism could have saved Malraux from the misunderstandings" evident throughout the book.[8] "There is no affinity between the author, despite all he knows and understands, and his heroine, the Revolution."[9] Malraux's heroes, in fact, make strange communists.

For them communism is, largely, a chance for action. "Marxism isn't a doctrine," says Gisors to his students; "it's a form of will power. For the proletariat and its supporters, for you, it means the determination to know yourselves, to appreciate all it can do for you, and to make it your watchword in the hour of triumph. It is not for the justice of its arguments that Marxism should appeal to you, but as the road to victory which involves no forfeiture of self-respect."[10] It is a form of will power, a means of strength which "will make dignity possible for those who are fighting with me," says Kyo.[11]

---

[8] *N.R.F.*, April 1, 1931, p. 493.
[9] *Ibid.*, p. 489.

[10] *C.H.*, p. 81.
[11] *Ibid.*, p. 343.

But Gisors and Kyo, who talk more clearly than any of Malraux's other characters about it, are both uneasy. Gisors admits, at Kyo's death, that though to Kyo communism was a form of will power, in his own heart of hearts he had adhered to it because it is "a fatality, and my anxiety before death made me ready to accept a fatality."[12] Kyo, lectured by Vologuin, a pure communist, on the inevitable course of the Revolution, says that "each time fatality predominates over the will, I am uneasy."[13]

There is the rub. Fatality is one thing: the inevitable dialectic may be taking place; but there must be play for human effort and freedom. It is the communistic authoritarian disregard for freedom, by setting up a clearly defined and limited purpose for all action, which haunts all the chief characters in Malraux's "communistic" writing.

In *Les conquérants* the communist Borodin (not, by the way, a fictional character) looks on China as "prime matter" ready for forceful domination. "A man should be preoccupied with the real, with the difficulties of the exercise of power."[14] Borodin is ruled by the "unbearable bolshevik mentality, the stupid glorification of discipline."[15] There are for him no half-measures in the Revolution. Garine reacts, saying that "there are half-measures wherever there are men and not machines."[16] Borodin thinks Garine too human: "There is no place in communism for the man who first wishes to be himself, to live separated from others. . . . Individualism is a bourgeois weakness."[17]

L'espoir also has harsh words. "The communists, you see," Hernandez says to Garcia, "want to get things done, whereas you and the anarchists want to be something."[18] "For the communists, love of action, of organization, of intensive production

---

12 *Ibid.*, p. 166.
13 *Ibid.*
14 *Conq.*, p. 23.
15 *Ibid.*, p. 222.
16 *Ibid.*
17 *Ibid.*, pp. 225-26.
18 Malraux, *L'espoir*, p. 156.

and the like" are the sentiments that count;[19] they have all the virtues of action, and no others.[20] Their asceticism and impersonality revolt Alvear: "I like to consort with men for what they are, not for their ideas. I want loyalty in friendship, and not the kind of friendship that hangs on a political position. I want a man to feel responsible to himself . . . not to a cause, even if it is the cause of the underdog."[21]

The Malraux objection to communism is perhaps best expressed in Alvear's words: "A man devotes to any line of action only a limited part of himself, and the more the line of action sets up to be totalitarian, the smaller is the part of him involved."[22]

Apropos of Malraux's communists Sartre wrote in 1950:

> The new militant is . . . a creature of the Party. He will find the Party wherever he goes. The Party will be the intermediary between him and his intimate friends. "Bring your wife into the Party," he is told, "and you won't lose any time." . . . He has no depths, no secrets, not even the most humble of complexes. He is constructed on the most rigorously objective foundations, explained by his class and historical contingency; he is externally what he is internally. . . . It is only for convenience sake that he does not speak of himself in the third person. He is an individual only by his acts. . . . He serves, that's all.[23]

The communist, therefore, comes off badly in Malraux. The Revolution, however, is an opportunity to realize oneself. Beyond that, one could even conclude from Malraux's novels that his knowledge of communist doctrine is quite elementary. Not

---

[19] *Ibid.*, p. 279. See also *Conq.*, p. 158: "La Révolution, dit Borodine, brusquement . . . c'est payer l'armée."

[20] Malraux, *L'espoir*, p. 356.

[21] *Ibid.*, p. 232. That Malraux's descriptions of the communist sting the communist is evident in Garaudy, *Literature of the Graveyard*, pp. 42 ff.

[22] Malraux, *L'espoir*, p. 232.

[23] Jean-Paul Sartre, in the study preceding Stéphane's *Portrait de l'aventurier*, pp. 11-12.

that there is no doctrinal commitment: it is not true that Malraux uses the Revolution merely to bring out the tragic in man.[24] But the only really doctrinal reference to communism beyond the "fatality" idea is in Alvear's remark that "the Revolution plays, among other roles, the one formerly played by eternal life."[25]

We must now dip into the slender volume of Malraux called *Le temps du mépris,* which, despite all said so far, is purely and unequivocally communistic, and the least typical, certainly the least convincing, of Malraux's works. It is his first optimistic novel, and an interlude.

2. LYRICAL COMMUNISM

In his much-quoted preface to *Le temps du mépris* Malraux sums up its elements in a few words. "The world of a work like this, the world of tragedy, is the ancient world still—man, the elements, woman, destiny."[26] The specific turn given to these elements in the book is indicated in this explanation: "It is difficult to be a man. But it is not more difficult to become one by enriching one's fellowship with other men than by cultivating one's individual peculiarities. The former nourishes, with at least as much force as the latter, that which makes man human, which enables him to surpass himself, to create, invent or realize himself."[27] We are on the threshold of Malraux's discovery of the *other*, not as a temporary solace, but as a *toi* perfecting the reality of the *moi*.

---

[24] Claude Delmas, "André Malraux et le communisme," in *L'Age Nouveau,* February 1953, pp. 51-62, suggests that communism for Malraux is merely material to express the tragic.

[25] Malraux, *L'espoir,* p. 252. See also *V.S.,* p. 482: "Les états totalitaires sont nés de la volonté de trouver une totalité sans religion," and Picon, *Malraux par lui-même,* pp. 94-95, where Malraux feels moved to write that he had never accepted the Marxist "class-struggle" idea as the key to history.

[26] *T.M.,* p. 541.

[27] *Ibid.,* p. 542.

We have before us destiny and its opposite, the human will, which gets strength and realizes itself in brotherhood, in *la fraternité*.[28] It will begin to become an end in itself, and Malraux's fascination with it will be one of the reasons he offers his solution to destiny within the limits of sheerly human activity.

This novel, the shortest and most uncluttered of them all, is a paean to the joys of fellowship, and the most lyrical of all Malraux's works. Kassner, a communist, suffers shortly after the rise of Nazism in a Hitlerian prison, is released because somebody gives himself up for him, flies back home to Prague in a hurricane, finds his wife and child again, and dreams of the fraternity of men,

> an eternity composed of his fellow prisoners of yesterday, of the child's trusting cheek, of the crowd loyally clinging to its companions in torture, of the face of the pilot in the hurricane, of the man who had given himself up for him, even of his forthcoming return to Germany, the eternity of the living and of the dead.[29]

The novel is a happy novel. The horrors of isolation in the Nazi cell are simply a fact, the justice of the Revolution is taken for granted, the nobility of man is worth fighting for:[30] the book is a psalm to communism, *à la Malraux*, and there is no arguing of a case. Briefly, the brotherhood of man is what man's fate is leading him to, and it is the responsibility of Kassner and other dedicated communists to accelerate its coming. "What is man's freedom but the knowledge and the manipulation [*organiser*] of his fate?"[31] Destiny means here the good days

---

[28] "Aux yeux de Kassner comme de nombre d'intellectuels communistes, le communisme restitue à l'individu sa fertilité" *(ibid.)*.

[29] *Ibid.*, p. 592.

[30] "Il pensait confusément que l'homme était parvenu à être l'homme, malgré les cachots, malgré la cruauté, et que seule sans doute la dignité pouvait être opposée à la douleur" *(ibid.*, p. 591).

[31] *Ibid.*, p. 580.

that are coming.[32] There is the fashioning of life to do: Malraux
is always a voluntarist, and in him, as in Sartre, man is what
he makes himself. But there is harmony here between what he
will inevitably become, a member of a conscious brotherhood,
and what he wants to work for. "If this night should become a
night of destiny, may it be blessed until the coming dawn."[33] A
clean idealism is offered by a temporarily hopeful author as the
way of release from destiny.

Bravery is on every page: the disciplined, selfless bravery
of the "true" communist. In prison Kassner remembers not to
work hard and wear himself out, merely for the sake of a little
extra food, lest when released he be unfit for organizational
work.[34] He will deny himself answering his jailers with memo-
rable words because he had to get away to resume his revolutionary work.[35] An unnamed comrade gives himself up for
Kassner, doing what is necessary,[36] perhaps because he considered Kassner more useful than himself.[37] And if he is to be
killed, Kassner, like Katow in *La condition humaine*,[38] resolves
to make his death useful by sinking his thumbs into the throat
of the first guard who entered, "without letting go, no matter
what happened."[39] He is frightened, has moments of despair
and feverish hallucinations, but fights insanity with an imaginary speech to his fellow prisoners. Even when he has been
released, it takes the eyes of his wife to remind him fully of
himself. "It came to him violently that his wife had just had an

---

[32] "Il semblait à Kassner, qu'englué de tout le sang qu'il venait de traverser, le
sens du monde naissait, et que la vie la plus secrète des choses allait être
accomplie" (*ibid.*, p. 592).
[33] *Ibid.*, p. 591.
[34] *Ibid.*, p. 546.
[35] *Ibid.*, p. 550.
[36] *Ibid.*, p. 573.
[37] *Ibid.*, p. 574.
[38] *C.H.*, p. 368.
[39] *T.M.*, p. 562.

extraordinary stroke of luck, as though it were she, not he, who had been freed."[40]

In all his sufferings he is sustained by the dream of brotherhood. He remembers the music of the "Internationale." "The music at last arose above its own heroic call. . . . Night fell on the universe, night in which men feel their kinship on the march or in the vast silence, the drifting night of stars and friendship."[41] He taps out the word "comrade" with an invisible prisoner in a neighboring cell; and when the other stops, Kassner, "deprived of brotherhood . . . waited in the silence which hung over the desires of hundreds of men in that termite's nest. He must speak for them, even were they never to hear him. 'Comrades in the darkness around me . . .' "[42]

Released, he meets the pilot who will fly him home. "He had a great capacity for friendship; and yet it stirred him even more deeply that they were united, not in their persons, but in their common devotion, as if each step toward the plane were bringing him nearer to an austere and powerful friendship of a sort rare on earth."[43]

The novel circulated freely in the Soviet Union. It is a moment in the evolution of Malraux's thought when, despite what he says in the preface, tragedy was not haunting him. Destiny is here defined in terms of the Marxist dialectic, and is the force of events which are slowly going to transform society and restore the human to man. When Gisors embraced communism, it was as a fatality in tune with his own fear of death. To Kassner it is the gospel of hope, promising the dawn of the brotherhood of man.

Judging, however, from the rest of Malraux's work, it would be naive to see in this book anything else than an accidental meeting at this stage in his career, of his growing fascination

---

40 *Ibid.*, p. 574.
41 *Ibid.*, p. 555.

42 *Ibid.*, p. 568.
43 *Ibid.*, p. 576.

with mankind as an eternal *anti-destin* and the promises of communism, which sings that "the International Soviet will be the human race." And just as the idea of a common victory, the meaningfulness of fighting together with others, assuaged in his earlier works the pangs of the loneliness of his characters, so here it meets communism in a temporary identification. The identification is, however, as brief as an eclipse.

3. LA FRATERNITE VIRILE

The sense of human community was present in the shadows in all the earlier work of Malraux. In the very beginning he had scoffed at it in the form of the *communauté des rêves* that gives Western man his force. "Our brothers are those whose childhood unfolded to the accompaniment of the rhythm of epics and legends that dominated our own."[44] This is a restricted *fraternité,* based on dreams of grandeur. Of Tcheng-Daï, the Chinese sage and man of action of *Les conquérants,* the arch-individualist Garine says: "With him, as with the Christian, action goes hand in hand with charity, but what is compassion among the Christians is in him the sense of solidarity";[45] and he says that the Terrorists work in fierce unity to "attain the sense of an existence that is more really human."[46] Neither idea is congenial to him, but he admits that he himself has "above all the need of a common victory."[47]

Garine, as a matter of fact, adventurer and ruthless heretic that he was, could love other men: his sympathy for the condemned Hong ("When I saw he was here, I almost stood up and said to him 'What's this all about?' the way you would to a boy who has played some child's trick"[48]), his affection for

---

[44] *T.O.*, p. 95.
[45] *Conq.*, p. 100.
[46] *Ibid.*, p. 120.
[47] *Ibid.*, p. 123.
[48] *Ibid.*, p. 202. See Kyo and Tchen (*C.H.*, pp. 153-54).

Klein ("I had for him the friendship of a man"[49]), and his farewell to the young Frenchman who is the narrator (who, seeking in Garine's eyes, finds nothing "but a hard and yet fraternal seriousness"[50]) are all evidence.

Actually, there is no chief character in Malraux who has not deep human sympathy, no matter how outrageously some may talk of their hardness toward life. Claude in *La voie royale*, trusting the boy he has engaged, says he is trying to enlist his loyalty. "Loyalty is one of the rare sentiments that do not seem to be corrupt."[51] He tells Perken: "If I accept a man, I accept him totally and like I accept myself."[52] The friendship between Claude and Perken increases, and in Perken's approaching death it becomes intense. There is in the look Claude throws at Perken "a deep complicity made up of poignant fraternity of courage and compassion, the animal unity of beings before flesh that has been condemned."[53] As Perken dies, Claude, all the time craving "to express by his hands and his eyes, if not in words, this desperate brotherhood which drew him outside himself, embraced Perken by the shoulder."[54]

So far, human affection is evident between individuals, though we have Garine's disturbing remark about needing a "common victory." *La condition humaine,* as we have seen, especially in the prison scene at the end, presents as a value the *community* of fighting and dying together for a cause.[55] Katow, pressing the hand of one of the prisoners to whom he had given the cyanide, is "beyond the meaning of tears, overcome by this sad fraternity without a face, almost without a

---

[49] *Conq.,* p. 207.
[50] *Ibid.,* p. 245.
[51] *V.R.,* p. 79.
[52] *Ibid.,* p. 83.
[53] *Ibid.,* p. 226.
[54] *Ibid.,* pp. 268-69.
[55] Even Tchen, the man apart, realizes that to fight side by side with the others is to forge the strongest of bonds between men. See *C.H.,* p. 108.

voice . . . which was being offered to him in the darkness, in return for the greatest gift he had ever made."[56] As Kyo's death had been "hallowed by a touch of common brotherhood" ("mort saturée de ce chevrotement fraternel"[57]), so likewise Katow walks to his execution followed by the compassionate eyes of his fellow prisoners.[58]

It is in *L'espoir*, however, that *la fraternité virile* moves out onto a wide field. The novel is long; has many characters— none dominant; and has almost no unity except the theme of hope, of belief in man if men fight together. The pure communism of *Le temps du mépris* is diluted; the party member appears only occasionally, and those characters who enlist the reader's sympathies are rather the intellectual, the ardent Catholic, the anarchist, the socialist, the republican—and the ordinary nonpolitical Spaniard. The communist is rather more often the foil for the thoughts of noncommunists.

It would be tedious to go into the book in detail. It is a series of brief scenes, sometimes blending into each other, at other times confusingly cut short and separated. Frohock has counted in the fifty-six chapters one hundred and forty scene units. Some critics brand the book as sheer reporting. Montherlant, on the other hand, apostrophizes "this remarkable and so little appreciated *L'espoir*—this book which, of all the books that have appeared in twenty years, one would most want to have lived and written."[59] All of this is as may be. The fact is that as far as "meanings" go, Malraux is at last preaching a positive message against destiny, the message of manly fellowship.

---

[56] *Ibid.*, p. 366.

[57] *Ibid.*, p. 362.

[58] *Ibid.*, p. 369.

[59] Quoted in De Boisdeffre, *André Malraux*, p. 54. Savanne waxes even more ecstatic: "[*L'espoir*] est un de ces livres dont on dit six cents ans plus tard: 'Vous voulez une idée de ce que fut la tragédie du XXe siècle? Lisez donc *L'espoir* d'André Malraux'" (*André Malraux*, p. 95).

The occasion of the book is, again, revolution. Some authors have seen it as an apologetic, demonstrating man before a new kind of *organized* revolution, the old form of the revolution of barricades and blocked-off streets now being an anachronism. A reading of *L'espoir* gives an entirely different impression: the theme is man (as in all of Malraux) brought to his feet and abruptly asked before the Revolution what he thinks life is all about. There are communists, with their communistic answer; but communism is clearly not the heroine of this book; it is necessary at the moment, in order that the Revolution win, that communists take over leadership. But the chief characters do not love it; for the individual in a free fraternity, fighting in order to realize himself, despite the small voice of destiny in his ears reminding him of the passingness of human things, is not a communistic character at all. He is, however, the Malraux character in *L'espoir*.

The eyes of the book are on the "quality of man." "The only hope that the New Spain has of keeping that for which you and Jaime and so many others are fighting," says Alvear to Scali, "is that somehow the thing we've been trying our best to inculcate year after year, may be preserved, the quality of man."[60]

It is lost when a man lives in humiliation. "This is how I see things," says Barca. "When we, our people, I mean, try to do something for humanity, we're working for our own kith and kin. But the others [the fascists] pick and choose. They sort folks out."[61]

Fraternity will restore this quality of man. "You spoke of hope just now," says Scali to Alvear. "Well, men who are joined together in a common hope, a common action, have access like

---

[60] Malraux, *L'espoir*, p. 233.

[61] *Ibid.*, p. 75. See also p. 146: "Quand les hommes sortent de prison, neuf fois sur dix leur regard ne se pose pas. Ils ne regardent plus comme les hommes. Dans le prolétariat aussi il y a beaucoup de regards qui ne se posent plus. Et il faut changer ça pour commencer."

men whom love unites to regions they could never reach if left to themselves."[62]

"The opposite of humiliation is not equality. You know the motto the French put on all their buildings: *Liberté, Egalité, Fraternité*. Well, they weren't such fools, since that's what fraternity means: the opposite of being badgered [*vexé*]."[63]

In *La condition humaine* the action of revolution was an antidote to the feeling of loneliness, dignity the opposite of humiliation. In *L'espoir* there is an advance: there is little of what has been called "metaphysical" loneliness, and the keen consciousness of the degrading effect of the disdain of one's fellows, of another class, is the demon in life which must be crushed, but not by equality, by fraternity. The besiegers of the Alcazar send in razor blades and cigarettes to the besieged to show them that they are not scorned; the same motive prompts Hernandez to forward Moscardo's letters to his wife. The communists have some contempt for the idea of fraternity because for them the important thing is to get people to *act*.[64] But for the vast number of soldiers in the book it is fraternity, clear as a revelation, that prompts their belief in the Revolution. One wonders if this is not clear only to a volunteer Frenchman . . .

The action of the book is actually a long, vivid argument, appealing to each character in turn until he rallies with realization to that which makes it possible for a man to be a man. Each character at some moment in the book utters the words of Puig the anarchist: "I never dreamt that such fraternity was possible."[65] *L'espoir* has no insensitive characters.

---

62 *Ibid.*, p. 233.

63 *Ibid.*, p. 75. See also p. 152: "Le contraire de l'humiliation, mon gars, c'est pas l'égalité, c'est la fraternité."

64 Malraux, *L'espoir*, p. 153. See Garcia's taunt to Magnin (p. 90).

65 *Ibid.*, p. 30. See Jaime, p. 35; Shade, p. 39; Manuel, pp. 57, 197; the aviators, p. 59; Ramos, pp. 68, 248; Vargas, p. 88; Scali, p. 105; Gonzalez, p. 171; Guernico, p. 226; Moreno, p. 264; Pol, p. 313.

Fraternity gives the sense of the quality of man. After a victory Manuel, at the end of the book (as Vincent Berger at the end of *Les noyers de l'Altenburg*), has a vision of mankind which is suffused with wonder at the marvel that is man. He had turned on a recording of a Beethoven symphony, and

> as the strands of the melody took form, interwoven with his past, they conveyed to him the selfsame message that the dim sky, those ageless fields, and that town which had stopped the Moors might, too, have given him. For the first time Manuel was hearing the voices of that which is more awe-inspiring even than the blood of men, more enigmatic even than their presence on the earth—the infinite possibilities of their destiny. And he felt that this new consciousness within him was linked up with the sounds of running water in the street and the footfalls of the prisoners, profound and permanent as the beating of his heart.[66]

The future, then, forged of the fraternity that gives a man his place as a man, will be a triumph of the ageless wonder that is man, in love, in sympathy, in courage, and in hope.[67] The executions at Toledo, the fighting before the university town, the last words of Unamuno, the return of the wounded aviators— all of these are men at their best. The book is a morality play of the "promise of a new world" of brotherhood.[68] And it is the world of men. As the German Klein in *Les conquérants,* each character in *L'espoir* stammers in wonder with his lips and his life the simple words: "Ein Mensch . . . a man."[69]

4. THE PRESENCE OF CHRIST

The moral is nevertheless cast in a troubled setting, and the spectator is constantly distracted by discordant voices in the wings: the many views on politics, the old theme of death as

---

[66] Malraux, *L'espoir*, p. 360.
[67] "La plus grande force de la révolution, c'est l'espoir" (*ibid.*, p. 39).
[68] *Ibid.*, p. 54.
[69] *Conq.*, p. 57.

destiny,[70] and most of all by the defiant honesty of the author in the scenes where Christ, priests, and the Church hold the center of the stage.

Except in *Le temps du mépris* Malraux has never presented a straightforward theme; he would seem unable even to leave unsaid the things that contradict his chief lines of thought. A man of deep human sympathy first, he seems to find enough justification in the pattern of tragedy to publish books that are emotionally disturbing and intellectually unclear.[71] He repudiates the great intellectual who is interested in absolute truth and the complexity of things. "He is . . . anti-Manichean by definition, by nature." Malraux is not an intellectual of that stripe; addicted to a message of action, he thinks that "all forms of action are Manichean . . . every true revolutionary is a born Manichean."[72] It is as though Malraux, long passionately believing in man, knows only too well that that belief will always be a bittersweet thing: an absolute humanism must necessarily be pregnant with tragedy.

In *L'espoir* Ximenes and Guernico are both avowed, believing Catholics; and they are fighting against Franco. They know, moreover, why they are fighting, and get their strength from their faith. They do not win any arguments: arguments are not settled in *L'espoir*. But the author's sympathy with them is evident. They are too eloquent and too convincing for it to be otherwise. There abides, in Malraux, a respect for Catholicism, wherever it is found in the world.

---

[70] Malraux, *L'espoir*. See pp. 166, 182, 185, 230-31.

[71] In his review of Hermann Keyserling's *Journal de voyage d'un philosophe* (*N.R.F.*, June 1, 1929, p. 886) Malraux had written: "La conception dramatique de la philosophie, plus puissante d'année en année dans tout l'Occident, et qui aboutira peut-être à une transformation profonde de la fiction, se défend beaucoup mieux quand elle pose le philosophe. Il importe peu, nous dit-on, que Nietzsche soit devenu fou. Il importe beaucoup, au contraire, et il faut savoir prendre le tragique où il est."

[72] Malraux, *L'espoir*, p. 279.

Both draw a sharp distinction between the clergy and the faith. "Let's assume the Church of Spain has fallen short of its duty to our countrymen. . . . The catechism's more important to me than St. Thomas," says Ximenes to Puig, the anarchist. Puig is incensed against the priests. "Those churches," says he, "where they've gloated over having thirty thousand men arrested, and tortured, and the rest of it—let 'em all burn, and a damn good thing too." Ximenes asks, "And Christ?"[73] There is no answer.

Manuel, later in the book, tells Ximenes that he finds that, the greater his efficiency and the better officer he is, the more estranged he is from his fellow men. "Every day I'm getting a little less human. But I expect you've been up against the same thing?" Ximenes answers: " 'All I could tell you, my boy, would be things you wouldn't understand. You'd like to lead men and yet remain their comrade. Well, in my opinion, no man's big enough for that.' He was thinking that fraternity of that kind was only to be found in the fellowship of Christ."[74]

Guernico is haunted by Christ. "I'm a Spanish Catholic. If theology were in your line," he says to Garcia, "I'd tell you I'm appealing to the soul of the Church against its body. . . . Faith does not imply a lack of love. And hope does not imply a world that would justify itself by making people worship again, like a fetish, that crucifix at Seville which they call 'The Rich Man's Christ.' . . . Nor is it looking forward to a Spanish empire as the be-all and end-all of the world, a regime in which no sound is heard because those who suffer must hide themselves to weep. Order can be found in a prison camp too. . . . What has Christ to do with such a world?" And the priests? "I said to you that for twenty years I've not heard Christ's words in Spain. But those priests [those ministering to the wounded] are being heard now. . . . Tonight Christ's gospel is a living pres-

---

[73] *Ibid.*, p. 31.   [74] *Ibid.*, p. 290.

ence.[75] . . . God alone knows the trials He is about to impose on the priesthood; but I think the priest's vocation *should* become hard once again. . . . As indeed every Christian life is hard."[76]

There is no talk of fraternity in the closed circle of men alone, when Ximenes and Guernico speak, nor is it mentioned in the parable told by the former monk.[77] The Spanish Catholic can love men more deeply when the love is rooted in Christ.[78] Malraux does not deny this; he has always recognized the force of a living Church in achieving "communion." "The art of a living religion," he writes in *Les voix du silence,* "is not that of an assurance against death, but that of a defense against destiny by an immense communion" linking a man to his neighbor and to all forms of pain and of life.[79] But Malraux, acknowledging that a man with love for Christ can by that very fact have a deeper love for man than he would have without Christ, records the fact, is touched—and moves on.

5. THE NATURE OF COMMUNION

Malraux, then, allows for a pluralism of the widest sort in politics and in religion, provided politics and religion *appeal to something deep in a man's soul* and provide him with the

---

[75] Malraux has spoken since of Christ as distinguished from the Church. See *V.S.,* p. 482: what the bourgeoisie lack most is Christ; *N.A.,* p. 40: Dietrich Berger is cut off from the Church but not from Christ. There is a lot of this in the air today. Herbert Butterfield in *Christianity and History,* p. 146 (London: G. Bell and Sons, 1950) ends his book saying: "We can do worse than remember a principle which gives us a firm Rock and leaves us with the maximum elasticity for our minds. The principle: Hold to Christ, and for the rest be totally uncommitted."

[76] Malraux, *L'espoir,* pp. 224-26.

[77] *Ibid.,* pp. 131-34.

[78] André Malraux, *Dessins de Goya au musée du Prado* (henceforth cited as *Goya;* see p. 224), p. xii (Geneva: Skira, 1947): "Au 'Christ, homme parfait' de Nicholas de Cuse, toutes les voix de l'Espagne répondaient que l'homme ne vaut que par ce qu'il porte du Christ."

[79] *V.S.,* p. 494.

opportunity for fraternity.[80] What is important is precisely the recognition by each man of the other's "quality of man." There is a relativism here of the frankest kind, but only because Malraux is convinced that there is something deeper than all beliefs. He will say of the twentieth-century acceptance of all art that "our pluralism, far from being an eclectism, a taste for a thousand forms, is founded on our discovery of elements *common* to works of art."[81] At the moment the honor of being a man is something each man worthy of the name discovers as common to himself and all other men. "To ask if 'man is dead' is to affirm that he is still man, not his scraps, to the extent that he demands to be put right again in terms of what is loftiest in him: that part of him which is rarely limited to himself."[82] It is something the German Vincent Berger experiences after the gas attack against the Russians in *Les noyers de l'Altenburg*, when he rushes to the Russian lines with the other Germans to save their victims. He picks up a Russian killed by the gas, and "his eyes shut, his whole body glued to his brother's body which protected him like a shield against all that he was running away from" struggles back to the German lines. Later, analyzing his actions, he asks himself if it was pity that drove him on. He finds that it was something a good deal deeper, an urge in which "pain and brotherhood were inseparably united"—as though

---

[80] Frohock, in *André Malraux and the Tragic Imagination*, I think misunderstands *L'espoir*. He says that "following the guidance of the titles, the reader may conclude that *Man's Hope* contains an unmistakable propaganda lesson: the Revolution must succeed; it can succeed only if organized; the only competent organizers are the Communists; thus the leadership must be handed over to the Communists at any cost" (p. 110). I would agree that in the book communism is a necessary instrument for victory, but would insist that to the extent it is necessary its use is, for Malraux, annoying. And Malraux does not know what to do with it, either in the action, or in any prophecy of the future made in the book. It would be highly erroneous, as a matter of fact, to look on communism as anything else than what is given in the case: the novel is in an historical setting. The communists were there. Ergo.

[81] *V.S.*, p. 555.

[82] *Ibid.*, p. 494.

the sheet of gas had yielded not those Russians, but only the friendly bodies of men in the same file.[83]

What is this *fraternité virile?* Negatively, it is finding strength against all forms of debasement, whether the injustice of class systems, the atomizing of the individual that is present-day Russian communism, or any forms of the state where the individual is so unconscious of himself, as a man and as a *freedom,* that he is "unauthentic." In all these cases there is no really human life, because the self is without virility. Positively, fraternity is the power individuals receive by fighting together to attain a full expression of the noble elements in them that they would not find separately.[84]

It is a case of the whole being greater than its parts, of each man awakening in another, by his earnestness and whatever degree of courage he has, the realization that the other too can be noble, can be brave, can be unselfish. (To this extent Malraux is faithful to the modern discovery of *l'autrui* as an agent that delivers the self to the self.) Camus has written a novel, *La peste,* about the rise in men, during a common affliction that has cut them off from the rest of the world, of the forces of love and unselfishness; something no one of them would have achieved alone. Rieux, the atheistic doctor, and Paneloux, the Jesuit priest, are the embodiment of a kind of hidden natural law which does not depend on the different ideologies each had em-

---

[83] *N.A.,* p. 243. Vincent Berger had liked war for one reason, "la camaraderie virile, l'engagement sans retour qu'implique le courage."

[84] Bespaloff, in *Cheminements et carrefours,* p. 54, writes: "Les romans de Malraux nous proposent une nouvelle image de l'homme seul retrouvant, à la faveur d'une rebellion commune, le sens mythique et religieux de la participation à l'humain. Ils nous dévoilent à une profondeur inaccessible aux contraintes sociales, le besoin primordial de communication qui noue, au coeur même du concret, la vie séparée à la vie collective. Cette solitude de combat, encerclée mais non submergée par des flots d'humanité, telle qu'ici elle est évoquée, devient le seul point stable dans notre désordre et notre délire. Tout ce qui subsiste d'intact, de pur, de non-contaminé dans l'âme individuelle s'y retire pour s'y fortifier."

braced and which comes into play the minute men suffer.[85] There is in all this the attempt at an ethic. Malraux and Camus find men at their best when they are united in a common battle against evil.

We understand the force of communion in action: nobility *is* infectious. But what of the periods in history, in an ordinary life, when the days must run their modest course and there is no incitement to battle? What of the millions of lives each decade which experience no privileged moment for action in a common cause? Is Mounier correct in saying that the high and royal weakness of Malraux is to call to a sort of paroxysm, and to leave us unarmed and at our wits ends before every-day existence?[86]

I think so (as I think that a chance for high and royal action was what appealed to Malraux in communism). The reader who may be convinced that the message of *L'espoir* applies to him would have to join some militant organization or go off to some war, like Malraux himself, who rushed to Spain as soon as the "Revolution" broke out. "The country of a man who can choose," he writes, "is wherever the clouds are darkest."[87] But the majority cannot choose; and are they by that to be immediately accused of ignobility?

Malraux has spoken of the community in action that a *faith* can give. "Thousands of human beings can be united by a faith or the hope of revolution, but (except in the language of propagandists) they are not then the masses, they are alike: united often by action, always by that which in their eyes counts more than themselves."[88] He knows, also, specifically, the power

---

[85] Albert Camus, *La peste* (Paris: Gallimard, 1947). The English translation, *The Plague*, by Stuart Gilbert (London: Hamish Hamilton, 1948), is out of print.

[86] Mounier, in "Interrogation à Malraux," *Esprit*, October 1948, p. 488.

[87] *N.A.*, p. 66.

[88] *V.S.*, p. 514.

of "communion in action which Roman Christianity carried in it" (adding that, though it recognized medieval castes, it alone transcended them).[89] He says that nowadays we do not know any such communion.[90]

Malraux so far refuses that faith. He sees its glory in the past only. He does not see it working in the present, as it once did, although it was a religion primarily of the present. "The fascination of Christianity in the early days," he says, "was not at all primarily in heaven; fewer scenes of paradise than of crosses are to be found in the first Christian paintings."[91] The message of Christianity, on the contrary, was founded on that which stood in greatest need of it—on suffering. "The West, that dares not pass by human suffering without shutting its eyes, has lost the power of realizing that something was even more needful than the promise of the next world to the beggar, the outcast, the cripple and the slave: deliverance from life's futility and from the load of sorrows borne in solitude. Early Christianity won the day in Rome because it told the slave woman, daughter of a slave, watching her slave child dying in vain, as it had been born in vain: 'Jesus, the Son of God, died in agony on Golgotha so that you should not have to face this agony of yours alone.' "[92]

There was once, then, a fraternity in Christ.[93] And it was among men who knew that redemption was not a thing for themselves alone, but was something called "good news" and worth martyrdom to spread in courage, and drawing on all that is noble in man. Negatively, this fraternity was hostile to the

---

[89] *Ibid.*, p. 224.
[90] *Ibid.*, p. 494.
[91] *Ibid.*, p. 279. We would qualify this by saying that the cross gave meaning to the present because, being lifted up, it drew the attention to heaven by the open arms extended over the world.
[92] *Ibid.*, p. 280.
[93] Malraux, *L'espoir*, p. 290.

meaninglessness of suffering. It was that which the Christians hated in the world—but never suffering itself, because the Redeemer had suffered. There was authenticity in all this; not a type of so-called authenticity that would refuse suffering, fight blindly against it, always struggle to produce a defiant world free from suffering. Christianity preferred to touch it with the fingers that put spittle on a blind man's eyes.

A philosopher of history has written that in the Western world the problem of suffering has been faced in two different ways: by the myth of Prometheus or by faith in Christ, "the one a rebel, the other a servant. Neither antiquity nor Christianity indulged in the modern illusion that history can be conceived as a progressive evolution which solves the problem of evil by elimination."[94]

Malraux would seem to have groped for a mitigated Promethean position. His sense of destiny would never allow him the hope that suffering could leave the world. He therefore accepts the tragic. He offers the answer of *fraternity*, failing to find the Christian answer. He says that the Mass "has found the only setting worthy of it in barbed-wire camps." He does not see that there is more than one kind of barbed wire.[95]

Some of the first atheists also wanted a fraternity. Feuerbach would never have conceived the unbrotherly Nietzschean Superman as an answer to life. His attempt to save what was for him worth saving in the ideal of Christian love is prophetic of Malraux's thought. If, as Feuerbach said, religion was alienation and nothing but man's projection of his own greatness into an illusion, the projection was to remain because man assumes true divinity, not by seeing in himself as an individual what he had attributed to God, but by rediscovering the distinction between

---

[94] Karl Löwith, *Meaning in History,* p. 3. Chicago: The University of Chicago Press, 1949.
[95] *V.S.,* p. 493.

the individual and mankind. The individual must go out from himself and, following the law of love, find himself in fellowship with those of his own species.[96]

This is, of course, replanting the tree in sand, and modern altruistic moralities are its withered branches. For what can I see in my fellow man that demands that I be just to him and love him, despite my natural selfishness, when neither he nor I are more than a whimper in the chorus of meaningless human voices? I can huddle together with him, so that we both have company. I can live with him in an instinctive loyalty. But I cannot sacrifice, and I cannot die, for him if his and my incorrigible insistence that there be meaning in life has thrust us both into an "unauthentic" idealism of some sort. I cannot do it out of sheer fidelity to the "quality of man" if that is to be found in a lucid acceptance of the absurd that is man and the courage to try to build a world of hope that is hopeless. No character in *L'espoir* in a moment of heroism prefaces his thoughts with "I know this is absurd"; he at least momentarily believes that what he is doing makes sense. And the fraternity which he feels comes from allegiance to something that "in his eyes counts more than himself." Can anything count, in Malraux's world? Or is Malraux moving away from his initial premises? We shall see.

---

[96] Feuerbach, *Essence du Christianisme*, p. 309: "La collectivité humaine, l'espèce n'est pas une pensée pure; elle existe dans le sentiment, dans l'énergie de l'amour. C'est l'espèce qui nous inspire l'amour, car son coeur à elle en est plein. Le Christ est donc, en tant que conscience de l'amour, la conscience de l'espèce. Un jour nous devons tous être unis en Lui. Celui qui aime l'homme pour l'homme lui-même, qui s'élève à l'amour universel correspondant à la nature de l'espèce, celui-là est chrétien, est le Christ Lui-même. Il fait ce qu'a fait le Christ, ce par quoi Il a mérité ce nom."

PART III

The Discovery
of Man

CHAPTER VI

Knowing Man

Malraux, at the opening of *Les noyers de l'Altenburg*, is a prisoner of the Germans in the cathedral at Chartres. "As a writer," he says, "by what have I been obsessed for the last ten years if not by mankind? Here I am face to face with our basic essence. And I think once more of my father's saying, which the constant presence of death has imposed on my memory and on which captivity relentlessly makes my thoughts run: It is not by any amount of scratching at the individual that one finally comes down to mankind."[1]

The essence of man, and mankind. Malraux has long abandoned violence and individualism; and as his thought has developed, it has passed from the nobility of the individual to the fullness of fraternity. Now it is going to fan out over history until it formulates an eloquent appeal to belief in mankind.

The approach in all the books so far has been through live characters; and since *Les noyers de l'Altenburg* is a novel, the same approach will prevail. But Malraux inserts at the heart of the book a thinly disguised treatise in the form of a discussion on man, which is a portent of things to come; for the long dialogue with art in *Les voix du silence* and the shorter one in *Le musée imaginaire de la sculpture mondiale* are the final

---

[1] *N.A.*, p. 29.

release of the novelist into a new form. It is as though an actor suddenly stopped acting and walked to the footlights to explain to the audience in burning words the hidden meaning of his lines.

From the beginning Malraux had been ill at ease with the idea of individualism, passionately (and absurdly) individualistic though his first works are. Ling in *La tentation de l'Occident* defends the Oriental ideal which Malraux will translate twenty years later into Western terms. Ling says:

> We do not desire to become conscious of ourselves as individuals. The action of our spirit is to sense with full clarity [*lucidement*] our fragmentary quality and to draw from it a sense of the universe, not in the way your learned men use scattered bones to reconstruct fossils, but more like looking at a name on a map and seeing in the imagination unknown landscapes lined with tropical creepers.[2]

Humanity, therefore, is not a total of individual nations and peoples: it is a haunting, mysterious presence, evoked by the fragments of it that are one's surroundings. Manuel in *L'espoir* felt it, and Vincent Berger's son feels it in an abandoned village during World War I.

> Like a man confronted for the first time with India, I can hear in this picturesque profusion the hum of the centuries buried almost as deep as last night's darkness: these barns bursting with grain and straw, these barns with their beams hidden by husks, full of harrows, canes, poles, wooden carts: barns which consist only of grain, wood, straw, leather . . . surrounded by the fires of refugees and soldiers, these are the barns of the Gothic age; our tanks at the end of the road are filling up with water, monsters kneeling at the wells of the Bible. O life, how old you are![3]

But it is not by any amount of scratching at the individual that one comes to mankind. We saw, when talking of the sense

---

[2] *T.O.*, pp. 111-12.   [3] *N.A.*, p. 288.

of destiny in Malraux, that he thinks we are doomed to failure if we are forced "to found our notion of man on the consciousness each has of himself."[4] There is nothing definite by which we can define the individual,[5] and self-examination does not reveal anything about man, but tells us merely about the man who is in the habit of examining himself.[6] To wish to give precision to the self is to scatter the self in probabilities.[7] Introspection is an overworked tool.

What of knowing another individual? Gisors says that the human being defies knowledge;[8] the most you can hope for is to feel sometimes that you know him.[9] There are hints: you can for instance tell something about what he is like by what makes him suffer;[10] but strictly speaking "the roots of a man's character rarely provide an immediate motive for his actions,"[11] nor do his public allegiances offer any important clues. To draw conclusions, for example, from the program of the party he belongs to would be much the same as setting out to deduce the psychology of Peruvians from their religious myths.[12] And since for us a man "is the sum total of his actions, of what he has done and of the things he may do yet,"[13] our knowledge of him will always be inadequate.

For a man's significance comes from what he does and not from his secret qualities,[14] so that we can say that a man is what he achieves.[15] Vincent Berger holds out savagely against the "secret theory," which he speaks of as he would of pickpocketing. "In the realm of secrets . . . men achieve equality too easily."[16] Too much can be read into their actions.

---

4 *J.E.*, p. 139.
5 *T.O.*, p. 103.
6 *N.A.*, p. 115.
7 *J.E.*, p. 143.
8 *C.H.*, p. 77.
9 *Ibid.*, p. 268.
10 *Ibid.*, p. 54.

11 *Ibid.*, p. 53.
12 Malraux, *L'espoir*, p. 279.
13 *C.H.*, p. 271.
14 *N.A.*, p. 50.
15 *Ibid.*, p. 90.
16 *Ibid.*

Why the apparent defeatism of Malraux in the field of psychology? His novels do not, for example, indulge in real character portrayal, and most of the characters speak very much along the same lines. Referring to his own work, Malraux wrote in 1953 that "the modern novel is, in my eyes, a means of privileged expression of the tragic in man, not an elucidation of the individual."[17]

The main reason that he has no interest in psychology, I suggest, is his ethical preoccupation. Malraux is trying to give a new value to twentieth-century man, perhaps too long fed with Proust, Gide, Freud, and many lesser writers who, under the pretext of giving a more complete knowledge of man, end by dissolving him into a series of fatalities, each more constraining than the former. "All psychology is a quest for an interior fatality," says Vincent Berger.[18] There are certainly "subterranean elements in man"; they are, as much as anything, what injects anguish into the heart of life. But as in the study of artists it is their quality and not their psychoses which give them their value,[19] so "it is a mistake to appraise men by what is lowest in them."[20]

"The *coup d'état* of Christianity was its establishment of a fatality *inside* man, its foundation of it on our own nature. . . . The Christian interiorizes his myths into demons, and original sin concerns everybody."[21] It is, in fact, our struggle with the devil which makes us confuse our knowledge of man with knowledge of his secrets.[22]

None of this is the concern of Malraux, except as an object of attack. "The accusation of man's estate leads . . . to the destruction of the forms which accept it."[23] Psychology has done nothing but increase the weight of destiny: "From the man of

[17] Picon, *Malraux par lui-même*, p. 66.
[18] *N.A.*, p. 94.
[19] *V.S.*, p. 418; see also p. 304.
[20] Malraux, *L'espoir*, p. 30.
[21] *N.A.*, p. 125.
[22] *Ibid.*, p. 126.
[23] *V.S.*, p. 538.

Rousseau to that of Freud it is not liberty that has increased."[24]
No; if we are to have a valid knowledge of man's real worth, let
us look at his acts, his fight *against* fatality, and let us champion
his exercise of free choice in this fight.

And if we are to love man, we are to do so, not because of
our knowledge of psychology, but because we sense the wondrous eternity of human efforts and human strivings through all
the ages. "Fundamentally the mind only conceives of man as
eternal," says Gisors. And Malraux, himself lying in the shadows of Chartres, watches every morning his thousands of fellow
prisoners in the restless light of dawn, and muses: "It's mankind. . . . These men I am with, these very men have been living
from day to day for thousands and thousands of years."[25]

Is there, then, nothing we can learn from the individual
which can offer some reason for falling in love with humanity?
We have to know some of the "possibilities" in men, revealed
in act, before we can be tempted to even the vaguest "faith" in
man. We have to have at least glimmers of the noble in him to
know "that man was not originally other than he is now,"[26] and
that it is therefore an honor to be a man.[27] It would be hard for
a Christian to believe in an eternal happiness if he never knew
happiness in this life. Does Malraux give any samples of this
nobility in action, or in thought?

He does. Bravery was one from the start,[28] even if in its
least likely form, which is lucidity in the face of absurdity.
There is also detestation of misery and indignity. There is love
of one's fellow man. All these Malraux presents as facts readily
discoverable among men. There are, besides, the brief moments

---

[24] *Ibid.*
[25] *N.A.*, p. 28.
[26] *Ibid.*, p. 114.
[27] *V.S.*, pp. 266, 639.
[28] Malraux, *L'espoir*, p. 30: "Pour Ximenes comme pour Puig le courage . . .
était une patrie."

in which other fine traits gleam forth—almost always in men of no religion.

In *La condition humaine* Kyo, liberal though he meant to be, felt pain at May's unfaithfulness, pain "in its most degrading form: pain which his self-respect dare not admit."[29] There is Tchen, saying to the minister Smithson: "I haven't much to say for the sort of kindness that comes from the contemplation of pain."[30] Hemmelrich, like a man who has confessed secrets under torture, knew that he would behave in the same way if it happened again, but he couldn't forgive himself for it.[31] Valérie says to Ferral: "I refuse to be regarded merely as a body, just as you would refuse to be regarded merely as a checkbook."[32] Gisors says at Kyo's death: "It takes nine months to create a man, and only a single day to destroy him."[33] In *L'espoir* two fascists concoct a lie, "a story as pitiful in the hearing as in the telling, like all obvious falsehoods."[34] There is Scali, suddenly conscious of that rather nauseous sense of superiority which comes from knowing that another man is lying.[35] There is Manuel: "In every village Franco takes, everybody gets more servile than ever. . . . That's why all the underdogs, in every walk of life, have joined our side."[36] There is the Negus: "It must be hard to bring yourself to burn a man who's looking at you."[37] Manuel again: "It struck him that to make oneself loved without courting popularity is one of the finest careers a man can hope for."[38] Scali again: "But there is always something repellent about anger, especially the variety that accompanies drunkenness."[39] Attignies "was struck by the way, when men are ashamed, a moral rot sets in."[40] Gustavo: "Repentance—it's

29 *C.H.*, p. 62.
30 *Ibid.*, p. 200.
31 *Ibid.*, p. 215.
32 *Ibid.*, p. 258.
33 *Ibid.*, p. 403; see also *N.A.*, p. 251.
34 Malraux, *L'espoir*, p. 66.

35 *Ibid.*, p. 105.
36 *Ibid.*, p. 70.
37 *Ibid.*, p. 100.
38 *Ibid.*, p. 128.
39 *Ibid.*, p. 206.
40 *Ibid.*, p. 231.

about the best thing a man has in him."[41] Garcia: "No incitement must be given to the brute that slumbers in the heart of
man";[42] and finally Manuel again, when he saw a small boy dip
his forefinger into the blood of a fallen fascist and scrawl on the
wall "Death to the fascists": "When we are building a new
Spain, we shall have both alike to contend with. And one will
be no easier than the other."[43]

It should be clear from the above citations that the thoughts
of the individuals are *right,* and can come only from men
with a basic decency bred of esteem for the human being. In
fact, there is not what could be called a disreputable character in Malraux's work unless it be Clappique in *La condition
humaine*—and yet he is more of a tragic clown than a mean
character. It is safe to say that what Malraux has honored in
his characters has always been something that any moral code
based on the intrinsic dignity of man has honored. He may
therefore be propelled across history in his search for mankind,
but his instincts have first taught him to find the noble in individuals, regardless of his asseverations to the contrary. It is by
some scratching at the individual that one comes to a hope that
mankind is worth the study.

---

[41] *Ibid.,* p. 132.
[42] *Ibid.,* p. 220.

[43] *Ibid.,* p. 67.

CHAPTER VII

The Intellectual

Malraux's thought, from *Les noyers de l'Altenburg* on, becomes more and more difficult to unravel because he continues to talk to his reader in the same concrete, poetic terms that belonged quite naturally in the novels, but which, when he becomes "doctrinal," render the thought that much more impenetrable at first reading. Were he, of course, to become philosopher-sans-poetry in his direct discourse, he would lose much of his force; but the reader sometimes pines for some straight, prolonged explanations instead of flashes of intuitions in fiery language. Malraux could plead his case by quoting his remark that "every confrontation of the ephemeral and of that which the writer sees as eternal belongs to poetry."[1] Indeed, the confrontation in Malraux is a questioning of the universe by a historical individual with "immortal longings." Malraux senses an "eternal": not his personal immortality, not a God, but something somehow eternal which is man. In that case we will have to permit him his poetry. This sense of the "eternity of man" is, after all, a poetical experience.

Were Malraux more of an intellectual than a poet, the reader searching for clear lines in his thought would have an easier task, but not a more rewarding one. If "Hamlet is the poem of

---

[1] Malraux, preface to Sperber, ". . . *qu'une larme dans l'océan*," p. xix.

a banal interrogation written by a genius,"[2] the reason is that the interrogation has human meaning only when cast in a full human context. To express it in abstract terms would be to deprive it of that human meaning. The genius is the man who casts a new, warm light over the banal series of human events, with a magic all his own. "Doubtless all true poetry is irrational in that it substitutes for the 'established' relation between things a new system of relations."[3]

It could be that all Malraux is doing in *Les noyers de l'Altenburg, Les voix du silence,* and *Le musée imaginaire de la sculpture mondiale* is to "reveal the presence of a mystery, not bring the solution of an enigma."[4] There will be mystery because there is always destiny.[5] (There is mystery in Christianity, too—that of God.) One can live with mystery and be enriched by it, and Malraux is searching for this way of life. To destroy mystery is to become an intellectual who is anti-Manichean, who oversimplifies, who systematizes chosen elements in life, ignoring the rest. Sartre and Marcel do not write plays merely for royalties. Their plays are necessary for the presentation of their philosophy. The *mysterium iniquitatis* or the mystery of transcendence strikes vertically into life, smashing any sheerly intellectualized system into fragments. Rationalism did not fail only because of the atom bomb. Man is wiser than that. Life is not, and cannot be, fundamentally rationalized. The individual cannot be explained in terms of the abstract.

The "poet," then, is the valid intellectual for Malraux: and Malraux remains a poet (as did Nietzsche) even when he an-

---

[2] *Ibid.*

[3] *V.S.,* p. 61.

[4] Malraux, preface to Sperber, ". . . *qu'une larme dans l'océan,*" p. xv.

[5] *N.A.,* p. 127: "Notre fiction . . . drame, roman,—implique une analyse de l'homme. Mais il est clair que cette analyse, seule, ne serait pas un art. Pour qu'elle le devienne, il faut qu'elle entre en lutte avec la conscience que nous avons de notre destin."

nounces the new absolute. Therein lies his strength—and his enormous danger.

It is interesting to pause here and examine Malraux's thoughts on intellectuals. He has gone on record with one definition of the right kind of intellectual, in the words of Vincent Berger's son: "I know now that an intellectual is not only a man to whom books are necessary; he is any man whose reasoning, however elementary it may be, affects and directs his life."[6] It is characteristic of Malraux that when thoughts do not become actions he finds nothing to admire.

Other types of intellectuals annoy him. The anti-Manichean rationalist, as we have seen, falsifies reality. Malraux will never accept as valid the type who is top-heavy with thinking, nor the oversimplifier, nor the man to whom everything makes clear sense.[7] "It is my opinion," says Gisors, "that taking an intellectual view of things is an attempt to compensate; to arrive at an understanding through intelligence is to make a vain attempt to anticipate time."[8] Shade, the American realist, finds the communists distasteful because "everybody's brainy [a une grosse tête]. . . . That's why I'm not a communist."[9] Their brains push the communists to a ruthlessness and a disregard for the complications of life. "The idea of totality is a sort of mania with our intellectuals. . . . As for the truth about things in general, the only man who aims at a 'totalitarian reality' is, precisely, the intellectual. . . . Perhaps he's the only fellow who needs it." But he is not himself needed today. "The close of the nineteenth

6 *Ibid.*, pp. 27-28.
7 In his essay on Laclos ("Laclos," p. 420), Malraux remarks that the French admiration for intellectuals stems from the fact that "le monde, saisissable par la raison, est objet des lois. L'homme supérieur est celui qui doit établir ces lois, celles de la France ou celles du coeur humain. Robespierre ne sera pas sûr que Montesquieu n'ait été capable de faire une Constitution mieux que lui."
8 *C.H.*, p. 268.
9 Malraux, *L'espoir*, p. 149.

century was an entirely passive epoch, whereas activity seems
to be the keynote of the new era."[10]

The self-righteous intellectual is one of the few types of
men who comes in for real scorn at the hands of Malraux, and
precisely in the book where he holds the floor in debate. Intellectuals are like women—soldiers make them dreamy;[11] on the
whole they are chatterboxes;[12] they do not like one of their
number being involved in action; but if he makes a success of
it, they are more curious about him than anyone else.[13] The
professor and Wurtz are "enemies" to the German field captain
in the trenches; men of words and figures, intellectuals who
wanted to do away with courage.[14] (Malraux will say repeatedly
in *Les voix du silence* that intellectualism did away with art.)

For Malraux the world of ideas is therefore inadequate
without action. The best a man can make out of his life is to
convert as wide a range of experience as possible into conscious
thought.[15] To arrange thoughts in rational sequence is not
enough, because those thoughts have to be fed with the food
of life.

Frohock, with his customary perception, says that Malraux's
ideas "are deeply felt, but, not, properly speaking, *thought*.
Rarely has he chosen—or perhaps been able—to develop them
discursively."[16] Part of the difficulty in understanding Malraux,
in fact, comes from insisting on using a strictly intellectual ap-

---

[10] *Ibid.*, p. 281. See also *Conq.*, p. 153: "Le Chinois inculte, le Chinois qui ne sait
pas lire les caractères, remonte et commence à dominer celui qui lit les livres
français et anglais."

[11] *N.A.*, p. 102.

[12] *Ibid.*, p. 107.

[13] *Ibid.*, p. 126.

[14] *Ibid.*, p. 179. In his preface to Sperber, ". . . *qu'une larme dans l'océan*" Malraux
remarks on the habit of intellectuals of incarnating in humble humanity "les
valeurs qu'ils ont perdues" (p. xviii).

[15] Malraux, *L'espoir*, p. 282.

[16] Frohock, *André Malraux and the Tragic Imagination*, p. ix.

proach. If he is a poet who has enriched his intuitions with personal experiences of great intensity, this approach is as unfair, and as unrewarding, as studying Shakespeare, for example, for his grammar. The blend of sensibility and thought must be left intact, as it should be in the case of Dostoevski, because man "thinks" with his sensibilities also. The presence of mystery (whether the mystery of evil or the mystery of God) is *felt* with the sensibilities, and mystery must be included in any portrayal of human life. Add to the both of those, to sensibility and thought, the experience that action and decision have brought, and you have the despair of the logician—but the richness that is Malraux.

In *Les noyers de l'Altenburg* the oversimplified "totality" contentions of the intellectuals will be refuted by human experience, as false aesthetics will be refuted in *Les voix du silence* by the adventure of art.

CHAPTER VIII

The Lived Approach

Permanence and metamorphosis in man is the theme of the famous discussion of the gathered intellectuals in *Les noyers de l'Altenburg*.[1] Möllberg, a renowned anthropologist,[2] instead of propounding a doctrine of man's permanence under change, shocks his listeners by bringing his conclusions from his African studies into support of the Spenglerian thesis of organic, discontinuous, meaningless civilizations.

Möllberg's conclusion is not Malraux's, and to identify Möllberg and Malraux is utterly to misunderstand the book. Malraux, in fact, comes to the opposite conclusion: that there is a meaningful permanence in man, underneath all civilizations.

In Part I the soldier named Berger,[3] a prisoner of war at Chartres, is overcome with the realization that the men around him are as much Gothic as modern. Part II recounts the life of Berger's father, Vincent, especially his adventures in the Near East in collaboration with the Young Turks. His plans had failed, but his experiences had given him a deep sense of the

---

[1] This book first appeared under the general title *La lutte avec l'ange*, the present text constituting the first part. The Gestapo destroyed the second part. The first publisher was Skira, 1945.

[2] C.-E. Magny ("Interrogation à Malraux," *Esprit*, October 1948, p. 523) identifies Möllberg with the anthropologist Frobenius, the author of *L'histoire de la civilisation africaine*.

[3] The name Malraux used in the Resistance.

111

unity of mankind and had set him in strong opposition to Möllberg's thesis.

Part III is the dispute among the intellectuals. At the inter-mission,[4] though silenced by Möllberg's arguments and learn-ing, Vincent Berger remains unconvinced and wanders off across the fields to the "big trees."

> The magnificence of the venerable trees was due to their great bulk, but the strength with which the twisted branches sprang from their enormous trunks, the bursting into dark leaves of this wood which was so heavy and so old that it seemed to be digging down into the earth and not sprouting from it, created at the same time an impression of free will and of endless metamorphosis.[5]

In Part IV Vincent Berger is on the Vistula front in World War I, and witnesses a poison-gas attack against the Russians. Assaulted with a rush of pity for the victims and bristling with horror at the brutality of the gas ("man was not born to rot"),[6] with the rest of the Germans he runs to the rescue. Men are brothers even despite wars.

In Part V Vincent Berger's son engages in a tank attack in World War II. Surviving, he walks with his companions into a village and finds a peasant couple sitting on a bench. They are too old to flee with the others. He looks at the woman:

> Open doors, washing, barns, man's imprint, biblical dawn in which the centuries jostle, how the whole dazzling mystery of the morning deepens into the mystery cropping out on those wasted lips of hers. Let the mystery of man emerge from that enigmatic smile, and the resurrection of the earth becomes nothing more than a pulsat-ing backcloth.
>
> I now know the meaning of the ancient myths about the living snatched from the dead. I can scarcely remember what fear is like; what I carry within me is the discovery of a simple, sacred secret.
>
> Thus, perhaps, did God look on the first man.[7]

---

[4] The discussion is never resumed.
[5] *N.A.*, p. 151.

[6] *Ibid.*, p. 228.
[7] *Ibid.*, pp. 291-92.

Les noyers de l'Altenburg is Malraux's testament of his discovery of the unity of man. "The human element, the quality of
man"[8] has come in to him as a revelation. And each section
of the book enigmatically says the same thing. Man is the noble
factor of the universe. In the Chartres camp the author hears
"in this den of ours, drowsy in the noonday sun of eternity, the
whispering voice of prehistoric man."[9] More than once in the
book there is the feeling of release, of great liberty, of joy
before this discovery.[10] Back in Europe after years in the East,
Vincent Berger senses the hum of eternal humanity: "He felt
released . . . with a raptuous liberty which was undistinguish-
able from license."[11] Home again at Altenburg, "he looked at
the infinite repetitions of this commonplace countryside, listened to the prolonged rustlings of Reichbach as it came to life,
just as in his youth he used to gaze beyond the constellations at
smaller and smaller stars until his sight failed. And the mere
presence of people passing hastily by in the morning sunshine,
as alike and as different as leaves, seemed to yield a secret that
did not spring only from the death which still lurked behind
him, a secret that was far less the secret of death than of life—
a secret that would have been just as impressive if man had
been immortal."[12]

Malraux is filled with wonder and exhilarated by the discovery that the "only animal that knows it is to die"[13] on earth

---

[8] Malraux, *L'espoir*, p. 233.

[9] *Ibid.*, p. 26.

[10] Not the lost feeling of Scali in Malraux's *L'espoir*, who, at the striking of the
clock, had "une telle impression d'indifférence et d'éternité; tout ce qu'il
pouvait dire lui sembla si vain qu'il n'eut plus envie que de se taire" (p. 107).

[11] *N.A.*, p. 79.

[12] *Ibid.*, p. 93. See also p. 98, after the Nietzsche incident. There is in all this
something like the joy Kassner felt: a feeling "auprès de quoi le mot joie n'a
presque pas de sens" (*T.M.*, p. 590). It is all a far cry from the intoxication
before death felt by Tchen which needed "un mot plus fort que joie"
(*C.H.*, p. 179).

[13] *V.S.*, p. 639.

toward the end of the second millenium of the Christian era[14] is in deep rhythm with "the kind of ape who for the first time felt a mysterious brotherhood with the starry sky."[15]

This is the moment of Malraux's psalm to creation. Yet notice that creation as man-changed is his only preoccupation. He admires nature only when it is human nature, and *homo faber* is, to him, *homo sapiens* par excellence. He seems to understand that a world without man would be more mysterious than man himself!

---

[14] *N.A.*, p. 79.   [15] *V.S.*, p. 635.

History the Key

Although *Les noyers de l'Altenburg* is a refutation of the Spengler thesis, it is as emotional as that thesis itself. Nor does Malraux specify what he means by the "discovery of man." He senses the unity of the human race, the affinity all men have in their human wills despite all the sea changes of history; and *Les noyers de l'Altenburg* presents that sense through Vincent Berger and his son, both caught in awe by the mystery that is man.

The initial reaction to a reading of the book could well be this: "Yes, I've felt all that too; but it could be that Malraux and I are both guilty of a pathetic fallacy." As a matter of fact, if Malraux's presentation of man had stopped with *Les noyers de l'Altenburg*, this reaction would possibly be warranted. But he presents evidence of a sort in his subsequent work to reinforce his intuition that "man is a wondrous thing," and it is now our task to examine that evidence.

Malraux is on the threshold of a new kind of world. He had remarked in 1929 that a conversion requires a mediator,[1] and it turns out that Malraux has found his mediator. It is history. He has in history the means of liberating himself (and, he hopes, Europe) from the excesses of the weight of destiny.

---

[1] *N.R.F.*, June 1, 1929, p. 886.

"It is history's task to give meaning to the human adventure, as it was the task of the gods to relate man to the infinite."[2]

It would seem that for years Malraux had suspected the presence of this liberator. Early in life he had gone into Indo-China in search of Khmerian bas-reliefs, urged on by his interest in the art of other periods of history; and from the beginning an interest in arts of other peoples bursts forth from his work with sudden fire. He shows little interest in the history of events; his interest is rather in the *realia* left by other cultures, the history of values carved in rock, whittled into fetishes, wrought on tympans, chiseled into statues, painted on canvas. Gothic man to Malraux is the man of the Gothic cathedrals. It is to history as it remains in art that Malraux will turn to answer his questions about man. And he *must* turn to art, because art is all that remains of man the *doer*.

The "meaning of history" haunts modern thinkers. Among theologians, Catholic or Protestant or Orthodox, there seems to be perfect unanimity on the conclusion that "Christianity alone has given and can give a meaning to History, and that outside Judaeo-Christian revelation or Islam (which is to some degree a Christian heresy) there is no philosophy of history. They admit that there may be a physics of history, which analyses its laws and discovers its common elements, but there is no progress—we can say that time does not exist either in the destiny of the human race or in the destiny of individuals."[3] The basic reason in favor of this theological position is that Christianity is the only body of thought that is based essentially on a historical event, and the "modern idea, often wholly secular, which sees progress in the future—even a sheerly material future,—would have been impossible without the 'Christian fact.' "[4]

---

[2] *N.A.*, p. 140.

[3] Paul Henry, S.J., "The Christian Philosophy of History." *Theological Studies*, September 1952, p. 421.

[4] *Ibid.*, p. 424.

The secular views of history, on the other hand, follow two
general lines. One is the "cyclic" idea: the same happenings
repeat themselves, the analogous occurs in the diverse, there is
nothing new, and we learn to read our own times by discovering
our own proper parallel in the past. This view has been sardon-
ically expressed in the old saw "Plus ça change, plus c'est la
même chose."

Spengler embraces the "cyclic" idea with his "culture-
pattern" theory. "I see . . . the drama of a *number* of mighty
Cultures, each springing with primitive strength from the soil
of a mother-region, to which it remains firmly bound throughout
its whole life cycle; each stamping its material, its mankind, in
its own image; each having *its own idea, its own* passions, *its
own* life, will and feelings, *its own* death. . . . Each Culture has
its own new possibilities of self expression which arise, ripen,
decay, and never return."[5] History is not, for Spengler, *one*
linear history. It is a series of endless transformations, "of the
marvellous waxing and waning of organic forms."[6] But, though
unconnected, cultures can be like each other; and Spengler
makes predictions for the future on the basis of his analysis of
the past. Western civilization, he says, will fade out as soon as
it has thought "its economic world to finality";[7] our direction
"is set for us within narrow limits, and on any other terms life is
not worth living. We have not the freedom to reach to this or
that, but the freedom to do the necessary or to do nothing. And
a task that historic necessity has set *will* be accomplished, with
the individual or against him. *Ducunt Fata Volentem, nolen-
tem trahunt.*"[8]

Toynbee denies Spengler's organism theory, but invents his
own "sociological units," discovering nineteen or twenty-one of

---

[5] Spengler, *The Decline of the West,* Vol. 1, p. 21.
[6] *Ibid.,* p. 22.
[7] *Ibid.,* Vol. 2, p. 506.
[8] *Ibid.,* p. 507.

them. Radically he adheres to the cyclic idea, and also makes predictions for the future on the basis of the past.[9] He formally denies, however, the charge that his theory is a form of historical determinism by saying that "certainly, in the movement of all these forces that weave the web of history, there is an obvious element of recurrence. Yet the shuttle that shoots backwards and forwards across the loom of Time in a perpetual to-and-fro is all this time bringing into existence a tapestry in which there is manifestly a developing design and not simply an endless repetition of the same pattern."[10] The metaphor is appealing; and Toynbee, moreover, allows that Western civilization can possibly save itself, hinting very strongly that it may be able to do it through Christianity.[11] But he builds better than he intended. There is an unmistakable accent of determinism in all his effort to find meaning in history.[12] The tapestry seems more of a Penelope's web.

Spengler and Toynbee are guilty, therefore, in different ways, of *leveling* history and depriving change of any value: man remains in a cyclic necessity, the victim of his circumstantial situation.[13]

The other secular view of history is the "progress" idea: the factual cycles are seen in their development and decline, first in isolation, then in mutual reaction. There is a common element discernible, which gives the key to a single meaningful pattern

---

[9] Arnold Toynbee, *A Study of History*, authorized abridgment by D. C. Somervell. Oxford: Oxford University Press, 1951.

[10] *Ibid.*, p. 253.

[11] *Ibid.*, pp. 530-32.

[12] See Karl Jaspers, *The Origin and Goal of History*, translated by M. Bullock, p. xv. London: Routledge and Kegan Paul, 1953.

[13] See Max Müller, *Crise de la métaphysique*, translated by Max Zemb, C. R. Chartier, and Joseph Rovan, p. 31 (Paris: Desclée de Brouwer, 1953): "On comprend bien qu'une telle conception et interprétation rencontre la protestation et le refus des consciences éveillées à l'histoire et soucieuses de découvrir une intelligibilité spécifique dans l'être-autre et dans le devenir-autre, bien au delà de la perennité d'un choix entre le même bien et le même mal."

in which all diversities have their place, leading into the synthesis, the goal of history. Thus Hegel. Here we have an attempt
to rationalize the irrational, to insert necessity into the contin-
gent, and to find liberty itself in the most absolute determinism.
In reality, it amounts to an actual denial of history.[14]

The impetus given to historical studies in the nineteenth century has, then, injected into philosophy a new question: Is there
in the *nature* of history as a process an intelligible direction
which gives it its own meaning? Modern philosophers are generally unhappy with either of the two general secular views of
history, because both are forms of determinism, the latter more
subtle than the former. In either case the individual human will
has little to do. And that, as a matter of *fact*, there was little
interest in finding a sense of history until Christianity does not
necessarily mean for the modern philosopher that he is therefore
to accept Christianity's sense of history. Some, in fact, reject
the Christian philosophy of history precisely for the same reason
that they reject the other two: with a providence, with history
being a history of grace, there is still, they think, no play for
creative human liberty. Troubled by the mystery of the divine
power face to face with human will, they would destroy the
mystery by eliminating one of its elements. Then man becomes
what he is not, God.

Malraux, among moderns one of the most sensitive to the
discoveries of archeology, ethnology, and history, has, surprisingly, seen in the intrusion of historical consciousness into modern man another, and the latest, *destiny*.[15] It is essential that

---

[14] See *ibid.*, p. 32: "Mais l'histoire ontologique de Hegel contredit à nouveau la
conscience historique, car sa démarche est construite a priori sur l'infini conçu
a priori et du point de vue du savoir absolu. . . . La conscience historique
exige, dans l'hypothèse d'une histoire réellement ontologique . . . qu'il y ait
une intelligibilité spécifique à l'histoire et partant un mode spécifique
d'expérience de la vérité historique."

[15] *V.S.*, p. 633: "La dernière incarnation du destin, c'est l'histoire."

we understand which concept of history he considers a new imposition of fatality on the modern mind. He says:

> To give a meaning to the flow of the centuries history either postulates a millennial identity of man with himself, . . . or affirms the existence of human constants, or tries to conceive successions of human types.[16]

The task of history is to find out

> whether our civilization . . . carries within itself humanity's past as a man carries within himself the child he once was, or . . . the sky is always the sky, whether it's overcast, or clear, or streaked with cloud; but the only common factor in the three cases is the one to which it does not owe its existence.[17]

There are, again, the two alternatives: history is either a progress, or it is a meaningless series of accidents, the only constant being that there are always civilizations.

Malraux is convinced that the "progress" idea has no play today. It is the meaninglessness of history which now weighs on us. With the death of the absolute and the rejection of any Christian meaning to history, we have plunged back into time, and come up with the poignant discovery that civilizations are unrelated, that they play their appointed time and lapse into nothing. We are now obsessed, not with man's permanence, but with his dissimilarity [*dissemblance*].[18]

It is Spengler's theory of history which Malraux considers the latest form of destiny.[19] "If mental structures disappear forever like the plesiosaurus, if civilizations succeed each other

---

[16] *Ibid.*, p. 621. The first two postulates would seem to be the "cyclic" idea; the third that of "progress."

[17] *N.A.*, p. 141.

[18] *M.S.*, p. 56.

[19] Frohock, in *André Malraux and the Tragic Imagination*, p. 151, note 2, refers to the dedicatory letter Emmanuel Cerf wrote to Malraux in his *La culture en péril*, in which he mentions that Malraux said in 1942 that "the most pressing of intellectual tasks is the refutation of Spengler."

only in order to cast man into the bottomless pit of nothingness, if the human adventure subsists only at the price of a
merciless metamorphosis, it's of little consequence that men
communicate their ideas and their methods to one another for
a few centuries; for man is a chance element, and, fundamentally speaking, the world consists of oblivion."[20] "Fundamental
man is a myth, an intellectual's dream about peasants"[21] if
history's anxious interrogation of the past reveals this form of
destiny.[22] "Humanity's successive psychic states are invariably
different. Fundamentally speaking, Plato and St. Paul can
neither agree with each other nor convince each other: they
can only convert each other. . . . I doubt if there's any communication between the caterpillar and the butterfly."[23]

Our historical consciousness has therefore delivered us to
a new destiny, which is the sense of the meaninglessness of the
past, and hence of the present. Since the mental structure of
each civilization has been a fatality, so much so that men are
"perhaps more thoroughly defined and classified by their form
of fatalism than by anything else,"[24] our own form of fatality
is history.[25]

Is Malraux's concept of history not, therefore, something
that enslaves him? How can history be the liberator we said it
was in the beginning of this chapter? How can historical awareness do anything but crush man?

For Malraux it is possible to accept Spengler's ideas and
by doing so discover a new antidestiny. "The force of history,
born of the weakening of Christianity and even of Christianity
itself, is not due to modern science, nor to historical inquiries
into the life of Christ or of Buddha, but to the fact that history
locks each religion into the prison of a circumscribed past and

---

20 *N.A.*, pp. 141-42.
21 *Ibid.*, p. 146 (Möllberg talking).
22 *V.S.*, p. 539.

23 *N.A.*, p. 148.
24 *Ibid.*, p. 139.
25 *V.S.*, p. 480.

snatches from the past its absolute."[26] History puts the absolute of religion in its place. "The reason that the German theory of 'cultures' as civilizations organically autonomous and mortal has succeeded is because, in subordinating religions to an organic life of the cultures whence they are born, this theory establishes a dialogue with religious civilizations which subordinates religion without restricting itself to mere forms."[27] That once done, the fear of not having a religious absolute dissolves, and a new sense of liberty sweeps over man. History then ceases to be a destiny, because with our new eyes we can at last take a long look at man, unhampered by any preoccupations with an absolute.

The man we finally see is not, however, the man of the historian. *He* remains locked up in the mental structure of his period. It is the man of art. The world of art is suddenly released to us with the fading in importance of civilizations.[28] "Often the *Decline of the West* seems a profound meditation which might have dwelt chiefly on artistic forms,"[29] because "when art becomes its own value, conflict disappears."[30] "If we may suppose that the civilizations that have disappeared are dead, their art is not; even if the Egyptian man of the old empire should remain forever unknown to us, his statues are in our museums, and they are not mute."[31]

"Let God on the Day of Judgment confront the forms of those who lived on earth with the company of the statues. It is not the world they made, the world of men, that will bear witness to their presence; it is the world made by the artists."[32] Our historical consciousness has done this marvelous thing: it has enabled us to discover an everlastingness in man that is fundamental.[33] Not that of the individual that history studies, but of

---

26 *Ibid.,* p. 607.
27 *Ibid.,* p. 617.
28 See *infra,* Chap. 13, "Art and History."
29 *V.S.,* p. 617.

30 *Ibid.,* p. 608.
31 *Ibid.,* p. 617.
32 *Ibid.,* p. 624.
33 *N.A.,* p. 145.

the "mysterious power, peculiar to great artists, of revealing man upon his highest level"[34]—the level of a challenger of destiny. Art is an antidestiny.[35]

Art has performed this gracious service: it has taught the gods a lesson. "Islam's true paradise is peopled not by houris but by arabesques. Florence's last agony is vibrant beneath the brooding splendor of Michelangelo's 'Night,' which is rather her soul redeemed than a symbol of her sorrows, and Spanish honor has a bright facet whose name is—Goya."[36]

It is in the world of art that we see, as in a vision, the glory that is man—not man as he may sometimes superficially appear, but fundamental man. History has been a liberator "who raises up the means to be free of itself."[37]

It should be remarked that Malraux is elliptical and exasperatingly fragmentary in the references that he makes to history and to history's function. If he maintains that history is the twentieth-century form of destiny and has taken away from us the last support we could have for belief in mankind, the reader might ask whether it could not be Hegel's concept of history that is in question. After all, Hegel uses the word "destiny," and the determinism that is Hegelianism could well be what Malraux means when he says history is a form of fatalism. In Malraux, however, the lie is given to history by the moments of freedom in history that are the works of art; and all his talk of history is centered around the incommunicability of one civilization with another. For Hegel, civilizations are not meaningless and unrelated. Rather, civilizations work in a dialectic, up to the moment when the perfect synthesis has been achieved. Freedom becomes determinism; but despite this determinism there is *progress*. In Malraux, on the other hand, there is no concept of progress; in fact, our discovery that there is

---

[34] *V.S.*, p. 627.   [36] *Ibid.*, p. 624.
[35] *Ibid.*, p. 637.   [37] *Ibid.*, p. 167.

no such thing, due to history, is what weighs heaviest on us today. But that was Spengler's concept of history.[38]

There is, when all is said and done (and Malraux is symptomatic of our age in this regard), a sweeping sense of the relativism of values pervading literature and philosophy today, and increasing tolerance on the one hand, while taking the zest out of things on the other. The long backward looks cast by sociologists, anthropologists, psychologists, scientists, historians are from such a dispassionate point of vantage that frequently the varying values of peoples all seem puny things, while the sameness of man himself impresses itself more and more. Values become merely extrinsic concomitants, distractions from the main issue. Yet what issue is there except values?

---

[38] Blanchet, in "La religion d'André Malraux," *Etudes*, June 1949, p. 299, agrees substantially with my interpretation.

PART IV

The Honor
of Being a Man

CHAPTER X

The World of Art

Malraux is talking with his own voice in his works on art. Though new novels have been promised, it will be surprising if he moves back into the world of fiction, so widely has he stretched himself into the world of art. For to Malraux "art is one of the fundamental defenses against our fate,"[1] and no one has spoken so passionately of it in modern times.[2] He has laid his talent at the shrine of world art with a dedication that is complete and unqualified.

In 1947 Skira published the first of his three volumes on *La psychologie de l'art,* called *Le musée imaginaire,* and in 1949 the second, *La création artistique.*[3] The set was completed in 1950 with *La monnaie de l'absolu.* Malraux's revision of these three books appeared in 1951 under the title *Les voix du silence,* which is a much more coherent and a much fuller work than its predecessors.[4] And in 1952 Gallimard produced his

---

[1] Quoted in Frohock, *André Malraux and the Tragic Imagination,* p. 150, from an interview given by Malraux in *Arts,* November 30, 1951.

[2] See Jean Onimus, "Malraux ou la religion de l'art," *Etudes,* January 1954, p. 3.

[3] The two were translated into English in 1949 by Stuart Gilbert, and published in 1949 by Zwemmer, London. They are now out of print.

[4] *Les voix du silence* appeared in Stuart Gilbert's translation in the United States in November 1953 (New York: Doubleday and Company) as *The Voices of Silence* (see *Time,* November 23, 1953, p. 37) and in England in February 1954 (London: Secker and Warburg).

Le musée imaginaire de la sculpture mondiale, which is four chapters of text and seven hundred illustrations of selected pieces of world sculpture.[5]

Later, in 1954, he published two companion volumes to this work on sculpture, to supplement it. They are *Des bas-reliefs aux grottes sacrées*[6] and *Le monde chrétien,*[7] again published by Gallimard in the same format as *Le musée imaginaire de la sculpture mondiale,* and a treasury of black-and-white reproductions of photographs from fresh angles, to revive the sharp meanings of the sculptors. It is expected that other volumes will appear: Malraux is convinced that it is a great service to print picture after picture of works of sculpture, and there is no doubt at all that a quiet paging through these three last-mentioned books shatters any preconceived notions about art that may have been entertained by the beholder. Man is too individual, and so are civilizations!

In addition to these major works there is Malraux's *Dessins de Goya au musée du Prado,*[8] with thirty-eight pages of introduction, and an enlargement and enrichment of this, called *Saturne.*[9] Malraux directed besides the publication of an elegant volume called *Tout l'oeuvre peint de Léonard de Vinci*[10] and a volume of Vermeer's paintings called *Vermeer de Delft* with a brief essay entitled "Un artiste à jamais inconnu."[11] Later he published *Van Gogh et les peintres d'Auvers chez le Docteur Gachet* (a collection at the Louvre), with a brief essay entitled

---

[5] Malraux prints the fourth chapter in *La Nouvelle Nouvelle Revue Française,* January 1953, pp. 27 ff., under the title "La métamorphose des dieux."

[6] Paris: Gallimard (Galerie de la Pléiade), 1954.

[7] Paris: Gallimard (Galerie de la Pléiade), 1954.

[8] Geneva: Skira, 1947.

[9] Paris: Gallimard (Galerie de la Pléiade), 1950.

[10] Paris: Gallimard (Galerie de la Pléiade), 1950.

[11] Paris: Gallimard (Galerie de la Pléiade), 1952. See Malraux, preface to Sperber, ". . . *qu'une larme dans l'océan,*" p. ix: "Avec la même confiance que j'ai écrit jadis de D. H. Lawrence méconnu, de Faulkner inconnu, qu'ils étaient ce que chacun sait aujourd'hui, j'écris que ce livre est un des hauts récits d'Israël."

"Fidélité."[12] All of these volumes are themselves works of art, but, unhappily, very expensive.

That Malraux finally dedicated himself to the study of world art comes as no surprise to the student of his other works. As early as 1926 Ling, in *La tentation de l'Occident*, meditates on the contents of European museums, on the difference between European (Christian) and Chinese arts, and the Chinese distaste for the *maladroite réunion* of the art in the Louvre.[13] He speaks of Greek art,[14] of animals in Asiatic art,[15] of the mouth in Occidental sculpture,[16] of the transformation of Greek art into Buddhistic.[17] And there is the ringing warning that Europe, searching always for new forms in art, is letting in the world "with all its present and all its past. . . . The great disturbing spectacle that is beginning is one of the trials of the West."[18]

It is in this invasion that Malraux sees, twenty years before his monumental work, the infiltration of a new idea on art. "Auriga of Delphi, sulking *Koré*, Romanesque Christs, Khmerian heads, Wei and Tang Bodhisatvas, primitives of all lands— these works are chosen first because we see in them the will not to seduce, and then for their almost emotionless architecture."[19] Greatness of spirit is incompatible with seduction, the old aesthetic is dying out, and our civilization begins to prefer all works that deny it. The invasion will liberate us, and give us, the inheritors of all the arts of all civilizations, a new vision of man.

---

[12] Published by the review *L'Amour de l'Art*, Paris, 1952.

[13] See *T.O.*, pp. 36-39, 54-59, 122; *C.H.*, p. 68; and *V.S.*, p. 124, where Malraux writes: "Aux yeux de l'Asie, le musée, s'il n'est un lieu d'enseignement, ne peut être qu'un concert absurde où se succèdent et se mêlent, sans entr'acte et sans fin, des morceaux contradictoires."

[14] *T.O.*, pp. 64-69.

[15] *Ibid.*, pp. 120-22.

[16] *Ibid.*, p. 131.

[17] *Ibid.*, p. 132.

[18] *Ibid.*, p. 143.

[19] *Ibid.*, p. 145.

The reader of *Les voix du silence* will marvel that Malraux not only had had an intuition of his basic message twenty years before writing that work, but has also remained faithful to his resolution to refuse faith in any value that reduces man to one of his less noble elements. The European spirit, he says, in accepting the resurrection of the past, is "led even to awaken to its need of a negative classicism, based almost entirely on its lucid horror of seduction."[20]

Claude Vannec in *La voie royale* has the same interest in the entrance into Western civilization of the works of art of the world. "Museums are for me places where the works of the past sleep, as myths . . . waiting for artists to call them to a real existence. And if they touch me directly, it's because the artist has this power of resurrection. . . . Every civilization is impenetrable to another. But the objects remain, and we are blind before them until our own myths are in harmony with them."[21] Here, as clearly put as he will ever say it, is Malraux's doctrine on *what* resurrects the different arts, what causes renaissances of periods of art. And the metamorphoses due to time, to history, to new ideas are also expressed: "What interests me is the decomposition, the transformation of these works, their most profound life, which is fashioned by the death of men,"[22] as is the basic intuition of Malraux that art is man's way of "defending himself against death."[23]

In *L'espoir* men active in a bloody war are never so active that they cannot be caught in discussions on art. (It may be truer to say that for some their interest in art is one reason they are fighting.) Painters need walls to paint on. "Yes, sir. We'll give our painters bare white walls. Get to work. Draw. Paint. The folks who're going to pass this way want you to *tell* them

[20] *Ibid.*, p. 146. See *J.E.*, pp. 150-51, and Malraux, "Laclos," p. 425.
[21] *V.R.*, p. 61.
[22] *Ibid.*
[23] *Ibid.*, p. 62.

something. . . . The cathedrals helped in the fight, all for all, against the devil. . . . Well, we, too, must help."[24] Obscurely, art is a weapon against destiny: "We may not turn out masterpieces, masterpieces are not made to order, but we'll create a *style*. . . . One day that new style of ours will catch on in the whole of Spain, just as the cathedral spread over Europe, just as Mexico's painters have given her a revolutionary fresco style."[25] The value for an artist is style, and style is an *anti-destin*. Hear *Les voix du silence:* "Nothing corrodes more deeply the idea of destiny than the great styles, whose evolution and metamorphoses seem like the scars left by the passage of fatality across the world."[26] A new style is the symbol of liberty. Says Lopez in *L'espoir:* "Spain's a graveyard full of tombstones, and we're going to turn them into works of art."[27]

Museums, resurrections, styles, conquest of destiny—these themes are the authentic Malraux. Walter Berger sums it all up in *Les noyers de l'Altenburg* when he says: "The greatest mystery is not that we have been flung at random between the profusion of the earth and the galaxy of the stars, but that in this prison we can fashion images of ourselves sufficiently powerful to deny our nothingness."[28] Certain men have that great gift, that divine quality, of finding in the depths of themselves, and then passing it on to us, the means of releasing ourselves from the bonds of space, time, and death.[29]

1. "LE MUSEE IMAGINAIRE"

"Même si l'Egyptien de l'Ancien Empire doit nous demeurer à jamais inconnu, ses statues sont dans nos musées, où elles ne sont pas muettes."[30] Any stroller in any capital of the world today is immediately captivated by the number of books

---

24 Malraux, *L'espoir*, p. 39.
25 *Ibid.*, p. 41.
26 *V.S.*, p. 44.
27 Malraux, *L'espoir*, p. 42.

28 *N.A.*, pp. 98-99.
29 *Ibid.*, p. 113.
30 *V.S.*, p. 617.

of artistic reproductions displayed in booksellers' windows. Each country is not only reproducing its own masterpieces, but there are books in English on Vermeer, in French on Hogarth, in Italian on Manet. "Obscure" painters and sculptors are also reproduced, not because the publishers are indulging in luxury items—publishers are usually smart businessmen—but because the fever of the times is art. Aesthetics is invading courses in philosophy, and a new metaphysics is being constructed under the title of art criticism. The ontology of style, as one writer put it, is replacing the ontology of concept. "It is to the mystery of art that men are turning, a mystery with the promise of the key, the explanation of man."[31]

The museum, once a collection, has become—and it alone— a kind of temple, says Malraux. The Annunciations do not evoke more prayerful recollection in the churches of Italy than in the National Gallery of Washington,[32] as any visitor to that museum will readily testify.

And of all the voices proclaiming the mystery that is art, André Malraux is *facile princeps*. It is the purpose of this chapter and those that follow it to present, as much in Malraux's words as possible, his thoughts on art.

The surgeon who removes a cataract does not translate the world for a man; he gives it to him or back to him.[33] Modern art is a surgeon; having found its own values, it has resurrected all the values that are stranger to it, and we are now the inheritors of the first universal humanism.[34] We are therefore the first people in history to have the grace of the vision of the quality of man.[35]

---

[31] Onimus, "Malraux ou la religion de l'art." *Etudes,* January 1954, p. 3.
[32] *V.S.,* p. 598. See also p. 493: "Tout ce siècle obsédé de cathédrales ne devait en laisser qu'une: le musée où l'on réunirait ses peintures."
[33] *Ibid.,* p. 606.
[34] *Ibid.,* p. 629.
[35] *Ibid.,* p. 638.

Our great boast, as men of the twentieth century, is that, freed as we are from the sense of any absolute which the art of the past may have served, we now have a new concept of art which can be applied to any great art of the past, and in that new concept we find our ultimate antidestiny. Art emerges with a life and a meaning all its own, free from the limitations of both time and place.

The cultures of the past are our inheritance. For a while, in the nineteenth century, it was the museums that gathered the past and began to change our relations with art. But museums had no stained glass, few frescoes, few great collections of tapestries. Napoleon could not transport the Sistine Chapel to the Louvre, and "no Maecenas will bring the Royal Portal of Chartres to the Metropolitan Museum of Art."[36] Even had a man been able to travel from one famous museum to another, he would have had only his memory to serve him in comparing a painting in Madrid, for example, with one in Rome. Also, sculpture had little place in museums.

It was photography (and be it remarked that photography is the product of technological advance!), succeeding engraving, with the perfection of color reproduction, which finally made world art available.[37] Framing and other techniques allowed into our "make-believe" museum tapestry, stained glass, coins, plates, amulets, miniatures, illuminated manuscripts, and all the painting and sculpture of the world, from prehistory to the timeless fetishes of Africa. Works can be reduced to a common scale, and a miniature compared to a tapestry, a painting to a stained-glass window.[38] Details and angles can be studied, and we have, ready at hand, all the data necessary for examination. A new *intellectual* understanding of the meaning of art is

---

[36] *Ibid.*, p. 13. John Pierpont Morgan or William Randolph Hearst may have dreamed of doing just that.

[37] *Ibid.*, pp. 15-44.

[38] *Ibid.*, p. 19.

now possible. The result is that our relation with art has become increasingly intellectualized for more than a century.[39]

What is it that prompts us to seek out all this art of the world? The zest of photography addicts is not what has produced our *musée imaginaire*. It is something else, something very deep, springing from our new twentieth-century mentality, that has called us to the quest of world art, and it is happily contemporaneous with modern skill in photography. What is this new fact that has removed the cataracts from our eyes, so that we can look around without prejudice at the conflicting arts of all times? It is a meeting of two elements: first, the death of the old academic "aesthetic," and, second, the positive element that is modern art. The first is the riddance of a distraction; the other a source of new vision.

2. THE DYING AESTHETIC

From the eleventh to the sixteenth century artists had been groping for the key with which they could release art from two dimensions. It was Da Vinci who found that key, and created the miracle of perspective. In doing so he changed the whole idea of art. Paintings from then on were to become something they had never been before, representations of beautiful subjects, not affirmations of an absolute. Gothic had been an affirmation.[40] "A crucifix of Giotto had been testimony: the Last Supper was a sublime tale."[41] The new idea of the "beautiful," the power to create illusions, to make a painting the representation of something fictional, "de l'imaginaire harmonieux,"[42] supplanted all other ideas of painting, and the Gothic artist, for one, was all of a sudden considered "an artist who would have

---

[39] *Ibid.*, p. 12; see also p. 575.
[40] *M.S.*, p. 38: "Les sculpteurs des crucifix du Rhin, celui du *Dévôt Christ* . . . veulent peut-être bouleverser, mais d'abord témoigner."
[41] *V.S.*, p. 70.
[42] *Ibid.*

liked to paint like Raphael, but could not,"[43] because in the time of Raphael "a masterpiece was considered the picture that could not be further perfected by the imagination."[44] The Italian *âge d'or* had dawned. It will perdure among most artists up to the nineteenth century.

The idea of beauty disengaged from time and history, the ideal of the "perfect work," gave rise to the myth of *eternal* style, and all previous styles were looked on as the childhood or decline of that style. For the first time in history, says Malraux, art escaped time.[45]

The Renaissance had thought that it had discovered another eternal style in Greece. In point of fact, we now know that the true art of Greece was not the art first discovered in the Renaissance, but was an earlier art, whose significance was in its attempt to reconstruct the universe according to human laws,[46] and was hence the first profane art of the world.[47] With its movement,[48] the smile,[49] with its nudes which finally became Nikés,[50] it was the first art that was in the pursuit of man.[51] "For many of us the fundamental discovery of Greece is its questioning of the universe"[52] and its replacing man for the absolute. Greek faces, for example, are "just the human face, free of demons, of death, of the gods."[53]

But at the time of the great European monarchies Greece was resurrected in its "baroque" period, its Alexandrian and

---

[43] *Ibid.*, p. 84; see also p. 18.

[44] *Ibid.*, p. 15.

[45] *M.S.*, p. 47. Malraux will say, however, that an "eternal style" is as impossible as an epoch outside of time: see *V.S.*, p. 405.

[46] *V.S.*, p. 84.

[47] *Ibid.*, p. 73.

[48] *Ibid.*, p. 74.

[49] *Ibid.*, p. 78.

[50] *Ibid.*, p. 79.

[51] *Ibid.*, p. 83.

[52] *Ibid.*, p. 72.

[53] *N.A.*, p. 98.

Roman imitations.[54] Thus the support it gave to the idea of the times that art could be a means of creating a fictitious world, expressing beauty.[55]

The times were susceptible to such an idea, *teste* Malraux, because with the Italian Renaissance "religion had ceased to be faith."[56] The world was, of course, still Christian: Italy made Roman columns as ornaments for its basilicas, not for battering rams to destroy its churches.[57] But from the day that Nicholas of Cusa wrote "Christ is perfect man," a Christian cycle closed at the same time as the gates of hell: the forms of Raphael could be born;[58] and religion and fiction became so confounded that Raphael quite naturally Hellenized or Latinized the Bible.[59] Goddesses and Madonnas became alarmingly alike.

With the Italian ascendancy, all other art was judged according to its "Italianism." It was in speaking Italian that one was admitted to the Academy of Eternity, even if one spoke with the accent of Rubens.[60] Formerly painters had known only

----

[54] In *M.S.*, pp. 25 ff., Malraux compares the "good" and the "bad" Greek art with illustrations.

[55] It is not possible to challenge Malraux on his preferred interpretation of Greek art as an "interrogation of the universe," for his answer would be to tell his critic to go and take another look at it. Socrates (who may not, admittedly, have understood Greek art) recommends to his interlocutors not to copy their models, but to take from each that which is *most beautiful* and recompose the whole into an image superior to reality, or at least to each reality taken separately. (See Xenophon, *Memorabilia*, Bk. 3, Chap. 10; also Chap. 8.) It is true that theories about art and their execution are frequently vastly different things: but are we justified in neglecting this contemporary evidence? Malraux remarks about Plato (*N.A.*, p. 112): "Malgré la recherche la plus attentive, les soins les plus zélés, nous ignorons encore l'idée essentielle que Platon se faisait de la musique, même de la beauté . . ."

[56] *V.S.*, p. 70. See p. 601: "Le grand art chrétien n'est pas mort de l'épuisement de toutes les formes possibles, il est mort de la transformation de la foi en piété."

[57] *Ibid.*, p. 268; see *M.S.*, pp. 45-46.

[58] *V.S.*, p. 84.

[59] *Ibid.*, p. 87.

[60] *Ibid.*, p. 16.

their points of departure and groped after new styles. Now it was expected "that they know where they are going, that they submit themselves to a preconceived idea of painting."[61] And since painting had become a beautification of realities and of dreams, the intellectual became for the first time the *arbiter elegantiarum*, because an intellectual can see in painting the representation of a fiction much more easily than he can see in it a specific language.[62]

Neoclassicism is thus on the scene, and the art of illusion gains strange champions. The Jesuits, for Malraux the arch-proponents of religion as opposed to faith, in their fight against Protestantism and later against the Enlightenment, found in painting a "means of action," and the style of *la plus grande illusion* was pounced upon by these champions of Catholicism as the most apt means of acting on the greatest number of spectators.[63] The art with which they covered the interiors of their churches became a means of propaganda, an instrument of *séduction* instead of an affirmation of a faith or a way of preaching. The rise of the theater and the Jesuits' ready use of it in their apostolate also influenced painting, and we thus have the furiously profane character of all baroque.[64] The women saints were neither fully saints nor fully women. They were actresses. The principal means of expression of the painter was no longer design or order, but the *personnage*.[65]

---

[61] *Ibid.*, p. 87.

[62] *Ibid.*

[63] *M.S.*, p. 44: "L'église impose le décor jésuite, exploitation des découvertes du baroque par la publicité de Paradis, aux peintres pour qui la peinture n'est pas une foi et dont la religion est devenue piété."

[64] *V.S.*, pp. 89 ff. See also Malraux, *Saturne*, p. 146: "Avec la Renaissance, l'art . . . était passé du service de la foi à celui de la civilisation, d'une image parée que l'homme se faisait de lui-même. Dans les formes italo-françaises qui avaient conquis l'Europe, les 'lumières' des philosophes ne s'opposaient nullement à celles des Jésuites, chez qui ils avaient fait leur rhétorique."

[65] *V.S.*, p. 90. The delirium of baroque leaves painting for good when the cinema is created, says Malraux (*ibid.*, pp. 119 ff.).

Hence romanticism, the art of poetry, becomes possible. "Up to Delacroix, the ideas of great painting and of poetry were inseparable."[66] Poetry, in turn, finally became enslaved by *official* painting, which subjected the artist to the service of the romantic and the sentimental, both often linked with the "fiction of history." Battles and heroes replace religion, and the art of the bourgeoisie rules in tawdry supremacy.[67] In brief, the decisive change of the function of painting which produced Italianism, the *beau idéal,* and the sentimental gets lost in the immense cemetery that is nineteenth-century *académisme.*[68]

After romanticism, itself a valid moment in art with great artists to its credit[69] because poetry had always been a possible means of expression and has never been entirely absent from painting,[70] the true artist was forging ahead on his own trail. Cézanne, Renoir, Gauguin, rejected the official art, and a historian of the years between 1870 and 1914 would be quite confused to find in the art of that period not only two schools, but even two concepts of the meaning of art. Cormon, Bonnat, Bouguereau, and Roll make strange contemporaries for Seurat, Van Gogh, and Cézanne.[71] All true painters were vomiting from their mouths the "Portrait of a Great Physician Performing an Operation,"[72] because that sort of thing was pandering to the bourgeois taste, which, as we have seen, was not built on true values. The bourgeois understood only the arts that satisfied his sensations, the arts that Malraux calls antiarts.[73] He had no absolutes, but was an *homme-du-fait.*[74]

---

[66] *Ibid.,* p. 52.
[67] *Ibid.,* p. 95.
[68] *Ibid.*
[69] *Ibid.,* p. 486; see also p. 97.
[70] *Ibid.,* p. 56.
[71] See *M.S.,* p. 25. "Production" and "creation" are often contemporaries.
[72] *V.S.,* p. 490.
[73] *Ibid.,* p. 523.
[74] *M.S.,* p. 41.

The real painter becomes a *peintre maudit,* and despising popular appeal as much as he is despised by the popular taste,[75] paints pictures that nobody buys,[76] sacrificing everything to his art. Even today we are inclined to look on the hungry artist in his garret as *the* type of artist. He is, in fact, rather recent in history. He had to be, however, because the official canons of the times were false canons, and his world had to be the world of his art. The *petit bourgeois* is defined by self-interest; Cézanne sacrificed everything to his work. The bourgeois is attached to his desires and is out of touch with anything that is beyond him; Cézanne submitted his life to a single value—painting,[77] and the bourgeois will still not accept him!

The old aesthetic of the beautiful is therefore long dead and gone, except in the textbooks and in some schools which "teach" art. We are once more free to found our concepts of art on the experience of art, and have done with subordinating art to concepts,[78] to rules imposed by any aesthetic.[79] Actually, *fiction,* the art of representation, is now for us only a moment in the long history of art, and one of the *means of style;* style is no

---

[75] *V.S.,* p. 598.

[76] *Ibid.,* p. 491.

[77] *Ibid.,* pp. 343-44. See pp. 492-93, 614. In *Sens et non-sens,* pp. 15-48 (Paris: Nagel, 1948) Maurice Merleau-Ponty shows that for Cézanne the only world worth living for was that of painting.

[78] *V.S.,* p. 446; see p. 88.

[79] I cannot resist quoting Toynbee, *A Study of History,* Somervell abridgment, pp. 245-46, talking of the breakdown of civilizations. What he says could be incorporated *mutatis mutandis* into the thought of Malraux. "These breakdowns [can be described] in non-material terms as a loss of creative power in the souls of creative individuals or minorities. . . . The piper who has lost his cunning can no longer conjure the feet of the multitudes into a dance; and if, in rage and panic, he now attempts to convert himself into a drill-sergeant or slave-driver, and to coerce by physical force [in art this would be, in our present case, the social pressure of the bourgeoisie] a people that he can now no longer lead by his old magnetic charm, then all the more surely and swiftly he defeats his own intention; for the followers who had merely flagged and fallen out of step as the heavenly music died away will be stung by a touch of the whip into active rebellion."

longer the means of representation.[80] It would be easy, as a matter of fact, to bracket the three centuries in which an aesthetic of beauty was dominant as a humanistic accident,[81] because, freed from it, the art of the world and of all history has so overshadowed those "three unhappy centuries" that they now seem themselves only an illusion.[82]

It must be remembered that through all this melancholy tale of the decline of the "aesthetic ideal" in art, there was also, for Malraux, a parallel decline of any belief in an absolute, and that, science and "progress" now being exposed as counterfeit ideals and optimism officially buried, neither belief in a providence or in the pretty little world of the bourgeoisie of the nineteenth century is of any interest to the man of today who "wants to make something out of his life."

The reader may be annoyed at what seems here an oversimplification. Admittedly, the decline of *the* aesthetic was inevitable in a world of human freedom: no artist with the inner dynamic to paint is going to submit for long to pre-established canons of painting, especially if they are imposed by intellectuals[83] or by the type of official who approved the cemetery that is the Pantheon.[84] But is the constricting effect of an official aesthetic necessarily bound up with the presence of an absolute? Must the absolute be killed if the aesthetic is to die? Gothic artists were at the service of an absolute, and Gothic is great

---

[80] *V.S.*, p. 331. See p. 518: "Le conflit entre les arts et leurs moyens n'est nullement éternel: en peinture, il commence à l'école de Bologne, donc à l'éclectisme. Il eût été inconcevable à l'époque romane."

[81] *Ibid.*, p. 180.

[82] *Ibid.*, p. 538. See p. 492, where Malraux says that the art in our museums is "une survie dont la beauté méditerranéenne n'avait été qu'une expression fugitive."

[83] *Ibid.*, p. 87. See *M.S.*, p. 33: "académisme . . . c'est-à-dire une rationalisation."

[84] *V.S.*, p. 596. See *M.S.*, pp. 43-44: "Asservir l'art est avant tout *imposer un style*; plus précisément, substituer à la recherche de style qui est la vie même de l'art, la convention ou la séduction: car l'art subit mille contraintes, se nourrit de plusieurs, et meurt d'une seule."

art. So is El Greco's, who discovered a "Christian style."[85]
Malraux is far from denying either fact. He says that in the
Middle Ages art was not at the service of the Church, but both
were in the service of God.[86]

We have already encountered Malraux's equivocal position
on the absolute. He seems to deplore decline of belief in an
absolute, and at the same time to find in that decline a release
for the human spirit—and the modern artist. Rather we would
say that the decline of such a belief made possible the bourgeois
set of false values, and that due to them the artist had to find
new values, thus saving himself from stagnation. That his new
values were independent of belief in an absolute is a fact. That
he would not have been a real artist had he rediscovered an
absolute, even one in a Christian form, Malraux himself would
have to deny summarily if he is to be consistent with his own
views on the superiority of Romanesque and Gothic art.

What is valid in this survey of the disintegration of the once
powerful aesthetic, therefore, is Malraux's accurate appraisal
of the bourgeois blindness to real art. It was this which nau-
seated the artist. "In his eyes, the power of the bourgeoisie was
usurpation, not because it had not conquered, but because it was
not justified."[87] Even fiction at the service of a high truth could
be great art. But once a unifying truth breaks into pieces, fiction,
which should serve art and not *be* art, becomes all powerful,
and spawns the *arts d'assouvissement*,[88] which appeal to the
lower part of man.[89] It was this that sent the true artist "far
from the madding crowd" in search of a new truth, and finally
effectively eliminated the old aesthetic from the world of art.
Its removal is the lifting of a curtain, and no longer is world

---

85 *V.S.*, p. 433.
86 *M.S.*, p. 44.
87 *V.S.*, p. 482.
88 *Ibid.*, p. 514.
89 He means the sensuality or sentimentalism of man.

art judged by its faithfulness or infidelity to the classical. We no longer see other styles negatively, by that which they lack of the classical, but we see them by what they mean themselves to say.[90]

What our new eyes see will be described later. But they have the same lucidity, as any *seeing* eyes for Malraux, as those of all the heroes of his novels, and they brighten with fraternal recognition each time they espy an art that is hostile to illusion,[91] to optimism,[92] to the miraculous,[93] to the petty world of appearances[94]—to the smile.[95] We become thus strangely sympathetic to sacred art,[96] and by that to all the art of all the world and of all time, because except between the sixteenth and the nineteenth centuries there was no *great* art of illusion, since men did not consider their religious beliefs illusions. Even the art of Greece rejected illusion. The Greek art which tricked the men of the Renaissance into an ideal of beauty was not the *great* Greek art. It was Alexandrianism.[97]

3. MODERN ART

Malraux says that, if Lorenzo the Magnificent had scanned the photographs of world sculpture gathered in *Le musée imaginaire de la sculpture mondiale,* he would not have seen them.[98] He would have been blinded by the old aesthetic. *We* are able to see them because that aesthetic is dead. But that is merely removing an obstacle. What is it that urges us to give them the examination they deserve? It is the new *value* in art which has been discovered by *modern art.*

The art of the past, that dictionary in which we are going to find the words with which to define our new humanism, has

90 *Ibid.,* p. 18.
91 *Ibid.,* p. 526.
92 *Ibid.,* p. 538.
93 *Ibid.,* p. 580.
94 *Ibid.,* p. 594.

95 *Ibid.,* p. 78.
96 *Ibid.,* p. 593.
97 *Ibid.,* p. 45.
98 *M.S.,* p. 56.

gone through a complex metamorphosis. We are inclined to forget, for instance, that Greek sculpture was colored, and yet the palette of an age is not less an expression of it than is its design.[99] Romanesque sculpture was a cinema of colors, and Gothic columns were striped in intense hues.[100] Much of the work of the past is in a state of decomposition, which frequently adds to its appeal: we would not, for example, now tolerate arms on the Venus de Milo,[101] or a head on the Niké of Samothrace. They are too much admired the way they are: they are now intact only if damaged!

But there is a more profound kind of change, one that has taken place within us ourselves, which modifies our attitude to the art of the past. Our knowledge of the history of an era, for example, has much to do with our views on its art. Medieval art, for one, means different things, depending on whether we look on it as part of the Dark Ages or as a powerful architecture of man.[102]

Our own historicity plays a great role in our appraisal of the past. It was not the same before and after 1789. Human experiences are different; the world has changed. And our appraisal of art depends very much on our appraisal of the artists themselves. What brought El Greco back was not research, but modern art. "What brought the antique statues to life, the diggers, or the masters of the Renaissance who opened their eyes? Who rendered the Gothic mute, if not Raphael? The destiny of Phidias was in the hands of Michelangelo, who had never seen his statues; the austere genius of Cézanne magnified the Venetians who made him despair. . . . It is in the light of the sorry candles that Van Gogh, already insane, stuck into the brim of his straw hat so that he could paint the café at Arles at night, that Grünewald appears. . . . Metamorphosis is not an

---

99 *V.S.*, p. 45.
100 *Ibid.*, p. 48.
101 *Ibid.*, p. 50.
102 *Ibid.*

accident; it is the very law of life of the work of art."[103] The masterpiece is not a sovereign monologue; it is an invincible dialogue with the past and the future. And it is we, with our own particular vision, who do the choosing and the exalting, leaving aside the rest.[104]

It is modern art which modifies our own historicity and suddenly gives life to statues and paintings which have long been among us, but have remained mute. Why? We saw, for example, that it is hostile to illusion.[105] "It is not long that Piero della Francesca has been considered one of the great painters of the world, but since he has, Raphael has changed a great deal."[106] But it is something deeper than hostility to illusion that is the preoccupation of modern art. It has discovered something special, the very core of the meaning of art, and it is due to that that we can look again at the past, suddenly finding the same secret in all art.

With the death of the exaltation that was Protestantism, the profane world enters the world of art.[107] Vermeer, following Hals, who had dared let painting take precedence over the model,[108] was left with only profane subjects, and proves, the first of all painters, that the painting of a world without a fundamental value can be saved by a solitary who gives it the fun-

---

[103] *Ibid.*, pp. 66-67. See p. 334: "Les oeuvres décisives flottent pour nous, en surimpression sur celles qui les précèdent; ce que l'art roman portait en lui de gothique serait plus obscur si le gothique ne nous le montrait pas." Malraux goes further in *M.S.*, p. 54: Granted that the works of art of the past have survived because they *are* works of art, "il serait pourtant non moins vrai, et plus instructif, de dire 'nous appelons art leur pouvoir de résurrection.'"

[104] *V.S.*, p. 65.

[105] This hostility is the main reason we are so impelled to look at primitives (*V.S.*, p. 495), and savage arts (*ibid.*, pp. 535 ff.) as well as at sculpture, which has always been hostile to illusion (*M.S.*, p. 54).

[106] *V.S.*, p. 50. Malraux is not partial to Raphael: see *ibid.*, p. 448.

[107] *Ibid.*, p. 473.

[108] *Ibid.*, p. 468.

damental value of painting itself.[109] Goya, though in his own
eyes painting is not the supreme value, is so free in his work
that he can be called one of the *accoucheurs* of the new value
in art.[110] But it is Manet who was to establish the first beachhead
of this new value, and of modern painting, in asserting "the
dominating presence of the painter himself" as against his subject[111]—and a new race of artists is born. The will of the modern
artist is to submit everything to his style. There is Van Gogh,
whose "Chair" is the symbol of modern art.[112] There is Cézanne:
"If the landscape and the still life, with nudes and depersonalized portraits, themselves still lifes, become the major themes
of painting, it is not because Cézanne loves apples, but because
there is more room for Cézanne in a picture of apples than there
was for Raphael in the portrait of Leo X."[113] There is Derain
and Soutine and Picasso and Léger and Matisse. They all *dominate* their canvasses, subjecting all to their art.

> Indeed this mastery is the common measure of all great works
> of art, however extravagant they may appear; it is the link between
> them and the rock-face figures of China, the pediment of Olympia,
> Romanesque statuary, the Sumerian priest-kings; and this style
> whose recognition synchronized with the "renaissance" of the
> art of savages is perhaps the greatest style the West has ever
> sponsored.[114]

All of this could look like the logical consequence of the
Protestant Revolt, since that was the rise of the individual as
against the Roman hierarchy.[115] But Protestantism was a reli-

---

109 *Ibid.*, p. 473. In *Vermeer de Delft*, p. 24, Malraux writes that Vermeer used
   members of his family as models for his paintings, adding "sujets, non
   modèles: moyens de peinture."
110 *V.S.*, p. 97.
111 *Ibid.*, p. 99.
112 *Ibid.*, p. 117.
113 *Ibid.*
114 *V.S.*, p. 580 (Gilbert translation, p. 582).
115 *Ibid.*, p. 468.

gious movement. Modern art, according to Malraux, is the negative side of sacred art, because for the moderns the sacred is
not true.[116] It is a *new* art, and at the service of an "obscure god
which one would like to call painting and which is called art."
A religious vocabulary is here necessary, because though "this
art is not a god, it is an absolute."[117] It is a faith, in the negative
sense, because it is a negation of the impure world of appearances.[118] Positively, it is bent on creating a new world, and that
is its reference to reality, because no forms are at the service
of nothing.[119] Yet the reality in which modern art is concen-
trated is precisely the reality of itself!

The new value, the discovery of modern art, the deeper
secret of it all, is the value there is "in the very old will
to create an autonomous world, *for the first time reduced
to itself.*"[120]

There we have it. It is due to this personal experience of this
power of autonomy that modern art, ceasing to subordinate itself
to any outside supreme value (like the Stoics, who made moral
values ends in themselves[121]), reveals the supreme value that is
lurking beneath all the art of history. Formerly, if the value
depicted by a work of art clashed with our own, we rejected
it. Now each value is relativized: magic, cosmic, religious,
sacred—the great works reach us from the past as so many
Zarathustras invented by so many Nietzsches.[122] For "when art

---

[116] *Ibid.,* p. 591. Modern art is "more or less openly against the Christian Masters"
(Malraux, *Saturne,* p. 112) but like sacred art in that it refuses three dimensions. A symbol of it could be the stain *(la tache)* one finds on ceramics: it
is as though it would be the art of one dimension (*V.S.,* p. 603).

[117] *V.S.,* p. 598.

[118] Our art "ne tient pour valables que les formes hétérogènes à celles de l'appar-
ence" (*ibid.,* pp. 592-94).

[119] *Ibid.,* p. 612.

[120] *Ibid.,* p. 614.

[121] *Ibid.*

[122] *Ibid.,* p. 617.

has no other end than itself, the most profound metamorphosis of the art of the past begins."[123]

The surgeon has performed the operation. Modern art has made the world of art now visible to us, in all its variety and all its contradictions.

A Roman crucifix was not first a piece of sculpture, the Madonna of Cimabue was not first a picture. Even the Pallas Athene of Phidias was not first a statue.[124] They each had some other function; and if works of art are not delivered from their historical functions, we cannot accept them.[125] How unite a Venus who was Venus, a crucifix which was Christ, and a bust? One can unite only three statues.[126] If we experienced the feelings of the first viewers of an Egyptian statue or of a Romanesque crucifix, we could not leave them in the Louvre;[127] if African fetishes were to find the full voice of their preaching, they would not invade the museum—they would burn it.[128] There must be a metamorphosis of these works if we are going to see them as art; and that is possible only with the death of the gods.[129] As long as artistic creation was the creation of sacred figures, the artist could not have known any arts of the past except of the past of his own art, because each of the great arts expresses some different part of the soul of man. In the Orient, for example, the statue "served" the fabrication of the gods, and art expressed a particular relation of man to the divine.[130] But now "to the mosaics of Byzantium, to the book which God the Father of the old Christian representations held in His sacred hands, to the illumination of the sacred texts which were destined less for the use of the celebrant than for the creator himself, to the purple book of the Gospels put on the knees of the corpse of Charlemagne and taken from his tomb

---

[123] *Ibid.*, p. 52.
[124] *Ibid.*, p. 11.
[125] *Ibid.*, p. 12.
[126] *Ibid.*, p. 51.

[127] *Ibid.*, p. 63.
[128] *Ibid.*, p. 541.
[129] *Ibid.*, p. 119.
[130] *Ibid.*, p. 64.

by Otto for the oaths of the future leaders of the Holy Roman Empire; finally to the cathedral in which human eyes did not distinguish statues from towers—there have succeeded *pictures.*"[131] The gods are now secularized because we do not believe any more,[132] and there is now the opportunity to seek deeper in the works of art for their real, secret meaning.

Only when we group them together does their language become clear.[133] We want no syncretism: our culture is made up of the irreconcilable parts of the past;[134] but all the values of the past are as different words put to the same music. Our pluralism, far from being an eclecticism, a taste for a thousand forms, is founded on our discovery of *common* elements in the works of art. The music of painting, finally isolated, by our lack of belief in any religion, from all the words in which it slumbered, is now clear to our ears.[135] Art is no longer for us one of the forms it once had; it transcends them all. This is the new fact of our times.[136]

The modern man, wandering in a maze, solicited by voices appealing to his sentimentalism and his sensuality,[137] an absurd inhabitant of an absurd universe,[138] is offered a new absolute, *art as the power of autonomy,* as the basis for the first universal humanism of all times.[139] He will have to practice a form of stoicism[140] and refuse to be seduced[141] even by his own sen-

---

131 *M.S.*, p. 45.
132 *Ibid.*, p. 48.
133 *V.S.*, p. 87.
134 *Ibid.*, p. 631.
135 *Ibid.*, p. 555.
136 *Ibid.*, p. 624. Malraux is so convinced of this that he went through 30,000 reproductions of world sculpture to select the 700 he publishes in *M.S.*, p. 16, "afin de préciser ce qui les unissait."
137 *V.S.*, pp. 518-21.
138 *Ibid.*, p. 523.
139 *Ibid.*, p. 629; see also p. 589.
140 *M.S.*, p. 66.
141 *V.S.*, p. 518.

suality,[142] and reject all forms of optimism.[143] But if he accepts Malraux's challenge, he can participate, promises Malraux, in a resurgence of Europe from bankruptcy and a new realization of the quality of man.

What will be the future of the great art of today? We do not know, because it is an art of *Great Navigators*.[144] "It is possible that the successor of what we have called modern art will be an art that is still more specific";[145] because the idea of art, now an open idea, has ceased to be preconceivable.[146] In any case art as an absolute, closed in on itself and serving no other absolute, is established as a fact by modern art, and those with eyes to see can reread the art of the past and there discover what made an artist an artist. In doing that they can see a supreme quality of man that is expressed in the artistic insistence on creating an autonomous world.

There is to be no mistake about the importance of *Le musée imaginaire* of world art in the thought of Malraux. Other eras had at least temporarily satisfying answers to questions on man and his destiny. We have none; and were the full truth to be told, Malraux holds art out as our only recourse. Our conception of the world, by its character of interrogation, is linked "to a question on man and not to a notion of man."[147] We need art to answer that question.

---

142 *Ibid.*, p. 54.
143 *Ibid.*, p. 538.
144 *Ibid.*, p. 602.
145 *Ibid.*
146 *Ibid.*, p. 607. See p. 318: "Quels que soient les dons que montrent les premiers essais auxquels il [l'artiste] s'arrête, et quelle que soit la forme de son apprentissage, il sait pourtant qu'il commence un voyage vers un pays inconnu, que cette première étape n'a pas d'importance, et qu' il doit arriver quelque chose."
147 *M.S.*, p. 56. See also p. 16.

CHAPTER XI

Style

Now that the scene is set, the temper of the times measured, our particular mentality defined, the cataract removed, we are able to turn our eyes to the art of mankind. (It is not by scratching at the individual that we can come to mankind.) Since our task is one of vision, "logic" has no privileged place in our study. Stendhal owes most of his errors on painting to the cult of logic, says Malraux.[1] He adds that his own "writings on art call for adherence, sometimes try to persuade, but prove nothing. . . . The capital works of the past being those which are united in our admiration, and not those which *should be* so united, our ambition is only to know what unites them."[2] With our *given* eyes, therefore, we scan the history of art.

Losing their nature as objects by confrontation in reproductions in our "imaginary museum," works of art suddenly become one thing, and only one thing: *style*. "It is difficult to see clearly what difference there is between our reading of a trag-

---

[1] *V.S.*, p. 353.

[2] *Ibid.*, p. 446. In his postface to *Conq.* Malraux, discussing "sentiment" in art, says: "Que telle oeuvre sentimentale soit artistique ou non, c'est un fait: ce n'est ni une théorie ni un principe" (p. 268). One must conclude that, if there is to be no *aesthetic* principle, no canon according to which real art is to be judged, one must attempt to go through the same experience as Malraux, allowing the works of art to play on him—and then agree with Malraux or not, depending on subjective reactions.

edy of Aeschylus and what it meant to an audience viewing it under the shadow of the Persian menace, with Salamis looming in the gulf. Yet we can feel the difference. Aeschylus is for us no more than his genius. And the figures which in reproduction lose their character as objects and their function, be it a sacred function, are nothing more than talent: are no more than works of art—it would hardly be excessive to say, moments of art."[3] But these different objects bear witness to the same search, to a re-creation of the universe in the face of creation.[4] "Painting tends less to see the world than to create another; the world serves style, which serves man and his gods. Style, then, does not seem to us to be merely something that the works of a school, or of an era, have in common. . . . It is for us the object of a fundamental search in art, and real objects are but its prime matter. To the question, What is art? we are moved to answer, That by which forms become style."[5]

Art, therefore, is a series of creations of a specific language, and these creations are free to follow their own destinies. The art of two dimensions, for example, so long regarded as imperfect art, is now visible to us, happily delivered as we are from the tyrannical "aesthetic," as quite compatible with style, as indeed is much of the seemingly "incomplete" art of the past. Baudelaire's words apropos of Corot, that "a work that is complete is not necessarily finished, nor is a finished work necessarily complete,"[6] are in harmony with our discovery of the Egyptian art of the old empire, of Assyrian and of Romanesque art. "Style was in those times the means of expression of an artist as much as his submission to illusion was later also style."[7] "Romanesque style may not have expressed the psychology or sentiments of the Christianity of the nineteenth cen-

---

[3] *V.S.*, p. 44.
[4] *Ibid.*, p. 13.
[5] *Ibid.*, p. 270.

[6] *Ibid.*, p. 106.
[7] *Ibid.*

tury, and the Christ of the twelfth century may be now far removed from artists and lovers of art; but Romanesque art, freed from its architecture and separated from its God, reveals that . . . art could subject the forms of life to the artist, instead of subjecting the artist to the forms of life."[8]

Coincident with the death of the old aesthetic, another change has taken place. A masterpiece is no longer what it was then, that which the imagination could not perfect further ("un navet réussi"),[9] but "the extreme point of a style, of the specificity and despoiling of the artist *par rapport à lui-même*. It is the most significant work of the inventor of a style."[10] "That which remains of a great artist, whether he believed himself at the service of God, of beauty, of himself, or of painting, is the *greatest density* of his art. . . . In the great expositions of the masters of the past it is this density which decisively designates the true masterpieces."[11] A masterpiece occurs, therefore, when the artist is *most* himself.

Book II of *Les voix du silence* is one of Malraux's two concrete proofs that art is a long search for style. It is entitled *Les métamorphoses d'Apollon* and is the story of the successive careers of the Greek style as it traveled into the Far East, into Byzantium, into Europe. Each time it is *conquered* by some other style, and *to be conquered* thus appears as the destiny of all styles: art keeps alive only as long as new styles crush those from which they are born.

Formerly, when Italianism reigned as the arbiter in art, the art that followed the fall of Rome was considered as *art regressé;* but either there was no mature art until the Renaissance or the art that spread over Gaul, Spain, Egypt, Syria, Arabia, Bactria,

---

[8] *Ibid.*, p. 105.
[9] *M.S.*, p. 38.
[10] *V.S.*, p. 17.
[11] *Ibid.*, p. 447. See Malraux, *Vermeer de Delft*, p. 24, explaining the principle on which he based the arrangement of Vermeer's work in this collection.

Gandhara was not *art regressé* after all: and whatever name you give to it, it was *not* like the art of the Renaissance. The "regression" is a form of art as widespread and as significant as that which begins at the Acropolis and ends with Constantine.[12] The word should be abolished.

Happily, we have stopped using the expression *art regressé* of all this art. Some of it *is* retrograde, of course; for retrograde art occurs whenever a style turns into a sign, an ideogram—such as appears on some coins. Then an art dies.[13] But more often a style is succeeded by another style, and then both are still art.

Malraux starts his *Les métamorphoses d'Apollon* by describing the fate of the head of Hermes struck on a stater for Philip of Macedon as it passes out into the world beyond Greece. Sometimes it is developed into a new style, as when it becomes, in Marseilles, a lion. "From degeneration to degeneration, the head of Hermes of Philip's stater is disintegrated, but this disintegration integrates into the head of a lion."[14] Sometimes it turns into a "sign," as in the coins of the Veliocasses, where it becomes "two plaits, a ring, a nose, an eye." The ensemble would be unintelligible if we did not know its origin. "There is no longer any metamorphosis here, but total regression; in this art, as in so many others, the triumph of the sign is the sign of death."[15]

What was it that changed the style of the Hermes stater? Not certainly the *maladresse* of artists—it can be supposed of every great artist that he always did what he meant to do[16]—but the fact that each period and each people had its own idea of man.

---

12 *V.S.*, p. 129.
13 Sometimes even sculpture becomes a "sign." Then its "langue sacrée" is silenced. See *M.S.*, p. 41.
14 *V.S.*, p. 137.
15 *Ibid.*, p. 142.
16 *Ibid.*, p. 129.

When sculptors fell to replacing the folds of Greco-Roman drapery by heavy, parallel, often hollowed-out folds, and when they gradually rediscovered symbolic representation (as it had been practiced for three thousand years, before being eclipsed during the six centuries of Greco-Roman supremacy), they acted thus because the Roman and Alexandrian concept of Man was passing away. Indeed, from Byzantium to Bactria, the dying Empire regarded the Aphrodites and Venuses much as we regard the wax busts in hairdressers' windows. They were not ignored, but unacceptable.[17]

1. APOLLO IN THE FAR EAST

The antique classical forms met Buddha in the Macedonian kingdoms of the East. Greece had made man the equal of his destiny, had exalted his liberty. Buddhism wished to deliver man from his destiny by suppressing the strenuous, the actively *free* acts of man. "Reincarnation had diluted all life with its eternity."[18] Yet central Asia found in Greek art a kind of liberation, because Buddhism carried in it a heavy sense of destiny. Greek art, becoming more and more Hellenistic as it crossed Asia, arrived at the Pamirs as a sun god. And it was as divinity that Buddhism embraced Greek art. The face of Buddhistic statues is that of a deliverance, that of the mediator.[19]

Greek art is rapidly metamorphosed by Buddhism.[20] The new subject of Buddhistic art is the sage, who had thus far been represented only by symbols. The first Buddhas of Afghanistan are copies of Apollo, with the addition of the signs of wisdom, a mark between the eyes and a protuberance on the head. But the metamorphosis did not stop there. There was a gradual freezing of movement, a lowering of the eyelids, and finally the conquest of mobility in any form. All of this is a refusal of the autonomy of man which had been the form of the Greek

---

[17] *Ibid.*, p. 144 (Gilbert translation).
[18] *Ibid.*, p. 147.
[19] *Ibid.*
[20] *Ibid.*, p. 149.

Niké.[21] The convent replaces the palace, the eyes are closed further, and the Buddhistic nude is not only immobile: it is delivered from movement.[22]

There is the Gothico-Buddhistic period, where the smile enters[23] when the Greek idealization is transformed into pity. Later, Greco-Buddhic art moves to China, where a true religious art arises, as distinct as Romanesque from the sacred art of the ancient East.[24] The pilgrim statues that reach the Pacific across the dry Gobi desert are touched suddenly with illumination.[25] "The eyes of the Wei dynasty are without precedent. They are the marks of a firm brush which draws spirituality from the sureness of its writing. But this spirituality is at the service of an architecture, which finds not the rigidity of death but immortality."[26] The Buddha of the Wei dynasty lowers his eyes on a universe where the vain cavalry of the Apocalypse sinks into the shadows.

> Over the voluptuous agony of the Hellenistic world, over the miserable agony of the Roman world, religious art, from Spain to the Pacific, was conquering, less by the lack of skill [*maladresse*] of primitives than by the passion of iconoclasts, the royal rights of the eternal; while to that which had been the smile of a woman before the Ionian sea, China was substituting the smile of men of silence on the mountain sides. . . .
>
> This whole adventure is not a history of the life of Hellenistic forms, but of their death. When, in India and China, they meet the powerful conception of the world of Indian and Chinese Buddhism, they are metamorphosized.[27]

The history of "influence" in art is really a history in reverse. One style conquers another. Seen in Asia, the life of Hellenistic art is that of "a liberator which raises up the means for other arts to liberate themselves from it."[28] And when

---

21 *Ibid.*, p. 150. See also p. 78.
22 *Ibid.*, p. 151.
23 *Ibid.*, p. 157.
24 *Ibid.*, p. 163.
25 *Ibid.*
26 *Ibid.*, p. 166.
27 *Ibid.*, p. 167.
28 *Ibid.*

the great conceptions of man die, so does art. The last meta-morphosis of Apollo is in the décor of the offices of the East India Company.[29]

2. APOLLO IN THE NEAR EAST

At Byzantium and in Christian Rome the new forms did not meet a powerful past, as in India and China, but encountered the Orient, at last freed of Roman legions.[30]

The Christianity of the catacombs had only a meager art. It had not witnessed a real art, because Rome, even before its conversion, had never had an art of its own.[31] And so Hermes Criophoros becomes Christ; he merely happens to be a more fitting representation of Christ than Jupiter or Caesar.[32] The Christian soul hides in antique forms as the churches are going finally to reside in imperial buildings. Out of humility the early Christian artist resorted, when he was specifically Christian, to symbols. But as soon as the Good Shepherd is no longer a sign, as soon as a woman with her child becomes a Madonna, the sacred gives promise of two means of expression. First, the arabesque of Rome is broken: the persecuted Christian lives in a form of tragedy, not sensuality. Second, the theatrical form which is the Mass enters into Christian life, not as "a question-ing by man of all that was beyond him, but as a questioning of man by all that which was beyond him, by what surpassed him, transcended or annihilated him."[33] And Christian art will be born when the "angular line will be put to the service of the eyes of the Orantes, fixed on the other world."[34]

---

29 *Ibid.*, p. 170.
30 *Ibid.*, p. 172.
31 *M.S.*, p. 42. See *V.S.*, p. 614, where Malraux calls Roman art "rhétorique," not "création."
32 *V.S.*, p. 172.
33 *Ibid.*, p. 178.
34 *Ibid.*, p. 179.

At Palmyra the gestures of Roman art were immobilized into a style of the eternal,[35] and in Middle Egypt into a style of death.[36] It was at Byzantium, however, that Roman art met its greatest challenge: not precisely by Christianity, but by the Orient.

It is high time, says Malraux, that we cease to see in Byzantium the decadence of the West. Byzantium, the only existing world power of the fifth century,[37] lasted over a thousand years, schismatic or not. And the conquerors of Roman art on the Bosporus were not disorder or sexuality: that to which Roman art yielded in Byzantium was the Oriental concept of God. "The murderous luxury which was opposed to the luminous ease of Greece, the spawning of the police so dear to tyrannies, the ingeniousness so often substituted for authority (except for the supreme authority)—all the mortuary *décor* that is Ottoman is but the latest mirroring of the millennial swell: the reflection of God."[38]

Byzantine art is a rediscovery of the divine, and it took as much genius to forget man at Byzantium as it did to discover him on the Acropolis. The Orient disdained the ephemeral, and a style had to be found to re-create the eternal.[39] Yet the superhuman had still to be expressed by the human, because Christian Byzantium knew Christ.

Christian Byzantium was proclaiming a truth, not a reality. In its eyes the life the Romans held for real is not the true life. To picture the true life the real had to be effaced. It is not

---

[35] *Ibid.*, pp. 180 ff.

[36] *Ibid.*, pp. 186 ff.

[37] *Ibid.*, p. 172.

[38] *Ibid.* This attribution of the Oriental profusion of splendor and rich gaudiness to a sense of the divine is an adventure Malraux allows himself into the psychology of a whole people. Like many of his intuitions, it is interesting; but apodictic and final though his manner be on such things, a still, small voice keeps cautioning the reader to be wary.

[39] *Ibid.*, p. 206.

a question of painting the world, but the other world. A scene is worth painting only to the extent in which it participates in the other world. Hence the backgrounds of gold, which create neither a true surface nor true perspective but another universe. Hence this style that it is impossible to understand as long as one seeks in it a reference to the real, for it is always a search for transfiguration. But Byzantium is also Oriental:

> It wishes to express the world as mystery. Palace, politics, diplomacy, all find again, as does religion, the old avidity for the secret and the lie that is the East. The art which portrays the emperors and empresses would be very superficial if it were only for the display of pomp: but it is the small change of the art of great mystery, the profane of this art which annexes it so quickly to the sacred. One has but to compare a bust of a Roman empress and the portrait of Theodora, or the St. Pudentiana Virgin, or the St. Agnes of Rome with the Virgin of Torcello. All the Byzantine incantation is in this latter figure, standing solitary in the background of her somber cupola so that nothing troubles her dialogue with destiny. Below is a row of saints and prophets; lower still the faithful at prayer. Above is the hereditary night of the Orient, the night in which the firmament is a derisory agitation of the stars.[40]

By the same paths by which Apollo had become Buddha, Jupiter has become Pantocrator. . . . Once again is established a style of the eternal.[41] And in none of this is there "regression"; there is only the living change that is art.

3. APOLLO IN THE WEST

The individualization of man, his redemption by an event of history, is the enemy of Greco-Roman art in the West. Divinities, emperors, heroes, Vestal virgins, barbarians, soldiers, all the figures of Rome are primarily natures; they are not biographies. The life of Venus is determined by her nature, that of the Virgin by the Annunciation. The recital of the life of Zeus

----

[40] *Ibid.*, pp. 210-11.   [41] *Ibid.*, p. 212.

is not a gospel. Mythology has no Sermon on the Mount and no crucifixion.[42]

"Christ on the cross *existed*. Sculptors did not require that a crucifix be more beautiful than another, but that it be more Christ. They sought less to 'create' than to approximate. It is impossible to think without emotion of the first artisans who dared bring into being with their hands the face of Calvary."[43] When in the museums we come to the rooms of Gothic art, it seems we are meeting real human beings for the first time.[44]

Romanesque art, contrary to popular opinion, is not the heritage of Byzantium, nor of the Irish or Carolingian miniature.[45] Romanesque art, like all art, is defined by what it brings and not by what it copies.[46] If we examine not merely what is kept of the past in the Romanesque, but also what it *destroyed*, and then its relation to Gothic, we can understand it. Romanesque is radically a humanization, if compared with the Byzantine;[47] it is profoundly religious, even if no longer sacred.[48] It

---

[42] *Ibid.*, p. 215.

[43] *Ibid.*, p. 221.

[44] *Ibid.*, p. 219.

[45] *Ibid.*, p. 228. See p. 130: "Un art vit de ce qu'il apporte, et non de ce qu'il abandonne."

[46] *Ibid.*, p. 225.

[47] *Ibid.*, pp. 223-24: "La Résurrection des villes, l'acharnement des ordres religieux à faire des figures chrétiennes une prédication . . . la puissance de communion *dans l'action* que portait en lui le christianisme romain . . . tout arrachait les formes byzantines à la crypte, tout les jetait en pleine lumière, et les contraignait à une métamorphose qui permit à l'art chrétien d'unir les hommes dans leur vie même, 'maintenant et sur la terre.' "

[48] Dom Claude Jean-Nesmy, in "Les chances de l'art sacré," *Témoignages*, January 1953, p. 7, writes that a "sacred" art is one separated from the profane world and opened entirely on God. "Cette définition permet déjà de bien saisir la différence entre un art d'expression de soi, qui peut être un art *religieux* et chrétien dans la mesure où il exprimerait une âme vraiment religieuse, mais qui n'est point un art sacré, pour autant que son souci n'est pas Dieu, mais d'exprimer la créature." But if religious art is not necessarily sacred, "sacred" art can also be non-Christian. For Malraux the only sacred Christian art is Byzantine. One wonders how, ultimately, the two are to be distinguished in the concrete.

is the entrance of the God-Man, as distinguished from the Byzantine, orientalized, deindividualized Pantocrator, into the world of art.[49]

> At Moissac, at Autun, at Vézelay Christ still dominates the tympan by His dimensions and position, by the fascination He seems to exert on every line; but above all because He has become the visible meaning of the prophets, of the dead and *of the living* who surround and contemplate Him; and without Him the signs of the Zodiac would be merely absurd constellations.[50]

Compared to Byzantine, Romanesque was the art of the New Testament; but compared to Gothic, it is still the Old Testament. It moves toward Rheims as God toward Jesus, as the Christ in majesty at Vézelay to the teaching Christ at Amiens, to the dead Christ of the "Pietà." As Christ becomes more man, Romanesque becomes more elaborate and individualized until the triumph it has in Gothic. "Gothic begins with tears. . . ."[51]—the face and its expressions; and the Christian man finds the only harmony he has ever had in all history. Abstraction is gone, the symbol is dead. A pure specimen of Gothic is the Christ of Rheims,[52] a king, contemporaneous with the kings of France, who has given a harmony to Christian life, because Gothic achieved unconsciously, but with passion, a *new style*, the style of the reconciliation of the two natures in Christ. Movement, expression, folds of drapery, come back into art. Art had once been the privileged language of man against what destroys him and also against what surpasses him. Gothic on the other hand was trying to become the language of the harmony between man and what surpasses him—the last act of the Incarnation.[53] Thus the smile came back into sculpture. As long as there was no real movement to reconcile man with God and both with the world,

---

[49] *V.S.*, p. 212.
[50] *Ibid.*, p. 236.
[51] *Ibid.*, p. 237.

[52] *Ibid.*, p. 240.
[53] *Ibid.*, p. 242.

the discoveries of Rheims were impossible: man had no need of anatomy, but a great need of theology. But to bring life back to a people sleeping in the antique statues, all that was necessary was that the first smile reappear on the first medieval statues,[54] the smile of Rheims, for example.

Giotto,[55] employing in his painting the sculptural style he had learned in the Gothic, adds a tenderness hitherto unknown in art, at the same time uniting his figures into "compositions"[56] where they look at each other, and not, as in Gothic, at the spectator.[57] Profoundly Christian in the love expressed by his figures,[58] he is also the artist of the profoundly human. "Giotto is the humanization of pain,"[59] as Gothic was the humanization of God.[60] "This honor of being a man will run under all Italian art as the muffled rumbling of a subterraneous flow,"[61] and Giotto's discovery of a new style will usher in the ultimate Christian humanization that is the Renaissance. "With the same rigor with which Byzantium stubbornly wrested from the Caesarian figures the immobility of the Virgin of Torcello, the West was wresting from Byzantine majesty the thin smile that was going to annihilate that majesty. As the Sassanian renaissance, as all renaissances, the Italian was quickly going to modify the forms it believed were its models, because these brought it the means to conquer its immediate predecessors and to accomplish the destiny of Christian art."[62]

---

[54] *Ibid.*, p. 249.

[55] *Ibid.*, pp. 251-68.

[56] *Ibid.*, p. 261.

[57] *Ibid.*, p. 260. See p. 224: "L'art byzantin attirait le fidèle dans l'église, le tympan roman crie à tous sur la place." Gothic took great account of the spectator. Giotto's figures look at each other (p. 260), and this grips the spectator more (p. 263).

[58] *Ibid.*, p. 259.

[59] *Ibid.*

[60] *Ibid.*, p. 239.

[61] *Ibid.*, p. 266.

[62] *Ibid.*, pp. 269-70.

This brief summary of Book II of *Les voix du silence* gives an idea of the basis for Malraux's definition of art as the quest for style. Of the Christian arts, Byzantine put the eye of the painter at the service of the sacred. Romanesque is the limning, Gothic the open expression, of the art of faith. In "sacred" art God alone figures; in the art of "faith" we have the reconciliation of God and man in Christ. Later in Giotto we have religious art, where man is to the fore. And the Renaissance will dedicate itself to beauty, the idealization of the human. (Centuries later, the "modern" *deformation* will be at the service of the individual.) In all these cases "progress" meant new styles, each a conquest of the one which stimulated it. "L'art est ce par quoi les formes deviennent style."[63]

Apollo has been metamorphosed in a continuous process, which is one of rupture each time Greek art meets another meaning of man. The new style destroys something in the previous one, and what it brings is at the service of a new signification of the universe.

The reader is invited to fix these points well in his mind, because Malraux is going to come dangerously close to saying later that the artist is one step beyond service: though his style may serve a special meaning of man in his relation to God, for example, he uses everything, man and God and the world, as raw material for his art. It is as though the purpose of the artist may incidentally serve the ideals of the time: basically his purpose is to create his *own* world.

To be noted also is Malraux's tendency to look on Christianity as *guilty* of individualism, even in art, because for him Christianity, searching deeper and deeper into means of expression in order to catch the fact of the human in the divine which is Christ, brought the human so naturally forward in Giotto that the Renaissance and all the further precisions of the sheerly

------

[63] *Ibid.*, p. 270.

human stemmed quite easily from the Christian fact. We have dealt with this point already.[64]

Finally, there is a matter Malraux has never made clear: what is this thing called "style" when applied to a whole period? He is going to define an artist as the creator of a style, and show in many cases how individuals of the same school have swung off each into his own style. Is there an over-all common denominator also true of a period? It seems that there is. In that case, where is the place for the high individualism of the single artist's vocation?

---

[64] See *supra,* pp. 20 ff.

CHAPTER XII

The Making
of an Artist

Book III of *Les voix du silence* is entitled *La création artistique*. It deals with the artist in the act of being an artist. If art is the conquest of style (and not of "beauty"),[1] the artist is the conqueror, and in forging his own style belongs to the royal company of creators. He is not an imitator, either of another artist or of nature.[2]

In *Le musée imaginaire de la sculpture mondiale* Malraux makes a sharp distinction between what he calls "production" and that alone to which he would give the name "creation." The former is the work of an imitator, an artisan. The latter that of the real artist. Before the Congress of Cultural Freedom in 1952 Malraux had said that "creation cannot be reduced to mere production; the latter can only ape creation. . . . This idea is not important in periods when a close harmony exists between the artist and the supreme value to which he dedicates himself, as

---

[1] See *M.S.*, p. 18: "Prenons garde à la beauté. Ses chefs-d'oeuvres ne sont plus que des présences par d'autres."

[2] *V.S.*, p. 308: "J'appelle artiste celui qui crée des formes, qu'il soit imagier comme Gislebert d'Autun, anonyme comme le maître de Chartres, enlumineur comme Limbourg, ambassadeur comme Rubens, fonctionnaire et ami du roi comme Velasquez, rentier comme Cézanne, visité comme Van Gogh ou vagabond comme Gauguin; et artisan celui qui les reproduit, quel que soit l'agrément ou l'imposture de son artisanat."

in the twelfth century;[3] but it becomes of paramount importance when creation and production are opposed to each other and when art is opposed in its most profound sense to the society in which it is born."[4] Production is based on a rationalization of art: and the failure of *académisme* is the ultimate proof of its being a second-rate art.[5]

Art is not production, whether in the service of canons of art, of public taste, or of a common culture. It is precisely because Russia puts artists under canons (something even the Church did not do in Gothic times),[6] because a communist painter has his style imposed on him "from without, *before* he has begun to paint, that there is not the slightest hope of his becoming a good painter, communist or not. There is not even a chance of his becoming a painter at all."[7]

We will study this uncontrollable individual that is the artist, *duce* Malraux, in his vocation and in his relation to other artists, to the real world, and to his time. We will find him surprisingly free from their positive influence.

1. THE VOCATION OF THE ARTIST

An artist's vocation is born of the world of art, not the world of things.[8] It is revealing, says Malraux, that no *mémoire* of a great artist records his vocation as due to anything but an emotion felt before some work of art. For the writer it is a play, a poem, or a novel. For the musician, music. For the painter, a painting he once saw. And the reaction of the man with the

---

[3] See *M.S.*, p. 31: "Sans doute la production semble-t-elle moins étrangère à l'art dans les âges de foi, car l'artisan suit et reproduit la découverte selon les valeurs du créateur."

[4] Malraux, "What Stand Will You Take?" *Confluence*, September 1952, p. 9.

[5] *M.S.*, p. 33.

[6] *Ibid.*, p. 44.

[7] Malraux, "What Stand Will You Take?" *Confluence*, September 1952, p. 8.

[8] At the time of the supremacy of the "aesthetic" Malraux says that "aux yeux du peintre seul, la peinture était peinture" (*V.S.*, p. 12).

vocation is "Et moi aussi, je serai peintre."[9] As a religious vocation is the response to a call from God, so is the artist's a
response to the call of art.[10]

We should carefully distinguish the vision of the artist from
that of anybody else. The vision of a man indifferent to art is
related to action, to what he does or means to do.[11] So is the
artist's: to the action of painting.[12] But between their two visions
the difference is one of kind, not of intensity. The artist sees
pictures when he sees the world, and is interested in the world
for that reason.[13] The nonartist fancies that the artist's vision is
merely sharper than his own, or more able to isolate a privileged scene and reproduce it with photographic exactness, or
more endowed with powers of the imagination: these three ideas
are due to the old classical aesthetic.[14] The fact of the matter is, however, that the first act of the painter is to change
the function of objects. The vision of the painter is that which
serves his painting, as the vision of the hunter is that which
serves his hunting.[15]

The artist is not necessarily more sensitive than others; he
is in fact frequently much less sensitive than a young girl. But
the greatest painters are not women. The artist is first and fore-
most a man who loves pictures.[16]

There are many reasons why the nonartist is led to conclude
that the artist is a specially sensitive individual, who sees more
in things than the rest of us. Basically, we have not shaken off
the old aesthetic that insisted painting be "beautiful representations" of real or imaginary things: and all our misconceptions
flow from that source.

We are tempted to think, for example, that the first artist
was faced with living forms and instinctively saw something

---

9 *Ibid.*, p. 279.
10 *Ibid.*, p. 315.
11 *Ibid.*, p. 273.
12 *Ibid.*, p. 277.

13 *Ibid.*, p. 276.
14 *Ibid.*, p. 277.
15 *Ibid.*, p. 278.
16 *Ibid.*, p. 276.

that was invisible to the rest of men. Actually, we know of no such art. The problem of first causes is not special to art.[17] Call the Magdalenian art found in Spain prehistoric if you will; yet what painter does not recognize an elaborate style in the buffalo of Altamira?[18]

Nor does the fact that children spontaneously paint prove anything. In the work of children there is no control, no imposition of a style.

> One can expect everything from the art of children, except awareness and mastery. Going from their images to painting is like passing from their metaphors to Baudelaire. Their art dies with their childhood. The sketches of the young El Greco are not separated from his Venetian canvasses by their lack of accomplishment: in the interim he had seen the Venetian masters.[19]

Popular and naive art suggests also that the artist wishes to represent what he sees. But a study of "popular" art shows that it too has its traditions and that, though sentimental, it is not instinctive. Rousseau *(Le Douanier)* for example, friend of painters and artists, loves, "imitates and builds his art on the naive art of the Second Empire," finally abandons that art and "discovers his own pictorial domain."[20]

The popularity of the portrait also gives weight to the "representation" idea, but only in Christian Europe, where the individualism of Christianity and then the Renaissance lend importance to the portrait. Also, there is the curious tradition that Chardin was on the lookout for the perfect peach, and Corot

---

[17] *Ibid.,* p. 280.
[18] *Ibid.,* p. 281.
[19] *Ibid.,* p. 285.
[20] *Ibid.,* p. 292. See pp. 506-12, where Rousseau's present popularity is explained by his discarding of old forms and his ability to speak a "secular" language. See also *Time,* December 28, 1953 (Atlantic edition), pp. 34-38, for an interesting article on America's ninety-six-year-old primitive, Grandma Moses. "Primitives are would-be realists whose charm depends on their very inability to paint photographically accurate pictures"! (p. 38).

for the perfect landscape. Actually, the Byzantine and the Chinese artist, among others, simply would not understand the portrait. Their art implied a representation *distinct from the real,* and this was as evident in their eyes (for other reasons) as to the sculptors of Babylon, Ellora, Lung-Mên, and Palenque. Likeness, for them, had no place in art; it belonged to identification,[21] and identification is a matter of signs.

Another "reason" in favor of the artist's being a man bent on a sensitive portrayal of reality is the avowal of some artists that they were rendering homage to nature. This, too, is misleading. Landscapes of Corot do give the impression of being very "true to nature"; but if each of them resembles the landscape it depicts, the landscape does not resemble it. That is why Corot had to "finish his paintings indoors." Like Chardin and Vermeer, he transcribes nature but is far from submitting to it; and we moderns, who rank these painters among the best, have no difficulty in seeing in their works the dawn, not of realism, but of modern art. All the great painters, Grünewald and Velázquez, Goya and Chardin, know of a special kind of unity, not always the same but always due to the relation of colors among themselves, which shines out brilliantly before the works of their imitators. The model of Vermeer's "Young Girl" undoubtedly resembled the portrait, but in the same way that La Champmeslé resembled Phèdre.[22]

The impressionists, despite their claim that they were being faithful to reality, were rather a revolt against the *ateliers.* The realists' submission to the real is as suspect as the fidelity of

---

[21] *V.S.,* pp. 292-93. Resemblance for the Chinese was a method of identifying an object, an ideogram.

[22] *Ibid.,* p. 296. Marie La Champmeslé (1642-1698) was a French tragedienne who triumphed in Racine's theater. See Malraux, *Goya,* p. x: "Goya affirmait n'avoir eu que trois maîtres: la nature, Velasquez et Rembrandt. Par la nature entendait-il la vérité? Il ne se soucia guère de l'autre. Il faut épuiser son oeuvre gravée pour y trouver un arbre."

impressionism. "The refusal of idealization by a great artist who painted a Virgin, a benefactor, had not been a submission to nature; it had implied using means of expression which are called 'realistic'—as other refusals demanded means called 'idealistic'—to bring this Virgin or that benefactor into a world that was unique and distinct from the real."[23] There is no realistic style; there are only realistic orientations of different styles. Every realism is a *rectification.*[24]

What of photography? Is it not also art, and at the same time most slavish representation? Only when the photographer "composes" his still lifes and by his lighting achieves an autonomous expression of the world do we call it art. When the photograph and the cinema become art, it is because a style is evident.[25]

The romantics held that genius was a great expression of sentiment. But this idea has died with the death of the myth of the "Great Artisan" of the Middle Ages. What gave that myth credence had been the anonymity of the medieval sculptors and our meager knowledge of the history of their work. All cathedrals were blocked together and called "Gothic."[26] But Gothic, a style with numerous artisans, is no more the creation of artisans than the Renaissance style would be if we lost the names of its great artists.[27] To say that the fervor and love of the artisans of the Middle Ages produced Chartres is as stupid as supposing that a painting by St. Francis of Assisi would have been superior to Giotto's.[28] Admittedly, faith and art both had

---

[23] *V.S.*, p. 299.

[24] *Ibid.*

[25] *Ibid.*, p. 300.

[26] See Malraux, *Saturne*, p. 113: "Peut-être pourrait-on définir le romantisme comme une tentative de retrouver le domaine irrationnel ou surhumaine que l'homme et le christianisme avaient perdu ensemble, et dont les formes chrétiennes n'étaient plus l'expression artistique."

[27] *V.S.*, p. 303.

[28] *Ibid.*

170 The Honor of Being a Man

the same values this once in history, but faith was not bursting out unconsciously into art. Artistic creation is not born of an abandonment to the unconscious, but of the aptitude to capture it. That the masters of Chartres were by no means unconscious of what they were doing is proved by their works. The artist is as unconscious as any man of the tide of humanity that is carrying him, but he is fully conscious of the control he exercises on it, even if this control be restricted to forms and colors. When a society speaks of artists of instinct, it does so primarily because it has an instinct for artists.[29] The artist is not in a compulsive world; he is not a "child of nature."

The word "instinct" should be used very warily in all talk on art. It has place, but never sole place, in discussions of fetishes and Celtic coins, for example. Yet the Polynesians did not carve one "Negro" statue. And one can trace the bars and balls and arabesques on Celtic money in direct line down to the abstractions of 1950. "A great artist abandons himself to his instinct only when he has conquered it; and the illusion of an all-powerful feeling in art, born of the Gothic resurrection, reappears each time that we find an art which cannot be explained by an aesthetic of beauty or by the nature-imitation theory."[30]

Neither a sensitive kind of vision, therefore, nor the welling up of instinctive response to values is the explanation of the artist and his genius.

> Genius has nothing to do with nature, except with what it takes from nature and makes its own. Whether the artist know it or not, whether his picture be premeditated or instinct play a large role, that which reveals a work of art to us is neither his vision nor his emotion, if style is absent. Even a Rembrandt, a Piero della Francesca, or a Michelangelo, at the dawn of his career, was not a man who scanned the profusion of earthly things with more intensity than others, but an adolescent who was fascinated by the

---

[29] *Ibid.*, p. 304.   [30] *Ibid.*, pp. 305-06.

pictures he was carrying around in his head, pictures which distracted him from the real world.[31]

Every society talks of painters as remarkable copyists of nature, as prophets, as esthetes or decorators: never as what they are.[32]

2.   THE ARTIST AND HIS PREDECESSORS

If art is born of art, in the beginning the artist is ordinarily tied up with the art of his time. "Neither Michelangelo nor Raphael began with antiquity. . . . The artist has need of living predecessors."[33]

We sometimes find it difficult to accept this initial dependence of the artist on other artists, because designing schools have created the illusion of a "neutral" style. There is, however, no such thing at the base of painting, any more than official documents could be the source of literature.[34] There is no more a neutral style than a neutral language, no more representation without style than thought without words.[35] The fact of the matter is that an artist is born the prisoner of some style: when Rouault pointed out some influence in an early canvas, Degas replied, "Have you ever seen anybody born by himself?"[36]

Even the subjects he paints are preassigned by the artist's time in history, because certain privileged subjects are used as vehicles for the styles that influence him. Out of all the infinite multiplicity of life a young artist saw, formerly, a youth, a Virgin, some mythological scenes, or a Venetian feast, as he sees today only a Harlequin or some apples; for he does not seek the representations of objects, he seeks only the objects which the style that portrays them has wrested from reality.[37]

As he works, he begins to find his own voice, his own style, and breaks with his masters. "It is at the rupture that art

---

[31] *Ibid.*, p. 306.
[32] *Ibid.*, p. 343.
[33] *Ibid.*, p. 315.
[34] *Ibid.*, p. 314.

[35] *Ibid.*
[36] *Ibid.*, p. 310.
[37] *Ibid.*, p. 317.

begins."[38] An artist's truth is the painting which frees him from his disaccord with the world and his masters. His vocation, born under the aegis of another's genius, brings him the hope of a future liberty, but also the sense of being a slave. "But his slavery is the slavery of an artist, a submission to forms and style; and his liberty is the liberty of an artist, his escape from that style. It is against a style that every genius fights, from the obscure *schema* which animates him at the beginning, up to the proclamation of the truth which he has conquered. . . . And the conquest of the style of every great artist coincides with that of his liberty, of which it is the only proof and the only means. The history of art is that of forms invented against those that are inherited."[39]

The idea of a "school" of painting is here treacherous. A "school" used to designate a common search. Later, however, due to the classical aesthetic, it became a place where masters taught the means to achieve beauty. But the true school comes into being when certain artists, disagreeing impatiently with the canons of their time, band together to produce, each in his own way, his own art.[40] The Renaissance was an appeal to artists in general. When individuals hearkened to it, "each of them answered the call with his own voice,"[41] and the art of each was a rupture with the art that preceded the Renaissance. It is that common spirit of rupture that forges the authentic school.

The rupture sometimes involves the accusation of former styles, as embodying means no longer valid. "The admirable refusal by modern painters of the art respected by the society

---

[38] *Ibid.*, p. 337. See Malraux, "Laclos," p. 424: "Comme tout écrivain, Laclos ne devenait maître de ses moyens que lorsqu'il échappait au style de l'époque."
[39] *V.S.*, p. 357.
[40] See *V.S.*, p. 414: "Les sorciers artisans copieront, les sorciers artistes créeront. Par sa seule présence, l'oeuvre magistrale appelle les premiers à la réplique en même temps qu'elle contraint les seconds à s'écarter d'elle."
[41] *Ibid.*, p. 359.

of their time enables us to see in art itself one of the highest forms of accusation."[42] Giotto, Rubens, Chardin, on the other hand, reject the styles which gave them their start, but are not pitted against their own world at large.[43] The rupture in art is then more necessarily a clash with former styles than with the values of society, although in given cases the values of society are as much blasted as former styles.

The history of art could well be the history of schools of art, in the original sense, because they allow for successors and not imitators.[44] In fact, great schools are families of ruptures, like young religions, or, better, like heresies.[45] The fact that we refuse the painting of even so perfect a forger as Van Meegeren proves that only in rupture with existing styles do we find the real artist,[46] for we require that genius be the *creator of forms*. "We want the work of art to be the expression of him who makes it, because genius is, for us, neither faithful reproduction of a scene nor a combination of elements, and is originality only because, classical or not, it is *invention*."[47]

An excellent example of the "influence" of one real artist on another is in the transformation of the black and red, and the volume, of Caravaggio into the nocturnal works of Georges de Latour.[48] Latour's art *filters* the art of Caravaggio.

> The line of the woman's profile in "The Cheat," that of the woman in "The Prisoner" and in the various Magdalens—now tracing a sweeping, all-embracing curve, and now broad, blunted angles—whose only precedent was the Florentine arabesque (very different however, because it moves less freely and serves to outline forms) ; that line which Caravaggio would have loathed as Courbet would have loathed it; that line which fluently adapts itself to trails of smoke and spirals, follows its ineluctable course, annexing

---

42 *Ibid.*, p. 339.
43 *Ibid.*
44 *Ibid.*, p. 362.
45 *Ibid.*, p. 365.

46 *Ibid.*, pp. 366-71.
47 *Ibid.*, p. 372.
48 *Ibid.*, pp. 373-98.

and transforming what it can annex, destroying all the rest, and draws its nourishment from things which, seemingly quite foreign to it, serve its turn, as a tree draws nourishment from the leafmold at its roots.[49]

The problem of "influence" in art is, therefore, as Malraux has said before, a problem in reverse.[50] The painter of stature always wishes to oppose his painting to that of another.[51] His moment of *kairos* arrives when he discovers that "he alone, of all who are delighted by these works [of others], must seek to destroy them."[52]

3. THE ARTIST AND THE REAL

The growth of the artist into his own style, is, therefore, as follows. The man who is going to become a great painter begins by discovering that he is more alive to the particular world of art than to the everyday world. He senses within himself the tyrannical need to paint. He knows that what he will paint in the beginning will doubtless be bad, but that he is entering into an adventure.[53] He passes through the period of the *pastiche,* generally imitating the latest masters, until he becomes conscious of an internal dissension between the "meaning" of what he is imitating and the paintings he feels within himself. He evolves

---

[49] *Ibid.,* p. 391 (Gilbert translation, p. 393). Malraux also works out Botticelli's "dependence" on Filippo Lippi (*ibid.,* pp. 397-404).

[50] *Ibid.,* p. 167.

[51] *Ibid.,* p. 345. Frohock, in *André Malraux and the Tragic Imagination,* p. 21, speaking of Malraux's first "surrealistic" writings, *Lunes en papier* and *Royaume farfelu,* denies that they are a revolt "of the imagination" and sanely concludes: ". . . the first writings use not a 'style of revolt' but a style against which he would revolt when the time was ripe for him to establish his own characteristic way of expression."

[52] *V.S.,* p. 357. Müller, in *Crise de la métaphysique,* p. 25, could be defining the artist's moment of realization when he defines "liberty in the highest sense" as "assomption dans la solitude d'une tâche qui se révèle à moi seul être la mienne, au moment où je l'accepte."

[53] In which he may suffer a great deal. He will certainly have to *work* to find his style. See *V.S.,* p. 341.

a personal *schema* which is going to liberate him from those masters, often turning to masters of the more distant past. (We shall see how he has recourse to reality.) When he has finally mastered, either successively or alternately, his color, his design, and his matter, and when what was a *schema* has become a style, a new pictorial meaning of the world appears. This the painter will modify and deepen more and more as he grows older.[54] There are exceptions: Picasso cannot even now be said to have his own style, except in the sense that he refuses to be fixed.

But if art is born of art and is irreducible to the real, it has nevertheless a special relation to the real because art is not a work of interrelated symbols, each taking meaning, like a deck of cards, from its relation to the others. No forms are at the service of nothing. What recourse has the artist to reality?

The answer is that, basically, artists are hostile to reality. Contrary to our illusion that the artist is first conscious of a meaning in the world and then expresses it symbolically,[55] the truth is that the artist devaluates reality "as the Christian world and every religious world devaluates it; and like the Christians, he devaluates it because of his faith in a privilege, because of his hope that man and not chaos carries in himself the source of his eternity."[56] The great artists do not transcribe the world; they are its rivals.[57] Styles, in other words, are not successive

---

[54] *Ibid.*, pp. 342-43. In pp. 419-35, Malraux makes an exhaustive study of the growth in El Greco from his Venetian days to those at Toledo, when "avid for God," he finds a Christian style. El Greco's evolution is then studied in comparison with that of one of his companions at Venice, Tintoretto, who moved out in another direction: see pp. 436-44. Also, the whole of *Saturne* is the story of an Italianized Goya becoming Spanish, of charm yielding to art, and "ensuite, commence la peinture moderne" (see p. 178).

[55] *V.S.*, p. 412.

[56] *Ibid.*, p. 318.

[57] *Ibid.*, p. 459. See p. 468: "Avec Hals commence . . . la rivalité du peintre et du modèle."

ornamentations of an unchanging world, but "the reduction to a human perspective of the eternal world which bears us into the mysterious rhythm of the drifting stars."[58] The world of space is more wonderful than our world; the world on canvas more surely captures the wonder of distance!

Whatever the artist himself might say, he *never* submits to the world, but always subjects the world to what he would put in its place. His will to transform the world is, in fact, part of his very nature as an artist. Not that he creates his style out of his own substance; his style is always the expression of a *signification* that he finds to be true, and he needs reality as grist for his mill. The world is not only a profusion of forms, it is also a profusion of meanings; but (and this is capital) it means nothing by itself, because it means everything.[59] Style is therefore the elucidation of one of those meanings; and until it appears in a work of art, that meaning simply does not exist, except in the vision of the artist. ("Les styles sont l'expression d'une signification particulière du monde: signification qui appelle une vision avant d'être enrichie par elle.")[60] Life is stronger than man in that it is multiple, autonomous, and charged with chaos and destiny. But each of its forms is weaker than man because no living form reveals the meaning of life. The Egyptian, for example, who finds in the world his link with eternity, reveals that link much less by his own features and his gait than by his statues.[61]

The essence of the importance of style is therefore this: style is the creation of the artist's special universe by use of those elements in reality which enable the artist to focus the shape of things on some essential part of man.[62] The artist, obsessed by this particular meaning, *filters* reality, employing his

---

[58] *Ibid.*, p. 321.
[59] *Ibid.*, p. 322.
[60] *Ibid.*, p. 319.

[61] *Ibid.*, p. 322.
[62] *Ibid.*

initially unsure style as a net in which to catch what he needs from the world.[63]

> A Byzantine painter decides to paint St. John the Baptist before looking at the faces of passers-by for material, and when he looks at them he is thinking of St. John. Da Vinci did not paint in order to represent faces lit up by the evening light: he observed that the evening light gave his faces a quality superior to any other. Corot is going to plant his easel before the bridge in Nantes or the Nerval ponds, not in front of factories.[64]

Delacroix calls nature his "dictionary." He meant that her elements are incoherent (or, more accurately, that they agree according to their own syntax, but not according to the syntax of art), and that it is for the artist to draw from among them.[65] The Buddhist sculptor who observes that a human face settles into the attitude of recollection when the eyelids lower will perhaps give that appearance of recollection to a Greek statue by closing its eyes; but he first wanted to change the Greek face, and discovered in the living face the means to do so. We are always to remember that the artist is working proximately on his own liberation from the forms of some other artist, and that he goes to nature only to find in its multiplicity some elements with which to metamorphose the forms already existing in art,—for example, eyes to close.[66] The artist will not find treasures in the rich cavern which is the world without his lamp, and his lamp is the new meaning he finds worth his dedication.

> Ingres advised his pupils to isolate and then design elements of ideal beauty, since talent for him consisted in welding them together. A perfect armless body called for a perfect arm. His

---

[63] In Picon, *Malraux par lui-même*, p. 58, Malraux, commenting on his own novels, writes: "L'image que je tente d'atteindre, avant d'être un portrait exemplaire ou embelli (ce dont je ne suis pas juge) est un piège où je saisis les éléments du réel dont j'ai besoin pour créer mon univers."

[64] *V.S.*, p. 346.

[65] *Ibid.*, p. 348.

[66] *Ibid.*

world, then, is filtered by the idea of classical beauty, then by the state of the work. The artist looks at the work through the hole left by the unfinished part of his puzzle. And if classical beauty be replaced by some other value, it is still always through this hole that the artist looks, much as a man who has lost his key looks around for something with which to force open his door.[67]

What is this "signification" that serves the artist's new style? We are not to think it is anything that he can rationalize, says Malraux. His forms are no more a rational expression of values than are musical forms. "To replace the arm for carrying loads, man did not invent an artificial arm, but the wheelbarrow: to express the world, the artist discovers a coherent domain of *significant equivalents*."[68] In other words, the artist, as artist, is not the same man as the one who goes to the café after painting, any more than the priest, *qua* priest, goes bowling after his prayers. His truth does not belong to the domain of the verifiable but to that of convictions. To the question, "Why are you painting that way?" the only answer he can give is, "Parce qu'ainsi, c'est bien."[69]

Art is, therefore, the world of forms conquering forms, and all meanings are inseparable from forms, which are "by no means the allegorical expression of a concept. The 'Last Judg-

---

[67] *Ibid.*, p. 350. In pp. 348-53, Malraux gives many examples of the different elements different artists used to express their "special" meanings of the world. It is interesting to note that the world is so rich to the artist that he will use the most surprising elements to complete his style. "If I had to paint battles," said Renoir, "I would keep looking at flowers; if a battle is to be good, it must look like a picture of flowers" (*ibid.*, p. 351). The same painter came up to a garage keeper on the beach at Cassis, and showed the garage keeper a picture of some feminine nudes bathing at quite a different place. Renoir "didn't seem to be looking anywhere in particular, and was only tinkering with one little corner of the picture." But the blue of the sea had become the blue of the brook of *Les Lavandières* (*ibid.*, p. 278).

[68] *Ibid.*, p. 354.

[69] Malraux cautions us not to take too seriously the artist's rationalizations to explain his work: see *ibid.*, pp. 340-45. The artist, in fact, is often rather unfaithful to his own rationalizations. With all their theorizing, compare the impressionists Manet and Monet!

ment' is born of a meditation on figures, not faith."[70] The meaning that is style shows

> how an artist of genius, whether he search for solitude as Gauguin or Cézanne, the apostolate as Van Gogh, or exhibit his canvasses in a booth on the Rialto, like the young Tintoretto, transforms the meaning of the world, whether he conquer it by reducing it to the forms he chooses or to those he invents, just as the philosopher reduces it to concepts, and the physicist to his laws.[71]

The artist's truth, consequently, is irreducible to any other language than the language of his forms; and if he is a good artist, he convinces, not by seduction, but by affirmation. Even the sculptor of the Acropolis *affirms* his interrogation of the world.[72] The world is filtered, transformed, conquered, annexed, rectified;[73] and if the modern artists suffer and accept their suffering, it is not for the glory of God, unless God here be painting,[74] and this despite the protestations of men like Rouault or Dali.

> Hals annexed "The Regents" to his universe. By his style Goya annexed demons to his. . . . Before his regents Hals is justified; before his Christs El Greco is the kind of Christian he wants to be; and as long as Goya paints Saturne he is free—as is Angelico when he has driven every trace of the devil from his pictures. The truth of the artist is the painting that frees him from his disharmony with the world and his masters: it is forms that evoke his *schema*, it is art which is summoned forth by his rupture.[75]

---

[70] *Ibid.*, p. 332. In pp. 322-29 Malraux discusses this masterpiece.

[71] *Ibid.*

[72] *Ibid.*, p. 357.

[73] It would be tedious to count how many times Malraux uses each of these words in his text. They are almost a refrain.

[74] *Ibid.*, p. 357. Of El Greco in his final period at Toledo, Malraux writes: "Représenté ou non, maintenant le Christ est toujours là. Il est devenu le plus puissant moyen de sa peinture: mais il est autant au service de cette peinture, que cette peinture est à son service. Style, Christ et cité sont indissolubles: le Greco vient de peindre le premier 'paysage' chrétien" (p. 435).

[75] *Ibid.*, p. 357.

The artist's relation to reality, according to Malraux, is specifically artistic: and in saying that Malraux absolves himself of further explanations. One feels that more problems are posed here than settled. Of course, if there is any specificity to art, if it is a form of creation, then all that Malraux says about the artist's long struggle for his *own* style, expressing his *own* meanings, is necessarily true. All forms of creation are in some way autonomous: otherwise they would not be creation. Nor would we deny that, whether they know it or not, artists put their faith or lack of it, their experiences and their prejudices, their *other* values all at the service of their creation, *when* they are creating. In this sense there is no "morality of art" as such. The *man* is moral or not: his morals or lack of them are then at the service of his work, and not vice versa. "The biography of an artist," says Malraux, "is his biography as an artist, the history of his transforming power."[76] The artist and the man are, surprisingly, two persons.

All of that we are ready to agree with, if there is any specific meaning to the power of human creation. But a deeper problem poses itself. Granting that there is a specificity to painting that is not that of music or poetry, and agreeing that it is in the realm of "design and color," we would still like to know what the "signification" is which style expresses. Malraux says this cannot be treated rationally. He has said that Greek art expressed an "interrogation of the universe," that Gothic had as its meaning the reconciliation of the human and divine, that Raphael meant to express ideal beauty. These are all things expressed, and are to that extent the *content* of the "thought" expressed in those works. Does Malraux now wish to retract those statements, or can he still consistently affirm them, adding, as he does, that the meaning of which he speaks simply does not exist until it is expressed by the artist?[77]

---

[76] *Ibid.*, p. 418.   [77] *Ibid.*, p. 319.

If he can, then the key question arises: What is art? And it is here that Malraux's thought crumbles. In his dynamic style Malraux thinks of art as the painter's reply to a challenge: the challenge of other paintings by other masters. But this is not enough. The simple fact is that Malraux has no theory of aesthetics. He will find in art an expression of human autonomy, in the manifold styles that run through history. But there are many expressions of human autonomy, of the power of creation: there is no less of the "human quality" in the harnessing of matter that produced the atom bomb, or the research that found penicillin, or the power of synthesis that produced the *Summa theologica* than there is in the hand that caressingly created the "Mona Lisa." There must be something different in art than there is in all these, just as physics is not biology, and neither of them is philosophy. Malraux *senses* art. He cheers, with the joy of a prisoner at long last liberated from the darkness of destiny and the meaninglessness of life, at the power of the artist. But he cannot tell us, except by printing reproductions of masterpieces, what is special to art. He can point to what he is hurrahing for. We can sense, too, what he sees. But he cannot, and has admitted that he cannot, give us a definition of art.[78]

One would forgive him this, one would even praise him for the honesty of this, if he did not take such a doctrinal approach to the world of artistic creation. He knows what art is not. The rest is a gesture of a guide who says, "Look for yourself."

---

[78] M. Nédoncelle, in his excellent *Introduction à l'esthétique*, p. 20 (Paris: Presses Universitaries de France, 1953), referring to an interview Malraux gave to Parinaud (reported in *Arts*, November 30, 1951) says that Malraux does not give a "ne-varietur" definition of art, because he is still looking for it and is not sure of having found it: there are so many styles which make up "l'humanisme planétaire qui se prépare."

CHAPTER XIII

Art and History

There is no art independent of time. Those who would proclaim the eternal primacy of a style forget that an artist belongs to his time, for the very banal but often neglected reason that he cannot belong to any other. Ingres may have been searching for a style outside of time, but we can date his "La petite baigneuse" at a glance.[1]

1. THE ARTIST AND HIS TIME

We are inclined, however, says Malraux, to conceive an artist as being too nearly the product of his epoch. The historical illusion teases us into lumping together artists and schools, all as expressions of their times. For example, Greece for us remains inextricably linked to her statues, despite what we know from other sources. "Though the Egyptologists look on Egyptian art as but one facet of the life of Egypt, everybody else looks on Egypt as a reflection of Egyptian art."[2]

The hostility we now feel for the classical aesthetic has undoubtedly moved us to accept the idea that art must be a particular kind of expression of a historical era. If there is no eternal style, then there would seem to be styles specific to certain periods of history. Doubtless, too, when, owing to the combined effect of metamorphosis and the lapse of time, a period

---

[1] *V.S.*, p. 403.   [2] *Ibid.*, p. 408.

of history has coalesced into a whole, it seems to have been expressed by its art as its symbol.[3] This is particularly true for us of Gothic times.[4] But it is fallacious to think that values produce their arts as apple trees produce apples. "Piero della Francesca and Andrea del Castagno belonged to the same moment of Florentine civilization, but expressed it in two opposite ways in their design, color, and spirit. Art is not necessarily the symbol of an epoch."[5]

Malraux grants, of course, that the artist is linked to the particular character of what it is his mission to destroy, and to the limits within which this destruction can become conquest: he is therefore forced to get his forms from the immediate past, in order to express the values that are in process of formation in the present or evoked by the future.[6] But while the artist is striving for his style, these values are unconceived, particularly by artists. "The painter does not express them as he would the character of a distant land he may have visited, but like a man condemned by sickness would try to express death: he is not expressing an experience, he is answering a call."[7]

Yet art is not necessarily the sign of the *coming* orientation of history. We are inclined to that idea because our civilization is still looked on as a conquering civilization. But if Praxiteles

---

[3] *Ibid.*, p. 410. Toynbee, in *A Study of History*, Somervell abridgment, p. 241, says: ". . . it is generally recognized that every civilization creates an artistic style of its own; and if we are attempting to ascertain the limits of any particular civilization in space or time, we find that the aesthetic test is the surest as well as the subtlest."

[4] Apropos of religious art that was in harmony with the beliefs of the time, Malraux writes: "Tout art qui atteint des masses est une expression de sentiments,— attendrissement, tristesse ou gaieté, patriotisme, angoisse, amour. C'est pourquoi tels sommets de l'art religieux où l'art s'unit à la fois à l'amour, et à la conscience de la dépendance humaine ou à celle de sa libération, trouvèrent dès leur naissance une audience immense" (*V.S.*, p. 276).

[5] *Ibid.*, p. 410.

[6] *Ibid.*

[7] *Ibid.*

and the sculptors of Olympia were announcing what was coming, history played them false, for they were followed by the
agony of Greece. The style, moveover, which preceded the Christian style was not that of Augustus, but a decomposing Roman
style. The artist, therefore, is no more "conditioned" by a future
whose spirit he would incarnate than by a past whose form he
would be seeking. Historical events act on him only in the measure in which they permit him, or impose on him, a new relation
with the world.[8]

There is, be it said again, an *irrational* that plays here. An
epoch stimulates "un domaine d'expressions imprévisibles."[9]
The reason? Because each artist is irreducibly himself, and
speaks his *own* language. "If we are surprised to see Delacroix,
Ingres, and Corot, all French and all contemporaries, answer
[the call of the Revolution] with voices that are so different, it
is because they did not break with the same elements of the era
that preceded theirs, nor for the same motives."[10]

It is because no era can stimulate a work which would ex-
haust its meaning that vast margins remain open on the sides
of even the most symbolic works: Raphael is flanked by Michelangelo and Titian. The plastic expression of a period is much
more subtle than its emotions. As for the expression of a culture, we find it only when the culture is about to hatch, and
sometimes when it has died. The motifs of the century of world
conquest by the machine and Europe are a dish of apples and
a Harlequin.[11]

A new style can therefore come to light, expressing some
new meaning hitherto unexpressed, because there are so many
possible meanings to express. This indicates that, if the artist
is linked to his time, he is not the symbolic crystallization of a

---

[8] See Malraux, *Saturne*, p. 155: "Goya n'est pas un prophète, mais un peintre."
[9] *V.S.*, p. 411.
[10] *Ibid.*, pp. 411-12.
[11] *Ibid.*, p. 412.

whole mentality. If art is born of the break with previous styles
and hence with the particular significations of those styles, and
if there are no neutral styles, it follows that there is no moment
in the evolution of an artist when he is sheerly himself and
that he is at every moment orientated by some signification—
not unconsciously, not rationally, but specifically.[12] In fact, if
there is any eclectic in any walk of life, it is the artist, and it
is so he has always been considered. His individuality is
more than the individuality of handwriting, his contribution
is more than an idiosyncrasy: but despite all this he still only
rearranges reality.

Every art is the expression of a fundamental feeling an artist
has before the universe (which is one reason why every living
religion impregnates profane works, and why there are no great
profane works until religion loses its force). Hence in breaking
with a previous signification, itself the expression of a "sentiment" before the universe, he must find another to express his
own. It may be in harmony with existing values, such as those
of religion. It may be a revolt against cheaper "values," such
as those of the bourgeoisie.[13] But the parade of forms is never
under the generalship of historical determinism.

As creator, the artist does not therefore belong to the col-
lectivity which lives under a culture but to the group which elab-
orates that culture, whether he be interested in doing so or
not. His creative faculty does not serve a fatality, be it the
fatality of his milieu. Rather it is a link between him and the
age-old creative power of man, to cities reconstructed on ruins,
to the discovery of fire.[14]

His own personal experiences, of course, modify his filter
of the world. But they have nothing to do with the quality of

---

[12] *Ibid.*

[13] In *Saturne,* p. 177, Malraux speaks of the anguish of Goya, who "avait dressé
contre toute la culture dans laquelle il était né son art solitaire et désespéré."

[14] *V.S.,* p. 414.

his work, with what makes him an artist.[15] "Comme l'histoire, la vie ne détermine pas les formes, elle les appelle."[16]

Creating in time, under the spell of current values or rebellious to them (in either case affected by them), and motivated by a ravaging desire to conquer other styles (and that is the chief motivation of the artist, according to Malraux), genius can be defined as *the power of autonomy whose expression is the density of his work, and whose privileged expression is the masterpiece.*"[17]

Soon other artists, not even yet freed from the attraction of the genius' voice, will give their lives to wrest from him the accent he has imposed on the world. From the first sculptor of the first god down to the modern painter most imperiously present in his painting, the great artist has always secretly aimed at the same kingship. And

> like the life of the genius, that of mankind gives ever rise, between the artists yet to be and the glorious jetsam of the past, to that pregnant disharmony out of which is born, world without end, the conflict between the Scheme of Things and the work of human hands. How strange is this far-flung world of ours, so transient yet

---

[15] Malraux has harsh words for the fascination of modern times with psychological determinism, and all forms of "conditioning"; they never explain *art* as such. See *ibid.*, pp. 416-18. See also p. 515: "Ce qui pour nous fait de la peinture un art n'est pas une disposition de couleurs sur une surface, mais la qualité de cette disposition," and this is not explained by "les conditionnements." See p. 416: "Le Moyen Age ignorait jusqu'au nom du peintre; la Renaissance l'étudiait comme les autres personnages illustres: son art et sa personne étaient distincts. . . . Notre époque croit aux secrets dévoilés. D'abord parce qu'elle pardonne mal son admiration. Ensuite parce qu'elle espère obscurément, parmi les secrets dévoilés, trouver celui du génie." (He admits in *Goya*, p. xi, that Goya's sudden deafness at least "occasioned" the eruption of his genius.)

[16] *V.S.*, p. 416.

[17] *Ibid.*, p. 456. On p. 459 Malraux says: "Le sentiment de création que nous impose l'oeuvre capitale est voisin de celui qu'éprouve l'artiste qui la crée: elle est une parcelle du monde qui n'appartient qu'à lui. . . . De même, elle est pour nous une parcelle du monde orientée par l'homme. L'artiste en a chassé les maîtres, il en a chassé la réalité."

so eternal, which, if it is not to repeat but to renew itself, stands in such constant need of man![18]

Thus, in barest outline, the hymn of homage Malraux pays to genius. Just as reality and his masters do not explain him, so neither does his milieu. He must, admits Malraux, have some "signification" to express. But that he expresses it the way he does is something so mysterious that it would be naive to try to explain it: genius is a given, art is a quasi person, talent is autonomous. What prompts the artist to break with previous styles remains a secret locked up in his own irrational dynamism. What inspires in him a new signification of the world, all his own, could partly be explained by other things than by the fact that he is an artist: but, Malraux insists always, that it be *this* and not *that* signification is not the important thing in art. That *style* triumph is what counts.

We would agree readily that Goya's liaison with the Duchess of Alba does not give the key to his painting any more than the tactics of Napoleon at Waterloo are explained by his adultery with Marie-Louise. Psychological determinism is not the answer to what makes Goya a great painter. The "creator" is not to be explained by forces *working on* him. That he turn to a given value, in this world or out of it, is of course something that *can* be explained more nearly by his life. But Malraux goes further. He says expressly that the artist frequently does not know what that value is going to be. He may find it in the very action of trying to express himself. But El Greco was looking all the time for a Christian style: *his* value was always known to him.[19] There is much that is unclear here.

In any case the important element in genius remains an *irrational*, and the principal drive in the genius is to subordinate everything, his former masters, reality, his milieu, his own

---

[18] *Ibid.*, p. 464 (Gilbert translation, p. 466).
[19] *Ibid.*, p. 433: "Il cherche—et il trouve—un style chrétien."

experiences, to *one* value, the value of the autonomous world of art: *his own world.*

Malraux would seem to want genius to be conscious of this drive. He concedes, of course, that in the old East statuary served the fabrication of the gods; that in Greece sculptors wrested their gods from the domain of terror, death, and the nonhuman, and served humanization.[20] And he insists that *we*, at least, now subordinate everything in art to one value, that of art itself. "Nous les [images] subordonnons toutes à la art."[21] Would it therefore follow that the artist was consciously doing the same thing? Or is it not more likely that those artists who *thought* they were serving some other value were the richer artists, the more successfully autonomous, by the fact that their genius was in a perpetual dialogue with a value higher in their minds than the value of being independent? Would Malraux really mean seriously his claim for modern art that it is "the greatest style the West has ever sponsored"?[22] Would he in fact be able to prove that "modern" art is so divorced from all values except that of art?

The artist may express himself in order to create,[23] and not vice versa. Malraux has not been caught by any silly infatuation with the fad of self-expression for its own sake. But the power to create is itself the power only of a man, and no man can subsist for long playing Narcissus to his own reflection. There is more than one question that Malraux refuses to answer. Can he refuse, however, to recognize the troubling presence of this one question: Where is the nobility, the honor in being a man, if its highest expression is carving out a face on a rock? Are

---

[20] *Ibid.*, p. 64.

[21] *Ibid.*

[22] *Ibid.*, p. 580.

[23] In writing of novelists Malraux remarks: ". . . je pense qu'il [le romancier] s'exprime pour créer, comme tout artiste" (Picon, *Malraux par lui-même,* p. 58).

we really convinced that the type of immortality Cicero craved in posterity is to Cicero's credit?

2. ART AND HISTORY

Closely allied to Malraux's defense of the artist against any historical determinism is his sharp distinction between the march of history and the course of art through history.

Our new pluralism, due to the resurrection of many forms of the past, seen together for the first time as forms and not as representations of values, is still a pluralism despite our discovery of a common denominator in all art, because no language is empty of content.

> Whatever were the sculptural qualities of the divine figures of India or Mexico, they were not cubistic or abstract, and they could never have been such; for in the eyes of the artists who discovered them abstraction in art is still abstraction from *something*, and not the object of its own search. It is illicit to conclude from the fact that there is no "content" in art distinct from the forms that express it, that the "Flayed Ox" of Soutine is distinguishable from Rembrandt's only by talent, and we would hardly tolerate the notion that a Negro mask is like a sculpture of Picasso.[24]

Content, therefore, is always present in real art. Genius, though not the power to represent or to design symbols (some modern art is, however, the vehement passion precisely to express nothing), is orientated by *something*.

This is puzzling if we are persuaded that modern painting is at the service of nothing. As we have seen, however, there is a truly fundamental value that orientates modern painting. "C'est la très vieille volonté de création d'un monde autonome, *pour la première fois réduite à elle seule.*"[25] And it is because it is subordinated to no other value that it suddenly reveals the fundamental value in all the history of art. Once the modern

---

[24] *V.S.*, pp. 608-10.   [25] *Ibid.*, p. 614.

painter reveals this power of autonomy in the art of the past, we are able to see it in itself, and therefore able to see much more clearly something else: the other value that the artist of the past was *also* expressing,[26] because that other value was the *means of conquest* used by this autonomy. An artist needed a signification to express this autonomy because each art is inseparable from some particular value. "But to artists and sculptors the kings of Chartres, *le dévôt Christ*, the Christ of Grünewald, all say that faith was at the service of art, although they know what these works owe to faith. . . . And the crowd from which modern art has removed the cataract welcomes what is suggested by these rediscovered works, in the same way as the romanticists welcomed the confused meanings of Gothic and Romanesque works when they discovered their forms."[27] The surgeon declares the operation a success!

The order is reversed for once and all. Far from being in the service of some value, the creative faculty makes use of magical, cosmic, religious, and sacred values as *means* of achieving its own eternal autonomy.[28]

Hence art and history follow different paths. History records the particular mentalities and values of particular periods of the past—the elements that art bent to its own will in achieving the *one* value it championed, its own autonomy. We speak of the past as though it abides in our civilization in the same way that ancient monuments linger in a modern city: but we know this is not true. For a small number of specialists the past is an object of interrogation; but for all the rest of men it comes to life only in becoming a vast fiction, a legendary story, based on monuments, statues, poetry.[29] The cinema brings back Joan of Arc and Henry V only by giving them the gestures of paint-

---

[26] One is moved to ask how the two can be distinguished.
[27] *Ibid.*, p. 615.
[28] *Ibid.*, p. 617.
[29] See *V.R.*, p. 61: "Toute oeuvre d'art, en somme, tend à devenir mythe."

ings, miniatures, or statues.[30] It is not the historian who assures the life of the past. "It is the grip the artist has on the dreams of men. His forms suggest a history that is not true, but humanity is nourished on them. The great Romans would not have had the effect on the Convention that Plutarch had."[31] The myth of the Renaissance would have been less powerful without the Sistine Chapel, and an insistent poetry emanates from the obscure zones of the past where history has not entered—such as from the enigmatic "Warrior" of Capestrano,[32] or the bison of Altamira or Lascaux.

Actually, our *musée imaginaire* renders superficial the historical knowledge it recalls because art is saying something more important about the past than is history.

> Every historical attempt to render the past intelligible makes of it an evolution or a fatality, charged with hope or death for those to whom the explanation is addressed; but a history of art (which is not a chronology of influences) would be no more a history of progress than that of an *éternel retour*.[33]

When we discover, as we have, that the key of artistic creation is in its break, its "rupture," then art is linked to history in a far different way than any historian would suspect. When the history of the entirety of art becomes the history of genius, it becomes a history of deliverance. For history, the modern-day destiny, "tends to transform destiny into a conscious thing; art to transform it into liberty."[34] And make-believe museums are the chant of history, purified of its sordidness, its cruelty,

---

[30] *V.S.,* p. 408.

[31] *Ibid.,* p. 618.

[32] A Proto-Etruscan sculpture.

[33] *Ibid.,* p. 621. Malraux is referring to the "éternel retour" of Nietzsche. A few pages before, he called the great works of art "autant de Zarathoustras inventés par autant de Nietzsches" (*ibid.,* p. 617). The story of art reminds Malraux of the Chinese funeral inscription in honor of the enemy hero: "Dans votre prochaine vie—Faites nous l'honneur de renaître chez nous" (p. 629).

[34] *Ibid.,* p. 621.

its mysterious elements.[35] "In the past of art, Sumer, Thebes, Nineveh, and Palenque have come to mean to us only the hymns arising from their abysmal darkness; the sordid annals of Byzantium are effaced by the majesty of Christ Pantocrator, the dust and squalor of the steppes by the gold plaques, the lazar houses of the Middle Ages by the Pietàs. I saw the fetishes of the Nuremberg Museum justify their age-old leer as they gazed down at the last wisps of smoke curling up from the ruins, through which a girl on a bicycle, carrying a sheaf of lilac, steered an erratic course amid the singing Negro truck drivers; yet had there been an art of the prison-camp incinerators, only that day extinguished, it would have shown us not the murderers but the martyrs."[36]

Art therefore sings of a triumphant *constant*, the creative power of man. "For us, art is a profound continuity, because it never destroys what it has inherited; but it is also a metamorphosis of forms . . . by the flow of time."[37] What effects the resurrection of the arts of the regression, what creates the audience for savage arts, what metamorphoses the art of the Sumerians, the archaic Greeks, the Wei masters, Grünewald, Leonardo, Michelangelo, Rubens, Chardin, and Goya is that they all act on us together, by a power that each of them possessed and none of them conceived: the specific power "qui révèle une haute trace mystérieuse de l'homme."[38] Each becomes an incarnation of what assures their hidden union, and perhaps of other unknown powers also.

Values change, men die, civilizations are transformed. The course of art has a hidden life of its own. It is the revelation of the human power of creation, autonomous before all else— and the book in which to read *the quality of man*.

---

[35] *Ibid.*, p. 622.
[36] *Ibid.*, p. 623 (Gilbert translation, p. 625).
[37] *Ibid.*, p. 625.
[38] *Ibid.*, p. 627.

CHAPTER XIV

The Quality of Man

Through art man seeks to find himself: "Art, often stranger to happiness and even to refinement, is not stranger to the obscure or clear effort of men to give some sort of supreme value to their lives."[1] But in this effort man is not wholly free. "When I say that every man is deeply conscious of the existence of fate," says Vincent Berger in *Les noyers de l'Altenburg*, "I mean he is conscious, and almost tragically so, of the world's independence of him."[2] For Malraux man is always an accident of the universe,[3] and there are always the age-old questions of death, old age, and all the forms of destiny,[4] including the twentieth-century form, which is historical determinism.[5]

It is the modern artist's fundamental acceptance, along with all thinking men of this age, of the fact of destiny that has driven him to an interest in what seems "fundamental" art (that of the insane, of children, of "popular" art) and in "savage" art.[6] The modern artist, engaged in a conflict between the su-

---

[1] *V.S.*, p. 622.
[2] *N.A.*, p. 127.
[3] *V.S.*, p. 637.
[4] *Ibid.*, p. 466.
[5] *Ibid.*, p. 510; see also p. 539.
[6] See *ibid.*, p. 540: "Mourante ou non, à coup sûr menacée, l'Europe, tout chargée des résurrections qu'elle embrasse encore, semble se penser moins en mots de liberté qu'en termes de destin."

preme value that he sees in art alone and what to his eyes are pseudovalues, usurpers, thinks he finds a kindred soul in the artist of the night, of the stars and of blood.[7] The world of destiny is a cold, hard, unavoidable fact, and the "devil" now exists again;[8] and the honesty of the arts that accept this fact, or portray it, is a world the modern artist understands. Indeed, the tragic depths in man have the value of founding most solidly the consciousness of being a man.[9] So the modern artist is dominated by the fierce desire to wrench away the "imposter fist" that has closed the mouth of destiny.[10]

But Vincent Berger also says:

> To me our art seems to be a rectification of the world, a means of escaping from man's estate. The chief confusion, I think, is due to our belief—and in our theories on Greek tragedy it is strikingly clear[11]—that representing fatality is the same as submitting to it. But it's not, it's almost possessing it. The mere fact of being able to represent it, conceive it, release it from real fate, from the merciless human scale, reduces it to the human scale. Fundamentally, our art is a humanization of the world.[12]

The entrance of consciousness, of man into the world of destiny, is the end of destiny: "Au destin de l'homme, l'homme

---

[7] We find, however, that, far from being subject to destiny, these arts are also its conquerors (*ibid.*, p. 570). For full treatment of an artist who bitterly acknowledged destiny see Malraux, *Saturne* in toto. Goya thought his deafness was his own fault. "Sourd maintenant, il craint de devenir aveugle. Il est entré dans l'irrémédiable. Un des charmants artistes du XVIIIe siècle vient de mourir," and real painting is the result.

[8] He paints, by preference, in two dimensions, and is the most eminent of the misunderstood artists of today (*V.S.*, p. 539).

[9] *Ibid.*, p. 574.

[10] *Ibid.*, p. 538.

[11] See *ibid.*, p. 628. We misunderstand Greek tragedy if we think it sent the audience home to "se crever ses yeux." The audience goes home resolved to come back to the theater. See also p. 73.

[12] *N.A.*, p. 128. One is reminded of Aristophanes' sardonic comment on Euripides, *Thesmophoriazusae*, ll. 450-51: "By representing the deities, he persuaded men that they did not exist."

commence et le destin finit."[13] The basic message of Malraux is in these words. Destiny is a fact, and men of our time know it. But "the *musée imaginaire* teaches us that destiny is menaced when the world of man, whatever it be, rises in the world. A subdued destiny paces or growls behind every masterpiece."[14]

Every great human conception of the meaning of life has been a different response to the voice of destiny. The Christianity of the West wrested the death of man from sheer death, and had given that conquest a form in its art.[15] But the artistic response can take many forms:

> The most profound experience of an artist is formed, and later acts, in many different ways. . . . The heaviest of human experiences, the consciousness of the irremediable, surely takes many forms. . . . There are no more predetermined forms of good fortune, or even of the irremediable, than there are of the meaning of the world.[16]

The values men construct vary with the times. All great painting expresses a fundamental value,[17] but because there are different elements in man, there are different kinds of values expressed. Statuary served the manufacture of the gods in the ancient Orient, and art expressed and doubtless enriched a particular relationship with the sacred. In Greece the sculptors also forged gods; but the artists wrested these gods from terror, death, and the domain of the nonhuman. If in these two cases

---

[13] *V.S.*, p. 73.

[14] *Ibid.*, p. 628. See *N.A.*, p. 97. Nietzsche's song in the train as it passed through the St. Gotthard tunnel produced in his companion, Walter Berger, an exhilaration: "Et dans ce wagon, voyez-vous, et quelquefois ensuite—je dis seulement quelquefois . . .—les millénaires du ciel étoilé m'ont semblé aussi effacés par l'homme, que nos pauvres destins sont effacés par le ciel étoilé."

[15] *V.S.*, p. 493. See p. 538: "Nulle civilization n'a empêché l'homme de mourir, mais les plus grandes ont été assez fortes pour métamorphoser parfois la mort à ses yeux, la justifier presque toujours."

[16] *Ibid.*, p. 416.

[17] *Ibid.*, p. 612.

art represented gods, it is only too clear that it did it by address-
ing itself to different parts of the soul.[18] Every real art puts
itself at the service of a part of man that is obscurely or ve-
hemently *élue*.[19]

Malraux is never concrete when he speaks of the "elected,
the chosen part of man." He is downright in his condemnation of
any appeal to the brutal, the sheerly sensual, or to the yen for
illusion. All arts pandering to those elements are "antiarts."[20]
But he leaves it up to us to see, through the great works themselves, what the "chosen part" of man is. There is a melancholy
reference to the "eternal part" of man: "This part exists, perhaps, but our civilization does not affirm it—it is looking
for it."[21]

Basically, however, there seem to be in Malraux's thought
two valid "chosen" elements in man: that which wishes to recompose the universe according to human laws, and that which
wishes to transcend the human to attain the sacred.[22] The latter,
a fundamental urge in man to wrest himself from the world and
link himself to the divine,[23] is true of art from Mesopotamia to
the Middle Ages, with the exception of Greece, whose art is an
example of the former element,[24] which itself begins in the
Christian world with Gothic.

It is because it does not seem, at least so far, to converge
toward expressing a "chosen" part of man that "popular" art

---

[18] *Ibid.*, p. 64.
[19] *Ibid.*, p. 523. See also p. 322.
[20] *Ibid.*, p. 523.
[21] *Ibid.*, p. 405.
[22] *Ibid.*, p. 84.
[23] *Ibid.*, p. 479.
[24] Yet Malraux says of Greece (*ibid.*, p. 479) : "Hormis peut-être la civilisation de
Rome, pas une de celles qui ont précédé la nôtre ne s'est plus fortement
définie que par son geste dont elle tentait de se lier au monde pour saisir
son éternité." See Malraux, *Goya*, p. xii: "Pour lui [Goya] . . . comme pour
le Moyen Age, l'homme ne valut guère que dans la mesure où il exprimait
ce que le dépassait."

is not important.[25] Conversely, the art of the beautiful and of fiction can have its place in the parade of art if it nourishes the highest part of man. It can do this when it occurs in a civilization already united in a truth: it is when the truth fails that fiction becomes false.[26]

This orientation of the *partie choisie* of man is always linked to a sense of *communion* of men among themselves. "Sacred and religious art require a community, and the death of this sense of community metamorphoses that art."[27] The art of a living religion is not that of assurance against death, but of a defense against destiny by an immense communion.[28] This is true of *Greek* art: it is not an art of solitude, but of communion with the cosmos;[29] of *Buddhistic* art: the victory of pity that made of the world a vast communion brought the smile to the face of Buddha;[30] of the victory of *Christian* art over that of Egypt: the Church is more favorable for communion than the cemetery; hence it is that Roman Christianity received its vocation,[31] for Roman Christianity carried in it the power of communion in action.[32] *Gothic* owed much to communion.[33] Further, *savage* arts, by roads other than those of the great religions, are means of a cosmic religion, a form of communion. Is their type of communion conceivable? Malraux thinks it was like that of Byzantium.[34] Finally, outside the world of art, it

---

25 *V.S.*, p. 233.

26 *Ibid.*, p. 514. It is when values die and none replace them that you have "les arts d'assouvissement." (See *ibid.*, p. 528.) See Malraux, *Goya*, p. xiii: "Goya découvre son génie le jour où il cesse de plaire."

27 *V.S.*, p. 600. All arts that do not reach the masses through the object of their communion are the direct inheritors of bourgeois painting (p. 521).

28 *Ibid.*, p. 494.

29 *Ibid.*, p. 633.

30 *Ibid.*, p. 157.

31 *Ibid.*, p. 195.

32 *Ibid.*, p. 224.

33 *Ibid.*, p. 615.

34 *Ibid.*, p. 565: Byzantium was more Oriental, Malraux thinks, than Christian.

is always a sense of communion (of fraternity) that gives exaltation, such as that of the eighteenth century in its fight against piety.[35]

Again we seek the secret Malraux finds in fraternity. He comes closest to explaining it when he writes that "thousands of human beings can be united by faith or the hope of revolution; but . . . then they are not the 'masses.' They are kindred: united often by action, always by that which counts in their eyes for more than themselves."[36]

Malraux is saying, therefore, that a man cannot live up to the honor of being a man[37] without the exercise of one of the superior elements in him:[38] his liberty, or his urge for the transcendent. Neither of these can be validly expressed except in a communion, which is itself impossible if those sharing in it make themselves their chief love. Is this saying that idealism engenders a need for kindred souls and that only then does a man achieve nobility, because only then does a man recognize his common nature with others, themselves in humble need of others like himself?

It is a fact that no authentic hero and no Christian saint was produced otherwise. A hero engenders a deep feeling of alliance in others, and is ready to sacrifice himself for them. The saint lives for others, all of whom he calls his "brethren" because of the vast communion of man, all made alike by being washed in the blood of Christ. "Cosmic communions" are another thing, though to feel part of the cosmos would seem impossible if the self came first. We should, therefore, grant Malraux his case as he has stated it here. We may grant, also, that "prayer in common is far from the common pleasure of going

---

[35] *Ibid.*, p. 480.
[36] *Ibid.*, p. 514.
[37] *Ibid.*, pp. 266, 417, 639.
[38] *Ibid.*, p. 639: "L'homme ne devient homme que dans la poursuite de sa part la plus haute."

to Mass on Sunday."[39] But whether the new communion he suggests will fulfill his own requirements for greatness is another
question altogether.

Malraux says that today we are not a united civilization.
"Our civilization is the first not to know the communion, be it
sentimental or metaphysical, that links man to his neighbor, to
all forms of suffering, and to all forms of life; but it is beginning to know it."[40] Where?

Inheritors as we are of world art, due to the absolutizing of
art by modern artists,[41] we have isolated for the first time the
noble element that runs through all great art: "la très vieille
volonté de création d'un monde autonome."[42] This is a constant,
and the second of the two chosen parts of man that are noble. If
the first, the desire to communicate with God, is present in some

---

[39] *Ibid.*, p. 528. We cannot, however, grant that modern Christianity "cannot give
a style to its Churches which permits Christ to be present" (*ibid.*, p. 493).
The communion that was Christianity is not doomed: the little church on
Broadway, "pseudo-Gothic in the midst of skyscrapers" (*ibid.*, p. 494), may
be a symbol of the destructive machine age, but the new interest in liturgy,
in cooperative Christian living, in mental prayer, and the sufferings and
"dematerializing" of thousands of Christians under modern persecution are
all bringing into being communities of the Church Militant, which do not
need geographical proximity to be united. Neo-Thomism is not the only force
in Christian life today. See on this whole question *Témoignages*, January 1953,
the entire issue entitled "Les chances de l'art sacré," especially p. 82.

[40] The modern artist has long known it. His art, being his sole *raison d'être* (*V.S.*,
p. 492), has made it possible for him to find his community "parmi ceux qui
sont, de près ou de loin, ses 'semblables,' dont le nombre s'accroit d'ailleurs"
(*ibid.*, p. 600). In *Van Gogh et les peintres d'Auvers chez le Docteur Gachet*,
p. 5, Malraux writes: "L'apparent fétichisme qui fit conserver le vase de Delft
et les bambous, c'est celui du temps où les vrais peintres étaient une secte
réprouvée, et ceux qui les admiraient, une communauté."

[41] *V.S.*, p. 599.

[42] *Ibid.*, p. 614. See pp. 459, 462. Albert Camus in *The Rebel (L'homme révolté)*,
translated by Anthony Bower, p. 226 (London: Hamish Hamilton, 1953),
writes: "Van Gogh's complaint is the arrogant and desperate cry of all artists.
'I can do very well, in life, and in painting, without God. But I cannot,
suffering as I do, do without something that is greater than I am, which is
my life—the power to create.'"

canvasses, the second is also arrogantly present, because each canvas is a reduction of the universe to human terms. And it is this "divine faculty"[43] like that of the sages and heroes and saints of the past[44] which is going to be the *accoucheur* of the new Man that is going to be born.

For art is the expression of this supreme power, this supreme value: "L'artiste crée moins pour s'exprimer qu'il ne s'exprime pour créer."[45] All the other values it expressed in the past are now subordinated to it.[46] Those values were always protections against some form of destiny. So now for us in art.[47] Each of the masterpieces of the world is a purification of the world, a reduction of it to the human scale, where the power of the artists dominates all else. "It is art in its totality, delivered by our own, that our civilization, the first to do so, raises up against destiny."[48]

No art succeeded in delivering "l'homme de n'être qu'un accident de l'univers." It is surely to the eternal that the great religions reply, but not to the eternal life of man.[49] Destiny is too strong. But our civilization too makes its own gesture: it finds in art the "power to oppose an eternity that is ephemeral to a life that is still more ephemeral."[50] In art our faith, like all other faiths, tends to embrace the eternal.[51]

The communion? Art is a chorus of the past, of other men drowning out the voice of the same destiny that crowds us. We are united with all the effort of the past, through art, to resist destiny, to make it man-sized, to give at least an ephemeral importance to life, because it is in this resistance to destiny that man is at his noblest. Thrilling to the chorus of art, we sense the possibility of "the first universal humanism" in history.[52]

---

[43] *V.S.*, p. 118; see pp. 318, 634.
[44] *Ibid.*, p. 489.
[45] *M.S.*, p. 62.
[46] *V.S.*, p. 523.
[47] *Ibid.*, pp. 44, 637.

[48] *Ibid.*, p. 631.
[49] *Ibid.*, p. 479.
[50] *Ibid.*, p. 556.
[51] *Ibid.*, p. 493.
[52] *Ibid.*, p. 629.

This humanism will not be a sort of cultural theosophy. There will be no attempt to reconcile elements of the past. Aristotle and the prophets of Israel will still exchange insults on the banks of the Styx. The past remains irreconcilable—except in art.[53]

Art, in its constancy and its metamorphoses, leads the way to the new humanism because it engenders a belief in man as a free, noble consciousness injected into a world ravaged by destiny. "The avenues of shadow which throughout their infinite recession impose the stamp of the human on that which seems least human—the void—seem a symbol of what the art of the past is coming to mean to us: one of man's very rare *creations*, inventive though man is. The feeling of being in the presence of something with a life of its own that we experience, when we are confronted with a masterpiece, is conveyed to us, though less vividly, by that never-ending process of transmutation running parallel to history which enabled the Egyptians to embody a people of the Dead, the Negro races the faces of their spirits, and so many others *des hommes semblables à des dieux.*"[54] We see man, the creator, giving to matter a life of its own, leaving his image on it, and each image only a partial reflection of his own infinite variety!

Our resurrection of the past is not, however, in the service of a preconceived humanism. It calls to a humanism not yet conceived.[55] The reason is that, although our art waved the wand that awakened the slumbering forms of the past, those forms, once awakened and active on artists, are going to transform modern art. "Whether we admit it or not, the West is going to be illuminated by the torch it carries, even if it burn its

---

[53] *Ibid.*, p. 555: "Qu'il s'agisse seulement d'art, le masque et Poussin, l'ancêtre et Michel-Ange ne sont pas des adversaires, mais des pôles." See p. 630 for summations of different values in different cultures.

[54] *Ibid.*, p. 625 (Gilbert translation, p. 627).

[55] *Ibid.*, p. 631.

hand; and what this torch will shine upon is every thing that can increase the power of man."[56]

Humanism is not to say, "That which I have done no animal would have done." It is to say, "We have refused the beast in ourselves and we wish to find man again wherever we have found what crushes him."[57]

Man and destiny will always move together. There is always this dualism.[58] Yet "there is beauty in the thought that this animal who knows that he must die can wrest from the disdainful splendour of the nebulae the music of the spheres and broadcast it across the years to come, bestowing on them messages as yet unknown."[59]

And men in the future will be grateful. "La postérité, c'est la reconnaissance des hommes pour des victoires qui leur semblent promettre la leur."[60]

---

[56] *Ibid.*, p. 638. The art of Great Navigators "ne survivra pas sans métamorphose, mais sa métamorphose peut être liée à la naissance d'une civilisation américaine, au triomphe du communisme russe, ou à la résurrection de l'Europe" (*ibid.*, p. 541). One wonders, then, how a universal humanism is possible. America or Russia or a Europe come to life again will certainly be in the line of some form of humanism; but, in the case of the first two, will not their art get its force from something specifically their own? "Les pays passionnés d'avenir, Russie, Amérique entière" (*ibid.*, p. 630) if they are going to *forge* that future in any way, would seem certainly to be in "danger" of finding some new value that again, like that of Gothic times, will be at least consciously primary, and subject the "pouvoir autonome" of the artist, if he is convinced, to a nonuniversally humanistic style.

[57] *Ibid.*, p. 639. In Vol. 2, *La création artistique*, p. 216, of the original version, *La psychologie de l'art* (Geneva: Skira, 1949), we read: "L'humanisme, ce n'est pas dire 'ce que j'ai fait, aucun animal ne l'aurait fait,' c'est dire, 'J'ai refusé ce que voulait en moi la bête, et suis devenu homme sans le secours des dieux.'" Malraux has changed the accent of his acceptance of the Death of the Absolute.

[58] Recall Kyo on communism. The dualism is the same: "Il y a dans le marxisme le sens d'une fatalité, et l'exaltation d'une volonté" (*C.H.*, p. 166).

[59] *V.S.*, p. 639 (Gilbert translation, p. 642).

[60] *Ibid.*, p. 462.

Reflections
and Conclusion

Generally the lines of Malraux's latter-day thought are clear. His writings are a fervid appeal to his readers to open their eyes to a world he loves passionately, even violently, and to see what he sees: the glorious triumph that is man. The triumph is ephemeral because there is no final answer for our questioning generation in its anguished search for the transcendental, *l'insaisissable*, for the absolute which satisfied the world for millennia despite its varying forms. If a man is authentic enough to recognize the heavy weight of destiny, Malraux sends him to art, which will share it with him. He will then be in the company of heroes, sages, and saints[1] in their fight against destiny, for the artist's work outlives them all, and art is the preferred embodiment of antidestiny for our age, which has few heroes, few sages—and seemingly can have saints only in concentration camps.

This is all terribly serious with Malraux. In fact, it is probably true that the great Berenson himself has not put more energy into the message of art than has the younger Frenchman. Yet as a general gospel Malraux has been condemned out of hand, especially in America, where the weight of destiny

---

[1] *V.S.*, p. 489. See *M.S.*, p. 60.

is something to talk about rather than something at long last deeply felt.[2] Not that America has rallied to any ennobling absolute; just that it has not been faced with any great "metaphysical anguish," because ordinary life seems to succeed only too well. In Europe, Malraux has been treated with exuberant respect; the reviewers and the more sensitive critics have long decided that *Les voix du silence* is a document of the age, one of the few great testaments of the twentieth century.

There are certain unfair approaches in estimating this book and *Le musée imaginaire de la sculpture mondiale*. One would be to expect of them a history of art and an accuracy of detail, although Malraux by no means intends the first and allows for disagreement in his judgments on different periods and artists.[3] Another carping criticism would be to demand that the books be written in a coherent sequence, so that the uninitiate in art would have more of a chance to learn about art, or the initiate would have more opportunity to pin down Malraux's theory of art. But the effect of Malraux's writings is to send the uninitiate reader to the world of art; and Malraux disclaims any "theory of aesthetics," as we have seen. He has not invited us into a world where he feels he can prove anything. He asks for response, not intellectual assent; and though this would automatically estrange many readers, it has never been more than a minority in a culture which has given itself to the world of art. A third approach would be to try to understand these books in isolation from the rest that Malraux has written: one of the purposes of this present study is to eliminate such a danger.

---

[2] See, for example, the *New York Times*, Book Review Section, November 22, 1953, p. 1, where the director of the Metropolitan Museum of Art writes of *Les voix du silence*: "This big and expensive book is not so much a contribution to our knowledge of the history of art as it is a dazzling reflection of the *Zeitgeist*—the Spenglerian sterility which has possessed Europe for the past half century and which, having produced Proust, Gide and Picasso, has ended in the Existentialist sub-cellars of the Boulevard St. Germain."

[3] *M.S.*, p. 16.

The reader is by now long familiarized with the two main
intuitions of Malraux: human liberty as our most precious
possession and destiny as our constant enemy; and be it said
that no philosophy of life worthy of the name, and certainly no
humanism, would ever try to blind itself to either element. If
various forms of existentialism are faulty, it is not because they
recognize man's ability to create himself or acknowledge the
limits of his humanity. His *facticité* and his *liberté* generate
his *angoisse*. Freedom and fatality—these are Vergil's *lacrimae
rerum;* and, even to the Christian, tears can be a quiet testimony
to the Creator on the cross.

The observations and conclusions which follow are, however, necessary if only to see whether or not Malraux has lived
up to his own requirements of a thinker: "It is not by his appro-
bation or his protestation that a thinker proves his worth, but
by his explanations."[4]

1. THE AUTONOMY OF THE ARTIST

For Malraux the artist is a rival of his predecessors and of
reality. This is as true as saying that each man is an individual.
Each artist will have his own language, as each human throat
has its own voice. Even an imitator, a restorer, or a forger will
betray himself.[5] Socrates may have insisted that an artist imitate
nature,[6] but he warned against copying it. Gauguin spent his
life trying to catch the exotic character of Tahiti: he would still
be Gauguin had he never left the Seine. We are not disposed,
therefore, to disagree with Malraux when he champions the
autonomy of style.

We are ready to agree with him also when he becomes im-
patient with attempts to reduce a style to events in an artist's

---

[4] Malraux, *L'espoir*, p. 280.
[5] *V.S.*, p. 369; see *M.S.*, pp. 26-27.
[6] Xenophon, *Memorabilia*, Bk. 3, Chap. 10.

life. An artist is, of course, first a man. He gets hungry; he does not detest (except rarely) the acclaim of others; he has noble and ignoble passions. Nonartistic motivation follows and precedes his work. And he belongs to a social group which more or less dictates his ideals and prejudices. But to reduce an artist's work to a discharge of his internal states, themselves all determined by heredity, experience, and milieu, is to leave the artist, as indeed it would be to leave every man, an object of positive science. Those who accept these forms of determinism as the full explanation of a *conquered* style will also renounce all forms of humanism that claim for humanity a privileged place in the world of nature.

There is, of course, a debt to nature in all art. Even abstract art abstracts from something. If art is a conscious process, it is wrapped in the world, as is all intentionality. "No form of art can survive on total denial alone. Just as all thought, and primarily that of non-signification, signifies something, so there is no art that has no signification."[7] But Malraux would not accept Merleau-Ponty's suggestion that an artist is giving us the *concret originaire,* is offering back to man "a visible object which without him remains locked up in the life separated from each consciousness: la vibration des apparences qui est le berceau des choses."[8] Nor would he admit as a universal principle that the artist unveils the secrets of the irrational world by using things of that world to perform his work.[9] For Malraux, both these ideas would limit the possible significations that lie exposed for the capturing hand of art. The idea of art is, for Malraux, an open idea, and what art should be is not preconceivable.[10] He feels that the discoveries of the vastly different styles of the past have proved that.

---

[7] Camus, *The Rebel,* p. 227.
[8] Merleau-Ponty, *Sens et non-sens,* p. 33.
[9] Thus Heidegger. See De Waelhens, *La philosophie de Martin Heidegger,* p. 287.
[10] *V.S.,* p. 607.

What, then, have the great works in common which allows the designation "works of art"? Malraux answers that they all have in common the evident autonomy of their styles. How distinguish autonomy from imitation? Malraux answers that we could be deceived in some cases, but that new discoveries of works of a given period will right that.[11] For whom? we ask. The answer seems to be that it is for "quiconque, aujourd'hui sait ce qu'est une oeuvre d'art."[12] Malraux is not going to be caught giving a definition of style.

Art is therefore not the world of metaphysics, born of the urge of the metaphysician to gather in the world with human concepts. Nor is it the world of science, which in its own way tries to do the same thing. But then the world of any human effort is a "humanized" world. Art is, for Malraux, quite simply itself, and looks after itself. The urge to act is deep in the artist. When he finds his style, it is an expression of some meaning which cannot be put into other terms. It is to reality what the poem is to a dictionary. In short, if there is a world of art, it is a special world where the irrational plays in tune with the human will to create, in some plastic form. The artist is not a creator *ex nihilo*. But he is a demiurge who transfigures the world; his defense against the question, "Why do you paint like that," is "Parce qu'ainsi, c'est bien."[13] And he points to his canvas with a gesture of finality!

Malraux's position is at least prudent. It leaves genius intact, and makes of a work of art a distinctive "quasi person." The intellectuals, whose previous contribution to art by *académisme* was to give it clients and take away the universe,[14] would do well to tread carefully. Aristotle composed his *Poetics* only after the experience of Greek drama. If an intellectual approach to art is possible, it will be after an open study of all the art of

---

[11] *M.S.*, p. 19.
[12] *Ibid.*, p. 16.

[13] *V.S.*, p. 354.
[14] *M.S.*, p. 45.

all the world, now present in reproduction. The idea remains open: for Malraux there is nothing more to say at this time.

Despite Malraux's brilliant defense of the autonomy of genius there are, however, serious lacunae in his thought, and there is the highly personalized accent that is nothing new to the student of Malraux, but is not, brilliantly personalized though it be, necessarily acceptable.

The chief complaint with the whole burden of Malraux's thought is what I should call its *negativeness*. He has never, it seems, conceived that which is *beyond*, outside of, man as in any way a grace to our nature, but always as a destiny. In treating of the "transcendental" he has conceived it either as an absolute without heart or personality or as God in the Christian sense, whose effect on humanity, in the final analysis, has been but to heighten the sense of individualism and therefore to intensify the series of frustrations of the man who would be like unto God. Reason and science, history and psychology, are also so many false gods, so many temporary distractions which have played mankind false: reason and science because progress is not a fact, history and psychology because they are new ways of fixing a fatality on man. That leaves us with the individual, endowed with a will and the possibility of being honest (authentic) before the litany of deceptions chanted by the intellectuals. For an example of the most imperishable and the most validly *human* of these individuals Malraux goes to the artist or, more directly, to the style he has thrust into the chaos of a world without purpose. The artist's domination of the world, by tying a parcel of it with his own hands and thus reducing it to the state of a *human* possession, is for Malraux a hopeful example (sometimes he speaks of it as though it were a messianic promise) of what a man of courage and dedication can do.

What is it precisely that the artist does? For Malraux, the artist treats reality with hostility, his predecessors with restless disrespect, his milieu—at least in modern times—with disdain.

And he treats destiny, the encroaching presence of all that he cannot control, as a wild thing he will tame and bring to toe. In painting on his canvas and forging his own style he will subject to his own purposes all that is not himself, all that he can tyrannize with his brush.

One is moved to ask why all of this must be thought negatively? Is the struggle with the angel a series of bouts in which the artist tries to conquer and make something his own, or is it a fervent attempt to climb the ladder to something that surpasses him? Is the artist defying the gods or showing them the most exquisite respect that man can show? Is Alvear right when he says, "It was not the gods who created music; it was music created the gods."[15]

How explain, for one thing, that the artist is never satisfied with his work when he has "found his voice"? Were he satisfied, he should stop painting. Nor is he satisfied with the work of other artists, or with the original dispositions of nature, or reality, at least *as* artist. Is this because he has something better, some rectification of his own style, of that of others, of reality, that will prove superior to them all and leave him winner of the field? Or is it not much more likely that what he and others have accomplished has not reached the utmost limits of what can be done, that in admitting present limits he admits there is more beyond? Is he not rather paying implicit homage to what is still beyond those limits of his own style? Is it not more true to say that no matter what he affirms about his purposes in working, despite all his equivalent denials in his own life, the artist recognizes that there *is* a transcendent in some form? It may take the form of an Oriental god, of the Christ of Christianity, of ideal beauty. Even the modern, who means forcefully to be present in his own canvas, is trying to dominate something that he knows is necessarily beyond him. Graham

---

[15] Malraux, *L'espoir*, p. 234.

Greene is not the only one who has discovered that to deny God is to accept His existence.

Malraux's distinction between human liberty and transcendence is, in fact, a neglect of the permanent relation between the two. If liberty is essentially ecstatic, a projection of myself beyond myself, it is the exercise of an effort to transcend myself: otherwise it would not be liberty, but imprisonment. But I do not will what is not to me in some way real. If an artist wills to burn his own style into his canvas, he wills to transcend what others have done, and what he has done, with a faith (Malraux himself uses the word[16]) in something more than himself, as a reality which is real at least for himself.

His restlessness, therefore, in the flourish of his "divine power" can be just as well, or is more accurately to be defined as, his will to attain to, to know, to find, to discover, to come into contact with some reality that is beyond him. To speak of the "old craving to create, for the first time reduced to itself"[17] is to speak contradiction. Not only must the artist crave to create; he must crave to create something not yet created, and that "something" is always beyond his reach. Hence the anguish of the artist, if he be *only* an artist, and the dynamism that keeps discharging new styles across the world. Hence the definition of man as the being who is restless until he rest in God. If the world stands in such constant need of man,[18] man *is* a need of the world, because that world, instead of being *la monnaie de l'absolu*, is the *vestigium Dei*. The coordinating value may now have broken into pieces for many modern artists:[19] it always will when gods are only what the music has created.

It is safe to say that for Malraux the tragedy of modern times is precisely its inability to put any hope into discovering a "coordinating value." But he does have the courage to say at

---

[16] *V.S.*, p. 598.
[17] *Ibid.*, p. 614.

[18] *Ibid.*, p. 464.
[19] *Ibid.*, p. 479.

the end of *Les voix du silence* that "for the believer, this long debate of metamorphoses and rediscoveries is but an echo of a divine voice, for a man becomes truly a Man only when in quest of what is most exalted in him."[20] If only Malraux could understand that real liberty implies a Reality that is transcendent, he could change the last words of those lines to say "a man becomes truly a Man only when in quest of what is most exalted *outside* himself." And with that, he would have his answer to destiny.

2. UNIVERSAL HUMANISM

Malraux has seen that *la fraternité virile*, a communion, is necessary if man is to reach a nobility that is truly human. He knows that the harmony of Gothic sculptors with the community of faith of their fellows gives Gothic a stature all its own. He admits, also, that sacred art is impossible today because there is no "communion" among men.[21]

But how can the modern *peintre maudit* be part of a communion? Malraux says our civilization is the first not to know a communion linking man to his neighbor, to all forms of suffering, and to all forms of life, but it is beginning to know it. Is the artist beginning to know it? Or must the modern artist be the midwife to someone else's child? He is certainly not part of a communion: if anything he is, in Malraux's own terms, a *strident* element of our times.[22] The Great Navigator is always *between* two communions.

Even in art, therefore, there is communion only among artists themselves; and the rest of civilization stands apart, watching uncomfortably until they catch something that the men of their times can understand. As for the rest of men, Malraux

---

[20] *Ibid.*, p. 639.

[21] *Ibid.*, p. 494.

[22] See *ibid.*, p. 605: "Au musée moderne comme en musique, en littérature, au ballet, au théâtre, la stridence fait partie de notre époque." See also p. 102.

thinks they are beginning to find a sense of communion: *due to the infiltration of world art.*

For Malraux art is a necessity. "The Imaginary Museum gathers together what pleases our taste and appeals to our sensibility, but also that which responds in some of us to a fundamental need."[23] Art is for some, therefore, the article of faith on which to found a belief in man. "One can wish the word art to mean an attempt to give men a consciousness of their hidden greatness."[24] No longer Christianized, man must look closer at hand for something to give meaning to his life. And when European (Western) man has discovered the redeeming presence of world art, he will rally, with an intense sense of the communion of all men, to a universal humanism.

It is here that it is difficult to take Malraux seriously. Doubtless, interest in art has become a phenomenon of our times. But is it from the story of triumphant styles that we are going to learn the greatness of man? Does painting play the role formerly held by the pursuit of the divine?[25] And in all this are we going to find the secret of a new brotherhood? How many men are there so able to intellectualize about art that they can abstract Malraux's common denominator?

Malraux says that "the true values are those for which men accept misery, derision, and sometimes death."[26] One would be almost embarrassed to ask Malraux if he sincerely means that the "quality of man" portrayed in great styles would solicit such loyalty and belief that it could justify a war. How many men would see what he sees? Could men really say, with Count Rabaud in *Les noyers de l'Altenburg*, that they can believe in eternal man because they believe in the everlastingness of masterpieces?[27] By what magic, one asks, has Malraux caught

---

23 *M.S.*, p. 17.

24 Preface to *T.M.*, p. 541.

25 *M.S.*, p. 64.

26 *V.S.*, p. 528.

27 *N.A.*, p. 113.

the imagination of thousands of readers to a hearing of his new message?

It should be acknowledged that the few, a minority, determine the general features of a culture. The saint does not engender only the saint. He helps ordinary men save their souls as well. The sage may speak primarily to the sage; but what he says filters down into the minds of men who never read his books. And the artist, if he has caught someone with the fervor and talent of Malraux, may well have engendered a new belief in man, or be in the process of doing so, as the importance of Malraux grows.

Toynbee's chapter on "Society and the Individual"[28] highlights brilliantly how social changes that abide are due to *someone*. This someone is a form of Superman, and "this creative personality is impelled to transfigure his fellow-men into fellow creators by recreating them in his own image."[29] The Superman can be embodied in a creative minority, but in any case he inspires some sort of identification with himself. For examples one can go from the divine become human which is Christ to the human aping of the divine that was Hitler.

Toynbee asks what produces an individual like this, and works out a fascinating pattern that is true of all great transformers of society.[30] The man who injects change into society passes out of action into ecstasy and then out of ecstasy into action on a new and higher plane. Toynbee calls this the process of Withdrawal-and-Return. Moses ascends Sinai and brings down a new law. The single prisoner released from Plato's cave has new things to say (and risks a hostile reception at the hands of his companions who have never been outside the cave). The

---

[28] Toynbee, *A Study of History*, Somervell abridgment, pp. 209-44.

[29] *Ibid.*, p. 213.

[30] This analysis by Toynbee is strikingly similar to that of Frohock in *André Malraux and the Tragic Imagination*, pp. 137-49, on the "shaman" in *Les noyers de l'Altenburg*. See *infra*, p. 215.

idea is in the allegories the human imagination has built portraying human life by the phenomena of withdrawal and return apparent in the life of the plants. It has thus wrestled with the problem of death, as did St. Paul when speaking of the resurrection of the dead, who were sown in corruption and raised in incorruption.[31] The resurrection of human beings is possible only in virtue of a transfiguration during a withdrawal. And Nazareth, the desert, the nights of prayer, the death of Christ, and His and our new life are all withdrawals and returns. Toynbee, who is not interested in the factuality of any of these examples, remarks that "this is evidently a theme of cosmic range; and it has furnished one of the primordial images of mythology, which is an intuitive form of apprehending and expressing universal truths."[32] But he finds, with characteristic Toynbee loftiness, that in the promise of the Second Coming of Christ "the timeless past of the foundling myth and the timeless present of the agrarian ritual are translated into the historical striving of mankind to reach the goal of human endeavour. In the concept of the Second Coming the *motif* of Withdrawal-and-Return attains its deepest spiritual meaning."[33] He then goes on to give examples of this motif in the lives of St. Paul, St. Benedict, St. Gregory the Great, the Buddha, Muhammed, and Machiavelli (!).

All of these transform their world, because the mass of men senses in them an illumination they have received during their period of withdrawal, and is moved to imitate them because they have been privileged with a precious secret.

These ideas on the creative individual or creative minority might help us in our effort to understand the appeal of Malraux's writings, and aid us in redeeming them from the charge

---

[31] 1 Corinthians 15:42-44.
[32] Toynbee, *A Study of History*, Somervell abridgment, p. 221.
[33] *Ibid.*, p. 223.

of being hopelessly aristocratic. Mounier calls Malraux's appeal an "appel kierkegaardien de l'exception à l'exception."[34] Is there in Malraux something of this appeal, which is nevertheless powerful to his readers at large and warrants an audience for his initially surprising message?

Vincent Berger in *Les noyers de l'Altenburg* is called a "shaman." He is a man who has gone apart, into the East, and returned to his fellows enlightened and charged with effectiveness. In the eyes of his tribe (the intellectuals grouped for the colloquy around his Uncle Walter) he enjoys a special status and is the object of unusual deference, while for the general public the newspapers have surrounded him with an atmosphere of mystery.[35] His message does not concern us here, but we are concerned to find some way to measure the strength of Malraux's message. Actually Malraux could be describing himself when he explains Vincent Berger's enthusiasm for Ottomanism. "It was mixed up with the need to get away from Europe, the lure of history, the fanatical desire to leave some scar on the face of the earth, the attraction of a scheme to which he had contributed not a few of the fine points, the comradeship of war, friendship."[36] Back from his wars, enriched by his wanderings in the East, established in his own mind with his own values, and looking up at his desk from reproductions of world art, much of which he has seen in the original, Malraux has discovered something: that mankind is a vibrantly powerful thing. And he has devoted all his talents to putting that discovery before us. He despises propaganda, but himself lived so fiercely in quest of what he has finally found that he is listened to with "unusual

---

[34] Emmanuel Mounier, *L'espoir des désespérés*, p. 71. Paris: Editions du Seuil, 1953.

[35] Frohock, *André Malraux and the Tragic Imagination*, p. 138. The author works out a description of the shaman and shows how many of Malraux's characters are just that (pp. 137-49).

[36] *N.A.*, p. 64.

respect." There is a vague mythology about his personal life. His voice is not like that of others. And what was his own experience he wishes to make a universal experience. He directs the publication of works of art, for our contemplation. He plays guide, and points out what we are to look for; he knows how to justify his captions for different styles. He is the shaman.

I suggest that the enlightenment and the feeling of conquest instilled in youth by the tales of the *conquistadores,* the preaching of the hermits, the words of St. Bernard at Vézelay, are, no more and no less, working on many youth today because they have listened to Malraux. He has withdrawn and returned; aristocrat and didact that he be, he has touched a chord of the times and the vibrations will continue.

The tragedy is that his words cannot long endure. Malraux has said himself that "it is not to art as such that the masses have ever been sensitive *(sensibles)*. . . . I call artists those who are sensitive to the specific nature of art; the rest are sensitive to the sentiment it expresses."[37] The crowds may have carried Cimabue's Madonna through the streets, but they were impassioned by the Virgin, not by art. To most men art will be unhappily what Malraux pleads it not be, an ornament of life.[38] Malraux's enthusiasm for art is sincere. He means desperately to move us to turn to it to find a new belief in man. His sincerity will gain disciples. But culture will never be a universal religion.[39] If Gothic art won universal response in its time, it was because it was in perfect accord with the "sentiment" of the time.[40] It did not do so because it was a *style.*

---

[37] Postface to *Conq.,* pp. 267-68. In *M.S.,* p. 42, he says that the nonartist is sensitive to production, not creation, because production is his proper art ("car la production est proprement son art").

[38] *M.S.,* p. 38; *V.S.,* pp. 310, 423.

[39] In *N.A.,* p. 115, the author notices the religious fervor for culture of the assembled intellectuals.

[40] Postface to *Conq.,* p. 268.

Malraux says that all art is born of "la volonté de transcendance." Modern art, moreover, is but the key "to finding in man's own nature that which formerly had been called his divine powers."[41] It is here that the work of Malraux finally fails, flatly and permanently. Divine power or not, the will to transcendence cannot long endure if there is simply no transcendent. Man will not long settle for man; Malraux has said himself that "a civilization of man alone does not endure a long time."[42] The will to transcendence is the absurd, if it is a capacity incapable of an object. Either man is what Malraux refuses to admit that he is, an animal fully explained by psychology, or he is a consciousness thrust into the world, whose will to transcendence needs an object. His permanence is ephemeral; his works are, in fact, less ephemeral. But neither is an answer to his will to transcendence. If "it is possible for a man to go on caring deeply—fanatically—about himself, even when he has already detached himself from life,"[43] it is because there is something more than life, whether he says he believes it or not. Lucidity is one thing; honesty is a great thing; but mankind will ever need a promise. Blind voluntarism is asking too much.[44]

Listen to Malraux ending his speech to intellectuals in the Salle Pleyel, in 1948, "au nom de mes campagnons gaullistes":

[41] *M.S.*, p. 66. Malraux could have lifted this line from Feuerbach.

[42] *V.S.*, p. 494.

[43] *N.A.*, p. 87.

[44] Camus, talking of rebellion and art, says: "Art disputes reality, but does not hide from it. Nietzsche could deny any form of transcendence, whether moral or divine, in saying that transcendence drove one to slander this world and this life. But perhaps there is a living transcendence, of which beauty [art] carries the promise, which can make this mortal and limited world preferable to and more appealing than any other" (*The Rebel*, p. 227). Is this noble stoicism anything more than a cult of consistency, based on postulatory atheism? One can be, and thousands are, lost in the limits of here and now, of the material, of the visible, of the pleasurable, and of the painful. That is the problem of evil. But a lucid statement that all of that is preferable to any other possible or impossible world seems, at least today, like literary, not human, courage.

We must first proclaim, not the unconscious, but consciousness; not abandonment, but the will; not stuffing the head with knowledge, but the truth. (I know that an illustrious man once asked, 'What is truth?' . . . In the field we are speaking of, the truth is that which can be verified.) And finally, the freedom of discovery. All that: not "toward what?" for we don't know at all; but "starting where?" as in the contemporary sciences. Whether we wish it or not, Europe will light its way with the torch it carries, even if it burns its hand. We wish to establish these values on the present.[45]

The fact of our "present" is the presence of world art. This is Malraux's Organization of the Apocalypse.[46] We are on the brink of the first millennium in history: the world will find its paradise!

The *promise* offered is, then, a new humanism. The earnest of the promise is what we already know about man from art. The rest is discovery. In his *Lettres à un ami allemand,* near the end of World War II, Camus, who has long settled for man, writes as follows:

We had to enter into your philosophy, we had to be ready to resemble you a little. You had chosen heroism without direction because it is the sole value left in a world that has lost its meaning. And having chosen for yourselves, you chose for the world and for us. We were obliged to imitate you in order not to die. But then we saw that our superiority over you was to have a direction. Now that this is going to end, we can tell you that we have learned that even heroism is not a very great thing. . . . The day will dawn when you will be conquered. I know that that heaven, which was indifferent to your cruel victories, will also be indifferent to your just defeat. I still expect nothing of it. But we will at least have contributed to save the creature from the solitude to which you

---

45 Postface to *Conq.,* pp. 271-72.
46 See Malraux, *L'espoir,* p. 90. For an American version of the same spiderlike building of a world see Thornton Wilder, *The Ides of March,* p. 37 (New York: Harper and Brothers, 1948) : "How terrifying and glorious the role of man, if, indeed, without guidance and without consolation, he must create from his own vitals the meaning of existence and write the rules whereby he lives."

wished to consign him. It is because you have disdained this fidelity to man that you are going to die by the thousands—alone.[47]

Fidelity to man! A new stoicism is among us, trying to become conscious of the noble powers of man and of his permanence,[48] in a fraternity that is against solitude, in a communion that is a new humanism.

One has the nagging uneasiness that all of this is rather a hopeless affair. The open future, *fully* to create, its only direction being "man," with the past as proof that man is a thing of power—is not this merely another form of a long-dying liberalism? How many of the disillusioned men of the present are going to look behind them, even into the privileged world of art, for inspiration? A hatred of the past is not uncommon today. To many the two World Wars are the fruits of the sins of their ancestors. They feel the need to build a brave new world; and therefore many, knowing, as they think, that they cannot escape the forces of time, embrace Marxism, which claims to rationalize the historical process.

> A Marxian can claim to understand the modern world, and the world which is to come. . . . This combination of intellectual certainty and the appeal to man's desire for justice, together with its promise of inevitable victory, is its strength. Many Western men are weary of the feeble, skeptical Liberalism which served well enough when the world was prosperous.[49]

The same disillusionment with the past of men has awakened many others to the eternal present of God, who is working out in history the kingdom of God: on earth, if men accept Christ; in any case, hereafter. Without Christ, Clio tends to be a tragic muse; but in Christ the temporal and the eternal can be recon-

---

[47] Albert Camus, *Lettres à un ami allemand*, pp. 75-76. Lausanne: Marguerat, n. d. (though it ends with the date 1944).

[48] See *V.S.*, p. 66.

[49] K. M. Booth, in *Month*, February 1954, p. 90.

ciled because the *historical* fact of the Incarnation gives meaning to history.[50]

Both communism and Christianity are interested in "universal humanism." Both champion an absolute, and both hold
out promises.[51] Neither is an invitation to open spaces, un-
chartered and inconceivable. Malraux does not see that most
men, due to the craving for certainty and the conviction that they
ought to be able to make something out of their lives, find a
sort of psychological attraction in some form of determinism:
and many men refuse to admit that any and every form of determinism is fatality. Even predestination confers on its devotees
a self-confident exaltation. To reject all order in the world, all
meaning to history, all absolutes, all providence, and then to
invite men to stand up and gather the broken pieces, *la monnaie
de l'absolu*, into their hands and to be content to do so because
they are working together, because at least they are exercising
their wills to recompose the universe—none of this is going to
appeal for any length of time. Many moderns, less masterfully
than Malraux, have tried to strike a smile on the face of Sisyphus. But Sisyphus, *salva reverentia*, was *not* happy.

3. RETORT TO MALRAUX

It has been suggested that Malraux, beneath all his modern
externals, is fundamentally a man of the Renaissance, a *condot-*

---

50 "Le mystère de l'Incarnation permet au chrétien une dialectique paradoxale, en
oui et non, qui le fait adhérer à la transcendance tout en l'insérant dans
l'histoire, qui autorise son consentement à l'inévitable tout en lui commandant
la lutte contre le péché et le mal, qui l'actualise dans le présent tout en
l'ouvrant à l'espérance, qui rejoint enfin la sagesse et la folie" (Rideau,
Paganisme ou Christianisme, p. 149). For the Christian there is a meaningful
now in Christ; for the Marxist all is in the future in a laicized Christian
hope: a negation of the finality and unicity of Christ.

51 Both are in the service of a value to be shared in common which is more than
the value of man's autonomy. If the idea of art on which Malraux's humanism
is to be based is the autonomy of man, how can this be but another form of
individualism? Where, in what, is the community, *la communion?*

tiere. Adventurer, man of culture, *arbiter elegantiarum,* aristocrat, humanist, master of his domain, endowed with a mind which sweeps over the known world and finds a relativism in values, imperiously subject to no man, and still the object of admiration and wonder of the world at large, and through all of this passionately addicted to all forms of human creation in art, Malraux steps before the twentieth century as a symbol of what it is not. One trait of the man of the Renaissance is lacking, however. Malraux is not even faintly tinged with skepticism. This is his touch of the *conquistador.* And as the man of the Renaissance strove to understand the message of Greece, so does Malraux write in modern terms of the Greek emancipation from the gods, the Greek questioning of the universe, with all the pagan accent of tragedy that lurked behind each Greek statue on the Greek stage. The elegance of Malraux's expression, the fiercely personal accent of his tone, the literary mastery of the man—all of these are reminiscent of another world. The *non serviam* of Malraux is not a ridiculous thing. To scoff is to admit one does not understand.

Where does he go from here? The evolution of Malraux's thought has reached a point, in his works on art, where it will either fan out farther and farther over the world of artistic creativity and, I fear, become repetitious or the specialized work of a critic of art, or it will regather itself for a question about man. One dare not predict which. At a certain age a man tends to settle for the values he has discovered. "One does not change one's religion at my age," said Vincent Berger's grandfather.[52] The Christian student of Malraux cannot but be haunted by the fearsome possibility that this writer (and man) of deep sincerity and courage will, no matter how much he works, have settled for good for man, in the unquestioning humanism that has caught half of Europe (if we are to believe a modern pe-

---

[52] *N.A.,* p. 40. See *V.R.,* p. 30.

222 The Honor of Being a Man

riodical[53]) and much of the rest of the world. There may still be in Malraux the force necessary to work the change in him that could open his eyes to the real *insaisissable*. But we dare not prophesy with many hopeful writers that Malraux will burst out of his refuge in art. It may be a makeshift, a poor substitute for the absolute; but what special insight entitles a writer to say that it is "the last distraction for a spirit that is too lucid and too sincere to remain happy with it"?[54]

Malraux has come far. The thirst for action, because of the value of courage in accepting the absurd, yielded early to action for estranged, humiliated mankind, which in turn engendered a faith in mankind that sent Malraux hunting mankind's great moments in art. There it is that he finds the rebuff to the "meaninglessness of history," and in the autonomy of the artist Malraux sings of a valiant *anti-destin*. The absurdity of a world without God remains; but Malraux is content with what here below carries some reflection of the absolute. He even calls it, ambiguously, *la monnaie de l'absolu*.

One therefore cannot resist asking this question of Malraux: If the bourgeois "values" were in *l'assouvissement*[55] and hence firmly to be repudiated because selfish satisfaction never elicits anything noble in man, what precisely, when all is said and done, has Malraux to offer instead? The "quality of man," he replies; and that, for him, satisfies our "will to transcendence." But how would he answer this further question: Is not infatuation with man, even though it be with man in his moments of admitted greatness in art, also a straight road to a satanic form of *l'assouvissement* that is not the sensuality of the bourgeois but the pride of the equally self-struck humanist? Is not the will

---

53 See *America*, December 19, 1953, p. 314: "No respecter of classes [the new 'atheistic' faith in man] is as much at home among the dockers of Bordeaux as it is in the French Academy."

54 Onimus, "Malraux ou la religion de l'art." *Etudes*, January 1954, p. 16.

55 *V.S.*, pp. 522-23.

to transcend myself, which finally produces deep within me a satisfaction in being a man, *in being myself,* a subordination even of the greatness that is art to my own fascination with myself? "The bourgeoisie craved a world ordered by no transcendence, and entirely subject to itself," says Malraux.[56] And the humanist?

---

[56] *Ibid.,* p. 490: "La bourgeoisie triomphante voulait un monde 'de faits,' que n'ordonnât aucune transcendance, et qui ne la soumit à rien."

C.H.: La condition humaine

Conq.: Les conquérants

Goya: Dessins de Goya au musée du Prado

J.E.: "D'une jeunesse européenne"

M.S.: Le musée imaginaire de la sculpture mondiale

N.A.: Les noyers de l'Altenburg

N.R.F.: La Nouvelle Revue Française

T.M.: Le temps du mépris

T.O.: La tentation de l'Occident

V.R.: La voie royale

V.S.: Les voix du silence

---

1. Works by Malraux

Malraux, André. "A l'hôtel des sensations inédites." *Marianne*, Decem-13, 1933. (An erotic scene lifted from the definitive version of *La condition humaine*.)

———— "L'art est une conquête." *Commune*, September-October 1934, pp. 68-71.

———— "Aspects d'André Gide." *Action*, March-April 1922, pp. 17-21.

———— "L'attitude de l'artiste." *Commune*, November 1934, pp. 166-75.

———— *Boukharine. Les problèmes fondamentaux de la culture contemporaine*. Paris: Association pour l'étude de la culture soviétique, n. d.

———— *La condition humaine*. Paris: Gallimard, 1933.

———— *La condition humaine*, édition revue et corrigée. Paris: Gallimard, 1946. Cited as *C.H.*

———— *Les conquérants*. Paris: Grasset, 1928.

———— *Les conquérants*, version définitive. Paris: Grasset, 1949. Cited as *Conq.* (The postface contains Malraux's "Address to the Intellectuals," given in the Salle Pleyel on March 5, 1948.)

———— "Les conquérants, fragment inédit." *Bifur*, December 31, 1929, pp. 5-15. (A scene in which Garine discusses Borodin at length. Never included in any printings of *Les conquérants*.)

———— *La création artistique*, Vol. 2 of *La psychologie de l'art*. Geneva: Skira, 1949.

———— "Culture." *Liberté de l'Esprit*, February 1949, pp. 1-2.

———— *Days of Contempt (Le temps du mépris)*, translated by Haakon M. Chevalier. London: Victor Gollancz, 1936.

———— *Days of Hope (L'espoir)*, translated by Stuart Gilbert and Alastair MacDonald. London: G. Routledge and Sons, 1938.

Malraux, André. *Des bas-reliefs aux grottes sacrées.* Paris: Gallimard (Galerie de la Pléiade), 1954.

—————— *Dessins de Goya au musée du Prado.* Geneva: Skira, 1947. Cited as *Goya.*

—————— "Dix ans après." *Liberté de l'Esprit,* June-July 1950, p. 103.

—————— "D'une jeunesse européenne." In *Ecrits,* with essays of André Chamson, Jean Grenier, and Henri Petit, and three poems by P.-J. Jouve; Vol. 70 of *Cahiers verts.* Paris: Grasset, 1927. Cited as *J.E.*

—————— "Ecrit pour un ours en peluche." *900,* Summer 1927.

—————— *L'espoir.* Paris: Gallimard, 1937. (Dedication "A mes camarades de la bataille de Teruel.")

—————— "L'espoir, film d'André Malraux." *Ecrits de France,* 1946, pp. 138-42. (Fragments of the film from the scenario made at Barcelona in 1938.)

—————— *Esquisse d'une psychologie du cinema.* Paris: Gallimard, 1946.

—————— An essay on Barrès among the *témoignages inédits* in Pierre de Boisdeffre, *Barrès parmi nous,* pp. 189-90. Paris: Amiot Dumont, 1952.

—————— Explanatory material for certain pictures in *Tout l'oeuvre peint de Léonard de Vinci.* Paris: Gallimard (Galerie de la Pléiade), 1950.

—————— "Exposition fautrier." *La Nouvelle Revue Française,* February 1, 1933, pp. 345-46.

—————— "La genèse des chants de Maldoror." *Action,* April 1920, pp. 13-14.

—————— "L'homme et la culture artistique." In *Les conférences de l'Unesco,* pp. 75-89. Paris: Fontaine, 1947. (Address delivered at the Sorbonne, November 4, 1946.)

—————— Introduction to Charles Maurras, *Mademoiselle Monk.* Paris: Stock, 1923.

—————— "Jeune Chine." *La Nouvelle Revue Française,* January 1, 1932, pp. 5-7.

—————— "Journal d'un pompier du jeu de massacre." *Action,* August 1921, pp. 16-18.

—————— "Laclos." In *Tableau de la littérature française,* pp. 417-28. Paris: Gallimard, 1939. (Preface by André Gide.)

—————— *Lunes en papier.* Paris: Simon, 1921.

Malraux, André. *La lutte avec l'ange,* I. Lausanne-Yverdon: Editions du haut pays, 1943. (First publication of *Les noyers de l'Altenburg.*)

—— *Man's Estate (La condition humaine),* translated by Alastair MacDonald. London: Methuen and Company, 1948.

—— "Mobilités." *Action,* July 1920, pp. 13-14.

—— *Le monde chrétien.* Paris: Gallimard (Galerie de la Pléiade), 1954.

—— *La monnaie de l'absolu,* Vol. 3 of *La psychologie de l'art.* Geneva: Skira, 1950.

—— *Le musée imaginaire,* Vol. 1 of *La psychologie de l'art.* Geneva: Skira, 1947.

—— *Le musée imaginaire de la sculpture mondiale.* Paris: Gallimard (Galerie de la Pléiade), 1952. Cited as *M.S.*

—— "N'était-ce donc que ça." *Liberté de l'Esprit,* April 1949, pp. 49-51; May 1949, pp. 86-87; June 1949, pp. 117-18. (On T. E. Lawrence.)

—— *Les noyers de l'Altenburg.* Paris: Gallimard, 1948. Cited as *N.A.*

—— "L'oeuvre d'art." *Commune,* July 1935, pp. 264-66.

—— *Oeuvres complètes.* Geneva: Skira, 1945. (Contains only the fiction.)

—— Preface to Bergeret and Grégoire, *Messages personnels.* Bordeaux: Bière, 1945.

—— Preface to William Faulkner, *Sanctuaire.* Paris: Gallimard, 1933.

—— Preface to William Faulkner, *Sanctuaire,* translated by R. N. Raimbault and Henri Delgove. Paris: Gallimard, 1949.

—— Preface to P. E. Jacquot, *Essai de stratégie occidentale.* Paris: Gallimard, 1953.

—— Preface to *L'amant de Lady Chatterley,* a translation by Roger Cornaz of D. H. Lawrence's *Lady Chatterley's Lover.* Paris: Gallimard, 1932.

—— Preface to Manès Sperber, *". . . qu'une larme dans l'océan."* Paris: Calmann-Lévy, 1952.

—— Preface to André Viollis, *Indochine S.O.S.* Paris: Gallimard, 1935.

Malraux, André. "Prologue." *Action,* October 1920, pp. 18-20. (A first version of the opening pages of *Lunes en papier.*)

———— *La psychologie de l'art.* Vol. 1, *Le musée imaginaire;* Vol. 2, *La création artistique;* Vol. 3, *La monnaie de l'absolu.* Geneva: Skira, 1947-1950.

———— "Qu'est-ce que le musée?" *Arts,* June 8, 1954, pp. 1, 9.

———— "Réponse à Léon Trotsky." *La Nouvelle Revue Française,* April 1, 1931, pp. 501-07. (After Trotsky's "La révolution étranglée" in *La Nouvelle Revue Française,* April 1, 1931, pp. 488-501, a severe criticism of the meretricious Marxism of Malraux's *Les conquérants.*)

———— Review of Marcel Arland's *Où le coeur se partage. La Nouvelle Revue Française,* February 1, 1928, pp. 250-52.

———— Review of Georges Bernanos' *L'imposture. La Nouvelle Revue Française,* March 1, 1928, pp. 406-08.

———— Review of Franz Hellens' *Documents secrets. La Nouvelle Revue Française,* April 1, 1932, pp. 915-16.

———— Review of Franz Hellens' *L'enfant et l'écuyère. La Nouvelle Revue Française,* August 1, 1928, pp. 291-92.

———— Review of Hermann Keyserling's *Journal de voyage d'un philosophe. La Nouvelle Revue Française,* June 1, 1929, pp. 884-86.

———— Review of M. Matveev's *Les traqués. La Nouvelle Revue Française,* June 1, 1934, pp. 1014-16.

———— Review of le Marquis de Sade's *Contes, historiettes et fabliaux* and *Dialogue d'un prêtre et d'un moribond. La Nouvelle Revue Française,* June 1, 1928, pp. 853-55.

———— Review of Alexandre Vialatte's *Battling le ténébreux. La Nouvelle Revue Française,* December 1, 1928, pp. 869-70.

———— *Romans.* Paris: Gallimard (Galerie de la Pléiade), 1947.

———— *The Royal Way,* translated by Stuart Gilbert. New York: Random House, 1955. (The original printing of this translation was by Harrison Smith and Robert Haas, New York, in 1935.)

———— *Royaume farfelu.* Paris: Gallimard, 1928.

———— *Royaume farfelu.* Paris: La Nouvelle Revue Française, 1928.

———— *Saturn: An Essay on Goya,* translated by C. W. Chilton. New York: Phaidon Publishers, 1957.

———— *Saturne.* Paris: Gallimard (Galerie de la Pléiade), 1950.

Malraux, André. *Scènes choisies*. Paris: Gallimard, 1946.

———— *Le temps du mépris*. Paris: Gallimard, 1935.

———— *Le temps du mépris*. In *Romans, André Malraux*, pp. 539-42. Paris: Gallimard, 1951. Cited as *T.M.*

———— *La tentation de l'Occident*. Paris: Grasset, 1926. Cited as *T.O.*

———— Tribute to Van Gogh in *Van Gogh et les peintres d'Auvers chez le Docteur Gachet*, pp. 5-6. Paris: L'Amour de l'Art, 1952.

———— "Un artiste à jamais inconnu." In *Vermeer de Delft*, pp. 15-24. Paris: Gallimard (Galerie de la Pléiade), 1952.

———— *The Voices of Silence (Les voix du silence)*, translated by Stuart Gilbert. New York: Doubleday and Company, 1953; London: Secker and Warburg, 1954.

———— *La voie royale*. Paris: Grasset, 1930. Cited as *V.R.*

———— *Les voix du silence*. Paris: Gallimard (Galerie de la Pléiade), 1951. Cited as *V.S.* (The definitive form of *La psychologie de l'art*.)

———— "Le voyage aux îles fortunées." *Commerce*, Summer 1927, pp. 95-131. (Almost the same as the first part of *Royaume farfelu*.)

———— *The Walnut Trees of Altenburg (Les noyers de l'Altenburg)*, translated by A. W. Fielding. London: John Lehmann, 1952.

———— "What Stand Will You Take?" Speech delivered before the Congress of Cultural Freedom, June 6, 1952. *Confluence*, September 1952, pp. 3-11.

———— and James Burnham. *The Case for De Gaulle*. New York: Random House, 1948.

2. Secondary Sources

Alberes, René-Marill. *La révolte des écrivains d'aujourd'hui*, pp. 11-62. Paris: Editions Corréa, 1949.

Baker, A. T. "Man's Quest." *Time*, July 18, 1955, pp. 24-30.

Bespaloff, Rachel. *Cheminements et carrefours*, pp. 22-58. Paris: J. Vrin, 1938.

Blaise de Saint Chef. "A l'ecoute du silence." *Témoignages*, January 1953, pp. 80-84.

Blanchet, André. "La religion d'André Malraux." *Etudes*, June 1949, pp. 289-306; July-August-September 1949, pp. 45-65.

Blanchot, Maurice. *La part du feu*, pp. 211-15. Paris: Gallimard, 1949.

Boisdeffre, Pierre de. *André Malraux*. Paris: Editions Universitaires, 1952.

——— *Métamorphose de la littérature, de Barrès à Malraux*, pp. 390-477. Paris: Editions Alsatia, 1953.

Butterfield, Herbert. *Christianity and History*. London: G. Bell and Sons, 1950.

Camus, Albert. *Lettres à un ami allemand*. Lausanne: Marguerat, n. d. (though it ends with the date 1944).

——— *Le mythe de Sisyphe*, édition augmentée. Paris: Gallimard, 1942.

——— *La peste*. Paris: Gallimard, 1947.

——— *The Plague (La peste)*, translated by Stuart Gilbert. London: Hamish Hamilton, 1948.

——— *The Rebel (L'homme révolté)*, translated by Anthony Bower. London: Hamish Hamilton, 1953. (Original version appeared in 1951.)

Collins, James. *The Existentialists*. Chicago: Henry Regnery Company, 1952.

Copleston, Frederick, S.J. *Friedrich Nietzsche*. London: Burns, Oates and Washbourne, 1942.

Czapski, Joseph. "Malraux and 'The Voices of Silence.'" *Encounter*, March 1954, pp. 60-64.

Danielou, Jean, S.J. *Essai sur le mystère de l'histoire*. Paris: Editions du Seuil, 1953.

Delhomme, Jeanne. *Temps et destin, éssai sur André Malraux*, troisième édition. Paris: Gallimard, 1955.

Delmas, Claude. "André Malraux et le communisme." *L'Age Nouveau*, February 1953, pp. 51-62.

Duthuit, Georges. *Le musée inimaginable*. Paris: Librairie José Corti, 1956.

Emery, Leon. *7 Témoins*, pp. 89-93. Lyon: Les Cahiers Libres, n. d.

Feuerbach, Ludwig. *Essence du Christianisme (Das Wesen des Christentums)*, authorized translation by Joseph Roy. Paris: Librairie Internationale, 1864.

Flanner, Janet. "The Human Condition." *New Yorker*, November 6, 1954, pp. 45-75; November 13, 1954, pp. 46-92.

——— *Men and Monuments*. New York: Harper and Brothers, 1957.

Frohock, W. M. *André Malraux and the Tragic Imagination.* Stanford: Stanford University Press, 1952. (See the laudatory review of this work in *Esprit,* February 1954, pp. 318-19, by Henri Talon.)

———— "Note for a Malraux Bibliography." *Modern Language Notes,* June 1950, pp. 292-95.

———— "Notes on Malraux's Symbols." *Romanic Review,* December 1951, pp. 247-81.

Garaudy, Roger. *Literature of the Graveyard.* New York: International Publishers, 1948.

Gombrich, E. H. *The Story of Art,* fifth edition. London: Phaidon Press, 1953.

"La grande aventure d'André Malraux." *Paris-Match,* June 26, 1954, pp. 34 ff.

Groethuysen, Bernard. Review of André Malraux's *Les conquérants* and *Royaume farfelu. La Nouvelle Revue Française,* April 1, 1929, pp. 558-63.

Henry, Paul, S.J. "The Christian Philosophy of History." *Theological Studies,* September 1952, pp. 419-32.

Hughes, Serge. "Culture in Fragments." *Commonweal,* May 4, 1951, pp. 92-94.

Lawrence, T. E. *Seven Pillars of Wisdom.* London: Jonathan Cape, 1952. (First printed privately in 1926. First printed for general publication in 1935.)

Löwith, Karl. *Meaning in History.* Chicago: The University of Chicago Press, 1949.

Lubac, Henri de, S.J. *The Drama of Atheist Humanism,* translated by Edith M. Riley. London: Sheed and Ward, 1949.

Marcel, Gabriel. *Being and Having (Etre et avoir),* translated by Katherine Farrer. Westminster: Dacre Press, 1949.

———— *Men against Humanity (Les hommes contre l'humain),* translated by G. S. Fraser. London: Harvill Press, 1952.

Mauriac, Claude. *Malraux ou le mal du héros.* Paris: Grasset, 1946.

Merleau-Ponty, Maurice. "Le langage indirect et les voix du silence." *Les Temps Moderns,* June 1952, pp. 2113-44; July 1952, pp. 70-94

———— *Sens et non-sens.* Paris: Nagel, 1948.

Mounier, Emmanuel. *L'espoir des désespérés,* pp. 11-81. Paris: Editions du Seuil, 1953.

Müller, Max. *Crise de la métaphysique*, translated by Max Zemb, C. R. Chartier, and Joseph Rovan. Paris: Desclée de Brouwer, 1953.

Nietzsche, Friedrich. *Ecce Homo*, translated by Alexandre Vialatte. Paris: Gallimard, 1942.

———— *Par delà le bien et le mal (Jenseits von Gut und Böse)*, translated by G. Bianquis. Paris: Aubier, 1951.

———— *Thus Spake Zarathustra (Also Sprach Zarathustra)*, translated by A. Tille and revised by M. M. Bozman. London: J. M. Dent and Sons, 1950.

Onimus, Jean. "Malraux ou la religion de l'art." *Etudes*, January 1954, pp. 3-16.

Picon, Gaëton. *André Malraux*. Paris: Gallimard, 1945.

———— *André Malraux par lui-même*. Paris: Editions du Seuil, 1953.

Pontcharra, Jean de. "André Malraux, révolutionnaire et romancier." *Etudes*, May 1938, pp. 451-65.

Reinhardt, Kurt F. *The Existentialist Revolt*. Milwaukee: Bruce Publishing Company, 1952.

Rideau, Emile. *Paganisme ou Christianisme*, pp. 137-42. Tournai: Casterman, 1953.

Riese, Laure. "André Malraux." *Canadian Forum*, June 1948, pp. 62-63.

Rousseaux, André. *Littérature du vingtième siècle*, Vol. 3, pp. 47-72; Vol. 4, pp. 174-95. Paris: Albin Michel, 1949, 1953.

———— and others. "Interrogation à Malraux." *Esprit*, October 1948.

Saint-Clair, M. *Galerie privée*, pp. 133-38. Paris: Gallimard, 1947.

Sartre, Jean-Paul. *The Diary of Antoine Roquentin (La nausée)*, translated by Lloyd Alexander. London: John Lehmann, 1950.

———— *L'être et le néant*, vingt et neuvième édition. Paris: Gallimard, 1950.

———— *L'existentialisme est un humanisme*. Paris: Nagel, 1952.

Savanne, Marcel. *André Malraux*. Paris: Richard-Masse, 1946.

Simon, Pierre-Henri. *L'homme en procès*, troisième édition, pp. 29-51. Paris: A la Baconnière, 1950.

Spengler, Oswald. *The Decline of the West*, translated by C. F. Atkinson, 2 vols. London: George Allen and Unwin, 1926.

Stéphane, Roger. *Portrait de l'aventurier*, précédé d'une étude de Jean-Paul Sartre. Paris: Sagittaire, 1950.

Talon, Henri. Review of W. M. Frohock's *André Malraux and the Tragic Imagination. Esprit,* February 1954, pp. 318-19.

Toynbee, Arnold. *A Study of History,* authorized abridgment by D. C. Somervell. Oxford: Oxford University Press, 1951.

Trotsky, Leon. "La révolution étranglée." *La Nouvelle Revue Française,* April 1, 1931, pp. 488-501.

Van Humbeeck-Piron, P. and M. "Plaidoyer pour l'art vivant." *Les Questions Liturgiques et Paroissiales,* September-October 1953, pp. 203-19.

Waelhens, A. de. *La philosophie de Martin Heidegger.* Louvain: E. Nauwelaerts, 1942.

———— *Une philosophie de l'ambiguïté, l'existentialisme de Maurice Merleau-Ponty.* Louvain: Publications Universitaires de Louvain, 1951.

INDEX

235